Before the Bible

Before the Bible

The Liturgical Body and the Formation of Scriptures in Early Judaism

———— ᴐⱱᴐ ————

Judith H. Newman

OXFORD
UNIVERSITY PRESS

OXFORD
UNIVERSITY PRESS

Oxford University Press is a department of the University of Oxford. It furthers
the University's objective of excellence in research, scholarship, and education
by publishing worldwide. Oxford is a registered trade mark of Oxford University
Press in the UK and certain other countries.

Published in the United States of America by Oxford University Press
198 Madison Avenue, New York, NY 10016, United States of America.

CIP data is on file at the Library of Congress
ISBN 978–0–19–021221–6

1 3 5 7 9 8 6 4 2
Printed by Sheridan Books, Inc., United States of America

To David

CONTENTS

ACKNOWLEDGMENTS

The research, writing, and production of a long-gestating scholarly book in the twenty-first century incur many debts. I doubt my ability to repay such generosity in full. The research for this book was munificently supported by a Standard Research grant from the Social Sciences and Humanities Research Council of Canada. I have also been supported by funding from Emmanuel College of Victoria University in the University of Toronto. Most recently, my time as a Starr Fellow at the Center for Jewish Studies at Harvard University provided important time and resources for me to complete the work.

Throughout the writing process, I have been deeply grateful to have had at my disposal the extensive University of Toronto library collection. It is a great privilege to have ongoing access to such a collection, but human resources are the most precious. I continually sing the praises not only of the larger library but especially of the gracious library staff at my beautiful "home" library at Emmanuel College, including chief librarian Karen Wishart. Digitization of books and other resources is a wonderful advance for the world of scholarship, but I always prefer to have a book in my very own hands to consult. In the close orbit of my office, I thank Mark Toulouse, former principal of Emmanuel College; Paul Gooch, former president of Victoria University, and William Robins, current president; and John Kloppenborg, chair of the Department for the Study of Religion, for granting the generous research leaves and other funding that enabled me to complete the manuscript.

I am indebted to graduate students (most now graduated!) for their fine work in research and assorted editorial tasks: Sherry Coman, Lelia Fry, Mariam Irshad, Nathalie LaCoste, Carmen Palmer, and Ryan Stoner. Nathalie LaCoste and Betsy DeVries offered invaluable indexing and proofreading help in the last stage. Gabriel Holt lent his creative editorial skills at various critical stages before and after graduation.

Wise scholars have read parts of this book and offered comments or discussed the research with me. I wish my father, Murray Newman, who insightfully discussed many of the book's ideas with me, had lived to see its publication. I hope others will forgive me for any sage advice I did not accept. I would like to thank George Brooke, Matthias Henze, Cynthia Briggs-Kittredge, James Kugel, Hindy Najman, Colleen Shantz, Eibert Tigchelaar, Leif Vaage, Rodney Werline, and Benjamin Wright. I have profited from the annual "Scrollery," a research gathering of scholars from the University of Toronto and McMaster University who work with the Dead Sea Scrolls, initiated by my esteemed colleagues Eileen Schuller and Sarianna Metso. I have no doubt absorbed important information from many others, students in classrooms and colleagues at conferences, that shaped the results of this work. Thanks to the unnamed!

I am grateful to the publishers Brill, Mohr Siebeck, and Walter de Gruyter for permission to include reworked parts of the following articles:

> "The Thanksgiving Hymns of 1QH[a] and the Construction of the Ideal Sage Through Liturgical Performance," in *Sibyls, Scriptures, and Scrolls: John Collins at Seventy*, ed. Joel Baden, Hindy Najman, and Eibert Tigchelaar, JSJS 175 (Leiden: Brill, 2016), 963–980.
>
> "The Reception and Composition of Jeremiah in (Daniel) and Baruch," in *Jeremiah's Scriptures: Production, Reception, Interaction, and Transformation*, ed. Hindy Najman and Konrad Schmid, JSJSup 173 (Leiden: Brill, 2016), 231–252.
>
> "Embodied Techniques: The Communal Formation of the Maskil's Self," *Dead Sea Discoveries* 22, no. 3 (2015): 249–266.
>
> "Covenant Renewal and Transformational Scripts in the Performance of the Hodayot and 2 Corinthians," in *Jesus, Paulus, und Qumran*, ed. Jörg Frey and Enno Edzard Popkes, WUNT II (Tübingen: Mohr Siebeck, 2015), 291–330.
>
> "Speech and Spirit: Paul and the Maskil as Inspired Interpreters of Scripture," in *The Holy Spirit, Inspiration, and the Cultures of Antiquity: Multidisciplinary Perspectives*, ed. Jörg Frey and John R. Levison, Ekstasis 5 (Berlin: De Gruyter, 2014), 241–264.
>
> "The Formation of the Scribal Self in Ben Sira," in *"When the Morning Stars Sang": Essays in Honor of Choon-Leong Seow*, ed. Scott C. Jones and Christine Roy Yoder, BZAW 500 (Berlin: Walter de Gruyter, 2017), 229–240.

Steve Wiggins, editor at Oxford University Press and himself a fine scholar, has been patient and supportive in waiting for the manuscript to be submitted. He has also offered helpful advice throughout the process. Last but not least, my greatest debt is owed to my most patient and faithful reader over many years, David Holt. A more attentive spouse is due to him, with interest.

Introduction

In the middle of the book of Daniel, events unfold that hold both narrative significance and broader import for understanding the formation of scripture in early Judaism. The exiled youth has received two visions about the unfolding of time, but even with angelic mediation, he cannot understand them. Then he tries a new technique: he reads from the scrolls of Jeremiah and finds a prophetic word about the length of time of Jerusalem's devastation. He afflicts his body and offers a long confession to the God of Israel. By praying, Daniel not only receives a new interpretation of Jeremiah's oracles from the angel Gabriel but also obtains the gift of wisdom so that he can perceive the meaning of visions. The action of prayer thus marks a transformation of Daniel's cognition. This cluster of actions—engagement of text, performance of prayer, and ensuing revelation—not only is crucial to understanding the unfolding of the rest of the Daniel narrative but also, more broadly, provides a key to understanding the means by which literary texts become scripture in the Hellenistic-Roman era.

In identifying the three elements of text, prayer, and revelatory discernment as central to our inquiry, I do not wish to imply that they are separate and discrete phenomena. Rather, my aim is to show how they are intricately interrelated. I argue in this book that the interaction between textual reception and composition framed through individual and communal practices of prayer transformed literary texts into scriptures. Texts become scripture to the degree they are understood to be connected to divine revelation in the service of the formation of self and community. Claims to divine revelation, and in particular its mediation, were clearly disputed among various communities, however, so not all communities had the same scriptures.

The transformation of texts into scripture can be tracked most clearly during the Hellenistic-Roman period. After the rise of the Hasmonean state in the second century BCE, and in part in reaction to it, we can see the development of various expressions of Judaism. Whether or not these can be equated neatly with the Pharisees, Sadducees, and Essenes mentioned by Josephus, let alone whether particular literary products can be ascribed to these groups, there were clearly different perspectives evident on a host of issues in the literature of this era. Most significant for this project are differing views on what constituted authentic revelation and who might serve as an authoritative learned leader mediating its message for the community. For example, the sapiential voice in Ben Sira looks askance at contemporary dreams and visions such as those depicted in Daniel. As we shall see, Ben Sira's own interpretive work and ongoing sapiential composition are themselves understood as revelatory. Yet during the centuries before the rise of Christianity, the textualization of Jewish religion, with its authoritative Torah of Moses and, for most, the Prophets, became a hallmark of the culture of all Judeans throughout the Mediterranean region, whether they could read these for themselves or not. Engagement in scriptural interpretation served the ongoing quest of shaping selves and communities. Such interpretation might be explicitly marked as such through quotation formulas; more frequently, we can see the implicit retrieval of textual tradition. This helps to explain why texts, once scripturalized, continued to be expanded, revised, and redacted for centuries long before the concept of a single Bible emerged. Before I substantiate this thesis in subsequent chapters, it will be helpful to discuss text, prayer, and revelatory discernment in turn in order to clarify the ways in which my project differs from other scholarship in objective and methodology.

I.1 BEFORE THE BIBLE: UNDERSTANDING TEXT IN LIGHT OF THE DEAD SEA SCROLLS

My argument runs counter to recent scholarly studies that trace the history of the Hebrew Bible from its putative origins as it moves toward fixity and canonical closure as a product of scribal culture. Most of this work has used the medieval Masoretic Text as a benchmark by which to construct a literary history of its development. David Carr's two learned volumes provide the most exhaustive treatment.[1] He approaches the Hebrew Bible like an archaeological tell, beginning with the presumed most recent "strata" of scripture and excavating to earlier layers to discover origins. Using traditional literary and redaction-critical tools as well as studies of orality, memory, and Hellenistic education, he details the presumed prehistory of the sources to posit an early form of canon, or in his terms, a "hardening" of a form of the Torah and Prophets for "education-enculturation" purposes during the Hasmonean period in order to rival the Hellenistic canon of Homer.

Most of this recent work on the formation of the Hebrew Bible emphasizes the role of scribes, in which two tendencies are observable. One set of scholars understands scripture as the work of a scribal elite attached to either the palace or the temple.[2] The second tendency recognizes the importance of oral culture as integral to the educational context in which the scribes were trained and worked.[3] Both trends in scholarship privilege scribal writing and editing work yet divorce it from other aspects of life. Thus, to understand the making of the Hebrew Bible involves little beyond exploring scribal modes of text production. To be sure, Carr offers a model that suggests that the origins of a proto-canon lay in a larger cultural context of anti-imperial hybridity, but while scribes are understood as connected with the economy of the palace and temple, and even as priests themselves, no attempt is made to connect the scribal hand to the scribe's other life activities. Rather, the social location of scribes within Jewish life in Judea is discussed broadly in political terms.[4] "Scribal schools" or "scribal elites" are posited without supporting evidence for this social construct.

1. David M. Carr, *Writing on the Tablet of the Heart: Origins of Scripture and Literature* (New York: Oxford University Press, 2005) and *The Formation of the Hebrew Bible: A New Reconstruction* (New York: Oxford University Press, 2011).

2. William Schniedewind, *How the Bible Became a Book: The Textualization of Ancient Israel* (Cambridge: Cambridge University Press, 2005); Karel van der Toorn, *Scribal Culture and the Making of the Hebrew Bible* (Cambridge, MA: Harvard University Press, 2007).

3. Philip R. Davies, *Scribes and Schools: The Canonization of the Hebrew Scriptures* (London: SPCK, 1998) and, among his more recent work, "The Hebrew Canon and the Origins of Judaism," in *The Historian and the Bible*, ed. Philip R. Davies and Diana V. Edelman (London: T. & T. Clark, 2010), 194–206; Carr, *Writing on the Tablet*; Richard A. Horsley, *Scribes, Visionaries and the Politics of Second Temple Judea* (Louisville, KY: Westminster John Knox, 2007). For a different argument that the high priests during the Persian and Hellenistic periods played a central role in "scripturalizing" the Torah, see the work of James W. Watts, most recently "Scripturalization and the Aaronide Dynasties," *Journal of Hebrew Scriptures* 13, no. 6 (2013), doi: 10.5508/jhs.2013.v13.a6. Watts's work, too, emphasizes the etic, politically motivated interests in promoting scripture rather than the emic.

4. For example, drawing on Ben Sira, Richard Horsley characterizes scribes thus: "The character requisite for service in the temple-state included rigorous personal discipline,

Not all scholars have focused solely on the Hebrew Bible. Another body of scholarship has treated the formation of the canon by considering the broader terrain beyond the "tell" of the Hebrew Bible.[5] Timothy Lim has provided the most recent entry in the discussion.[6] Rather than trace the history of the Masoretic Text alone, he takes seriously the linguistic and ideological diversity of Jewish communities in the Hellenistic-Roman era in order to identify "canons" that developed among different Jewish communities. He uses the term "canon" in the sense of a listing or collection of books, rather than, for instance, their particular order within a closed canon, as has been emphasized by Brevard Childs. While Lim recognizes that multiple canonical collections were circulating in the Second Temple period, by the first century CE a "majority canon" of the Pharisees, in all respects identical to the rabbinic numeration of twenty-four books, had become dominant.

Textual Pluriformity

One aspect that Lim does not address in detail is the shape of the text in relation to the lists of books in the canons he evaluates, but the earliest artifactual evidence in the eleven caves at or near Qumran has changed our understanding of the shape of these books and must be taken into account in reconstructing the development of the Bible. The material evidence points to considerable fluidity among works understood to be precursors to books of the Hebrew Bible. The case of the pluriform Hebrew texts of Jeremiah found at Qumran is well known, as with the varied collections of psalms, but such pluriformity relates also to the Pentateuch, typically considered the oldest part of the Bible.[7] The Dead Sea Scrolls, too, make clear

obedience to higher authority, and patience with superiors reluctant to listen to legal traditions recalled and advice given." *Revolt of the Scribes: Resistance and Apocalyptic Origins* (Minneapolis, MN: Fortress, 2010), 12.

5. There is now a large bibliography on canon formation and related issues in both Judaism and Christianity. Lee Martin McDonald offers a sound, up-to-date annotated overview in "Biblical Canon," *Oxford Bibliographies: Biblical Studies*, last revised April 29, 2015, doi: 10.1093/OBO/9780195393361-0017.

6. Timothy H. Lim, *The Formation of the Jewish Canon* (New Haven, CT: Yale University Press, 2013).

7. Eugene Ulrich's work on the Qumran manuscripts has substantiated this point; see *The Dead Sea Scrolls and the Origins of the Bible* (Grand Rapids, MI: Eerdmans, 1999) and *The Dead Sea Scrolls and the Developmental Composition of the Bible*, VTSup 169 (Leiden: Brill, 2015), 215–227. For the Pentateuch, discussion has largely focused on the "Rewritten Scripture" debate; see Molly Zahn, *Rethinking Rewritten Scripture: Composition and Exegesis in the 4QReworked Pentateuch Manuscripts*, STDJ 95 (Leiden: Brill, 2011); Sidnie White Crawford, *Rewriting Scripture in Second Temple*

that a version of the Pentateuch circulated in the late Second Temple period that contained many of the variants known to us from the Samaritan Pentateuch.[8] Moreover, the manuscripts of the so-called 4Q Reworked Pentateuch also display readings similar to this "Samaritan" version.[9] While other examples of such textual fluidity could be cited, it is clear that neither the Torah of Moses nor the Prophets display a uniform text during the late Second Temple era. Attempts to retroject notions of a fixed, stable text are actually an anachronistic symptom of a modern, post-Gutenberg print culture. The reality of life in antiquity was, rather, one in which the written text was in some sense secondary to the oral transmission of these discourses as part of a larger and living tradition in the process of continuous renewal, a phenomenon that the medievalist John Dagenais has described using the term "mouvance."[10] Such mouvance is evident in the many and varied written forms of the text.[11]

My approach thus differs from this prior work principally in two respects. First, I am concerned not with the Hebrew Bible alone, but with the development of scriptures more generally in early Judaism. I thus seek to avoid a teleological approach to scripture formation, which assumes that there was a gradual and inevitable process by which certain texts were elevated as scripture and were brought together as a collection. David Brakke has called attention to this problem in scholarship on the formation of the New Testament canon. As he puts it: "Historians continue to

---

Times, SDSSRL (Grand Rapids, MI: Eerdmans, 2008); Moshe Bernstein, "'Rewritten Bible': A Generic Category Which Has Outlived Its Usefulness?," *Textus* 22 (2005): 169–196; Hindy Najman, *Seconding Sinai: The Development of Mosaic Discourse in Second Temple Judaism,* JSJSup 77 (Leiden: Brill, 2003); Emanuel Tov, "The Significance of the Texts from the Judean Desert for the History of the Text of the Hebrew Bible: A New Synthesis," in *Qumran Between the Old and New Testaments,* ed. Frederick H. Cryer and Thomas L. Thompson, JSOTSup 290 (Sheffield: Sheffield Academic Press, 1998), 277–309; George J. Brooke, "The Rewritten Law, Prophets and Psalms: Issues for Understanding the Text of the Bible," *The Bible as Book: The Hebrew Bible and the Judaean Desert Discoveries* (London: British Library and Oak Knoll Press, 2002), 31–40.

8. George J. Brooke, "The Qumran Scrolls and the Demise of the Distinction Between Higher and Lower Criticism," in *Reading the Dead Sea Scrolls: Essays in Method,* SBLEJL 39 (Atlanta: Society of Biblical Literature, 2013), 10.

9. For an assessment of the Qumran materials in relation to the development of the Samaritan Pentateuch, see Magnar Kartveit, *The Origin of the Samaritans,* VTSup 128 (Leiden: Brill, 2009), 259–311, and Eugene Ulrich, "Rising Recognition of the Samaritan Pentateuch," in *The Dead Sea Scrolls and the Developmental Composition of the Bible,* 215–227.

10. John Dagenais, *The Ethics of Reading in Manuscript Culture: Glossing the* Libro de buen Amor (Princeton, NJ: Princeton University Press, 1994).

11. George Brooke has long argued for a new approach to textual criticism that abandons the quest for the "original text" for this reason, see for example, "The Rewritten Law," 36.

tell a story with a single plot line, leading to the seemingly inevitable *telos* (in Greek) of the closed canon of the New Testament."[12] In order to avoid this pitfall, I take seriously the material evidence available for shedding light on ancient texts, bearing in mind the fact that beyond the first level of physical fragments, the construction of manuscripts, compositions, and "books" and their boundaries are all hypothetical reconstructions.[13] I am also not concerned to tell the story of the closure of a canon or canons; I assume this process postdates the first century of the Common Era and involves the differentiation of Judaism from an emerging sibling religion, Christianity.

My second point of difference with current scholarship on the formation of the Bible in early Judaism relates both to orientation and to method. Rather than focusing simply on the scribal hand at work on written texts, I am concerned with the scribal body, or rather what I call the "liturgical body." In short, my argument shifts the debate away from both origins of scripture and closure of the canon. I place political contexts for understanding the development of scripture in the background in order to highlight the role of embodiment and ethical formation. While traditional philological and literary methods of textual analysis have an important role to play in understanding the development of scripture, as do theoretical frameworks of orality and collective memory, I shift the focus toward the uses and diachronic function of texts in their specific social contexts and linguistic registers mediated by the liturgical body. Yet this new orientation raises further questions. What do I mean by "liturgical body"? Both "liturgical" and "body" require some comment because I am positing a new methodological framework for understanding the formation of scripture in relationship to this liturgical body.

---

12. David Brakke, "Scriptural Practices in Early Christianity: Towards a New History of the New Testament Canon," in *Invention, Rewriting, Usurpation: Discursive Fights over Religious Traditions in Antiquity*, ed. Jörg Ulrich, Anders-Christian Jacobsen, and David Brakke, ECCA 11 (Berlin: Peter Lang, 2012), 263–280, at 265. See, too, Philip Davies's similar observation in shorter scope about the Hebrew Bible in the Prolegomenon to "Loose Canons: Reflections on the Formation of the Hebrew Bible," *Journal of Hebrew Scriptures* 2006, http://www.jhsonline.org/cocoon/JHS/a005.html.

13. For a careful description of the steps by which Qumran scholars move from fragments to manuscripts, see Eibert J. C. Tigchelaar, "Constructing, Deconstructing and Reconstructing Fragmentary Manuscripts: Illustrated by a Study of 4Q184 (4QWiles of the Wicked Woman)," in *Rediscovering the Dead Sea Scrolls: An Assessment of Old and New Approaches and Methods*, ed. Maxine L. Grossman (Grand Rapids, MI: Eerdmans, 2010), 26–47. The process of identifying which fragments belong to the same manuscript often involves guesswork, comparing the handwriting as well as the jigsaw "fit" of the individual pieces. A manuscript, while reflecting material evidence of text, thus frequently requires disciplined interpretive construction.

I.2 THE LITURGICAL BODY AND THE UBIQUITY OF PRAYER

At first blush, this liturgical turn may not seem new at all. The association of scripture and worship or liturgical settings has a long pedigree. This has been argued in different ways but has generally assumed a fixed text of scriptures used within the context of worship.[14] Reading "backward" from rabbinic texts, earlier scholarship often wrongly presumed an early fixed Jewish liturgy in a synagogue setting, assuming even a lectionary cycle.[15] That which is liturgical, however, cannot be separated from the scriptural so tidily in antiquity. They are in fact intertwined even at the compositional level, as texts were written and performed in communal settings. Most recently, George Brooke has drawn attention to the need for more scholarly attention to be paid to this nexus:

> To be sure there has been some substantial investigation of the way in which many liturgical texts use scripture and thereby reflect its already existing authority or imbue it with some, but there is room for further investigation of how liturgical texts contribute symbiotically to canonical processes. In particular it seems to me that in several ways liturgical texts assist in the institutionalization

14. Johannes Leipoldt and Siegfried Morenz concluded more generally that the common context for scriptural texts throughout the ancient Near East was their use in liturgy; *Heilige Schriften: Betrachtungen zur Religionsgeschichte der antike Mittelmeerwelt* (Leipzig: O. Harrossowitz, 1953). In terms of Jewish scripture, Henry St. John Thackeray argued even earlier that the Septuagint arose in connection with the celebration of Jewish festivals; *The Septuagint and Jewish Worship: A Study of Origins, The Schweich Lectures 1920* (London: British Academy, 1921). Gerhard Von Rad posited that the earliest piece of scripture was Deut 26:5–10, a "kleine geschichtliche Credo" that arose in the context of the celebration of the Feast of Weeks and gave shape to the Hexateuch; *Das Formgeschichtliche Problem des Hexateuchs* (Stuttgart: Kohlhammer, 1938). John Barton has suggested that the third section of the Tanakh, "the Writings," developed in contrast to that which was read in the liturgy; *Oracles of God: Perceptions of Ancient Prophecy in Israel After the Exile* (London: Darton, Longman, and Todd, 1985), 75–82. More recently, consider David Carr, who seems to have followed Barton in this; *Formation*, 162–163. Cf. also Konrad Schmid, "The Canon and the Cult: The Emergence of Book Religion in Ancient Israel and the Gradual Sublimation of the Temple Cult," *Journal of Biblical Literature* 131, no. 2 (2012): 289–305. While some degree of substitution for the Temple is surely observable, I find his contrast between cult (the Temple sacrificial system) and canon (Judaism as a "book religion") somewhat too starkly portrayed without considering the ongoing ritual elements of Jewish observance.

15. Cf. Jeremy Penner's monograph *Patterns of Daily Prayer in Second Temple Period Judaism*, STDJ 104 (Leiden: Brill, 2012), which argues against the idea that there were any fixed liturgical texts during the Second Temple period.

of scripture, but that at the same time the use of scriptures within liturgical texts encourages transformational experience in the worshipper.[16]

This is a helpful nudge toward a new direction in scholarship that considers the formation of the worshipper. It is also a notable contrast to earlier depictions of liturgical contexts that were limited by a pre-Qumran understanding of scripture. Brooke is informed by more recent scholarship that recognizes the pluriformity of scriptures and the nuanced ways in which scripture is interpreted in prayers and other freestanding "liturgical" texts. Yet in my view the understanding of "liturgical" still needs refinement. The underlying conception of "liturgical" operative in other, more recent scholarship seems influenced by later classical Jewish and Christian conceptions of liturgy that center on worship according to fixed liturgical texts that have come to replace the sacrificial system performed by priests at the Jerusalem temple. That is unnecessarily narrow, however, if one considers "liturgy" in light of its root meaning of (divine) service.

Redefining the Liturgical

Already in the Hellenistic-Roman period, Jews had found ways to provide divine service outside of the Temple, whether as individuals or in communal gatherings, as would happen in the developing Egyptian synagogues. Thus, I argue that the "liturgical" in this era should be broadened to include a constellation of practices, including prayers. Early Jewish liturgy, as Stefan Reif has pointed out, should be understood more comprehensively than the formal service of the gods in the temple. Rather, beyond the Jerusalem Temple and its sacrificial system, it includes the "whole gamut of worship in and around the study of sacred texts, the acts of eating and fasting, and of course, benedictions, prayers and amulets . . . Liturgy was expressed in many ways within Jewish society as a whole."[17] Daniel's fasting and donning of sackcloth and ashes after consulting the scrolls of Jeremiah should be understood as liturgical in this sense. The earliest tefillin and mezuzot

16. George J. Brooke, "Canonisation Processes of the Jewish Bible in the Light of the Qumran Scrolls," in *"For It Is Written": Essays on the Function of Scripture in Early Judaism and Christianity*, ed. Jan Dochhorn, ECCA 12 (Frankfurt am Main: Peter Lang, 2011), 33.

17. Stefan C. Reif, "Prayer in Early Judaism," in *Prayer from Tobit to Qumran*, ed. Renate Egger-Wenzel and Jeremy Corley, ISDCL 1 (Berlin: De Gruyter, 2004), 439–464, at 442. Reif assumes that the *ma'amad, shema'* are among examples of a more broadly based liturgical expression.

discovered at Qumran that contain not yet standardized scriptural passages offer another example of liturgical practice at the intersection of embodiment and scriptural reworking, entangled in text.[18] So too, the collection for the saints in Jerusalem that Paul would later exhort from his congregations in Corinth and Achaia should be considered liturgical. While the act of giving is not itself divine worship, it is legitimated with reference to scriptural texts.[19] Within this broader sense of "liturgical," then, which encompasses the performative and pedagogical dimensions of textual engagement, we can describe the "liturgical body."

I nonetheless focus in particular on prayers in relation to texts because prayer practices remain an unexplored link in the evolution and composition of early Jewish scripture.[20] The reason for this attention to prayer is straightforward. Prayer, as a communication with the divine, serves purposes of sacralizing discourse. Judging by its ubiquity in all early Jewish texts that have been transmitted to us, praying became a central feature of Jewish practice in the centuries following the Babylonian Exile when the scriptures were being composed, transmitted, translated, and transformed. More than two hundred prayers, psalms, hymns, and other "liturgical" materials were found among the Dead Sea Scrolls, and that is bracketing prayers that are contextualized in narratives. Prayers appear in all of the books that do eventually come to constitute the Hebrew Bible and the Septuagint.[21] The New Testament books likewise depict Jesus and Paul praying, and they include multiple prayers and hymns as well. Individual and corporate acts of prayer are simply a very prominent feature of Jewish practice during the Hellenistic-Roman period. While taking some cues from the Persian, Egyptian, Greek, or Roman pagan environments in which they found themselves, Jews and their prayers also developed distinctive formulations and habits during the Hellenistic-Roman period.

One characteristic feature of early Jewish prayer texts, as mentioned above, was the tendency to include wording and interpretations of earlier

18. Yehudah B. Cohn, *Tangled Up in Text: Tefillin in the Ancient World*, BJS 131 (Providence, RI: Brown Judaic Studies, 2008).

19. 2 Cor 8:15 quotes from Exod and 2 Cor 9:9 quotes from a form of Psalm 112:9, with allusions to Hosea and Isaiah.

20. I focus on kataphatic prayer; that is, affirmative, verbal prayer that is informed by words and images, as opposed to apophatic prayer, which seeks to empty the mind and body of images and affective attachments to a state of stillness. While "apophatic" and "kataphatic" are Greek terms most often associated with traditions of Christian prayer practice, there are aspects of both in most religions traditions and certainly in Judaism.

21. The notable exception is the Hebrew version of Esther, which was written nonetheless to commemorate the festival of Purim.

scripture.[22] Indeed, such reingestion and reworking of the scriptural tradition, through allusion, interpretation, and citation, was a hallmark of all early Jewish literary texts in the time well before the Bible came into being. As has now become widely investigated, the interpretation of earlier scripture became a fundamental activity during and after the exile, both as a means of extending older scriptures, as in the case of Isaiah, and in composing new works.[23] The use of scripture in prayer, however, does something distinct within this broader cultural phenomenon, in that prayers are a communication to the divine, what we might think of as a vertical dimension, according to the pervasive metaphorical understanding of God as dwelling in the heavens. Indeed, long before our period, prayer and sacrifice were correlated or equated, as can be seen in numerous psalms (e.g., Psalm 20:1–3, 50:14, 141:2).

Moreover, in antiquity, prayers could be offered by anyone, unlike sacrifices, whose offering was restricted to ritual specialists.[24] Such scripturalized prayers reflect an internalization of scripture, a performatively enacted kind of "Torah written on the heart." They thus can be understood to represent personal "offerings" of scriptural interpretation to God. While I detailed this phenomenon in my first book, my approach was literary and historical.[25] And there was something that I could not yet fully describe and analyze when I wrote that book: what was happening between the texts. I neither addressed the fuller range of texts available through the Dead Sea Scrolls nor tried to account for the phenomenon in sociological

22. My first book detailed the diachronic shift in prayer culture in early Judaism; Judith H. Newman, *Praying the Book: The Scripturalization of Prayer in Second Temple Judaism*, SBLEJL 14 (Atlanta: Scholars Press, 1999). Cf. such subsequent studies as found in *Prayers That Cite Scripture*, ed. James L. Kugel (Cambridge, MA: Harvard University Center for Jewish Studies, 2006); Adele Berlin, "Qumran Laments and the Study of Lament Literature," in *Liturgical Perspectives: Prayer and Poetry in Light of the Dead Sea Scrolls*, ed. Esther G. Chazon, STDJ 48 (Leiden: Brill, 2003), 1–17; Daniel K. Falk, "Scriptural Inspiration for Penitential Prayer in the Dead Sea Scrolls," in *Seeking the Favor of God*, ed. Mark J. Boda, Daniel K. Falk, and Rodney A. Werline, SBLEJL 22 (Atlanta: SBL Press, 2007), 127–157.

23. James L. Kugel, *Traditions of the Bible: A Guide to the Bible as It Was at the Start of the Common Era* (Cambridge, MA: Harvard University Press, 1998); Kugel, "Early Interpretation: The Common Background of Late Forms of Biblical Exegesis," in *Early Biblical Interpretation*, ed. James L. Kugel and Rowan A. Greer, LEC 3 (Philadelphia: Westminster, 1986); Michael Fishbane, *Biblical Interpretation in Ancient Israel* (Oxford: Clarendon, 1985); George J. Brooke, *Exegesis at Qumran: 4QFlorilegium in Its Jewish Context*, JSOTSup 29 (Sheffield: JSOT Press, 1985); Matthias Henze, ed., *A Companion to Biblical Interpretation in Early Judaism* (Grand Rapids, MI: Eerdmans, 2012).

24. Moshe Greenberg, *Biblical Prose Prayer as a Window into the Popular Religion of Israel* (Berkeley: University of California Press, 1983).

25. Newman, *Praying by the Book*.

or anthropological terms as an integrated feature of early Jewish life and practice.

The foregoing review raises questions about how to situate such scripturalized and scripturalizing prayer in religion to its social setting. How do we account for the traditioning process that can be seen between texts and their shared or divergent interpretive motifs? Who was transmitting these interpretations and for what purposes, and how did this result in different kinds of textual products, whether wisdom instruction, prophetic narratives, psalm-like poems, or letters? With that sense of attending to unfinished business, this brings me to the second half of my titular phrase, the liturgical *body*.

Embodiment and the Liturgical Body

How can we understand ancient bodies in prayer and their relation to textual production? Needless to say, academic studies of "the body" have multiplied since the seminal work of Peter Brown almost thirty years ago.[26] Moving far beyond assessing doctrinal disputes in writing the history of early Christianity, his work concerned the cultural significance of ascetical bodies for mapping society in late antiquity. My work here, however, has a different epistemological grounding than scholarship following in Brown's wake. I adopt a framework often termed "embodied cognition" that includes both anthropological and neurocognitive perspectives. Such interdisciplinary work integrating the empirical sciences and the humanities offers the possibility of reframing questions about individual and communal bodies in relation to social and material realities—and even ancient texts and contexts.[27] Embodied cognition developed as a response and reaction to the epistemology of Cartesian dualism, which assumes a strict separation of mind/consciousness and body/material reality. The field of embodied cognition argues for an integral tie among brains, sense organs, motor systems, and emotions as humans interact with others and their environments.[28]

26. Peter Brown, *The Body and Society: Men, Women, and Sexual Renunciation in Early Christianity* (Princeton, NJ: Princeton University Press, 1988).
27. The volume edited by Maxine Grossman offers another set of methodological perspectives on this corpus: *Rediscovering the Dead Sea Scrolls: An Assessment of Old and New Approaches and Methods* (Grand Rapids, MI: Eerdmans, 2010).
28. Thomas J. Csordas's work has been influential in the appropriation of embodied cognition in the field of religious studies, beginning with the volume he edited, *Embodiment and Experience: The Existential Ground of Culture and Self* (New York: Cambridge University Press, 1994), and informing his ethnographic work

The philosophy of Maurice Merleau-Ponty, with its emphasis on human perception in meaning-making and culture formation, has been particularly influential on a range of theories of embodiment, from anthropology to cognitive neuroscience. His foundational insight, itself with roots in Aristotelian ideas, is that the physical body is the medium through which human cognition operates; human thought itself cannot escape nor be separated from the phenomenology of human experience, from seeing, hearing, sensing, feeling—in short, "knowing" as a body-in-the-world. Even our language is deeply embodied, it has been argued, with conceptual metaphors that locate us in relation to how we experience our bodies in space in the world around us.[29] Prayers are conceived as offerings to God, who dwells "up above" in the heavens; thus the prayers, like the experience of smoke wafting upward from burnt offerings, ascend to God's nostrils and ears. This, of course, depends on metaphorical personification of God as one who dwells in the heavens "he" created, a concept rooted deeply in Jewish conceptions of divinity. Moreover, discussion of the body is complicated by the fact that Hebrew has a different semantic range of words relating to "body" than does Aramaic or Greek, thus suggesting somewhat different anthropologies at stake.

The influential essay on the "mindful body" by Nancy Scheper-Hughes and Margaret Lock provides a helpful entry into the discussion of embodiment. They distinguish three senses of body in modern anthropology. First is the phenomenological lived experience of the "body-self." This is the biological body that senses and interacts with its physical environment. The "body-self" is, to be sure, an etic construction, in that a biological framework for understanding the body is contemporary and not ancient, but it can prove heuristically useful, in any case. The second is the "social body," the body that is understood through its interaction with other bodies. Peter Brown's signal work on asceticism and that of Mary Douglas on the body as a "natural symbol" for thinking about relationships among nature, society, and culture are benchmarks here. Such a "body" is socially constructed and thus, unlike the biological body, which is a given universal, differs from culture to culture. The third is the "body politic," which they describe as

---

on Catholic charismatic and Pentecostal groups, *Language, Charisma, and Creativity: The Ritual Life of a Religious Movement* (Berkeley: University of California Press, 1997).

29. George Lakoff and Mark Johnson, *Metaphors We Live By* (Chicago: University of Chicago Press, 1980); George Lakoff, *Women, Fire, and Dangerous Things: What Categories Reveal About the Mind* (Chicago: University of Chicago Press, 1987); Gilles Fauconnier and Mark Turner, *The Way We Think: Conceptual Blending and the Mind's Hidden Complexities* (New York: Basic Books, 2002).

"an artifact of social and political control."[30] This is the way in which the body comes under the control of political or institutional entities. Michel Foucault's focus on the institution of the prison and its disciplinary system serves as their paradigmatic example of the body politic at work in controlling individual bodies.[31] The identification of three "bodies," the biological, the social, and the political-analytical, allows for a more multidisciplinary way of analyzing embodiment in relation to culture. Yet, as heuristic constructs for analysis, they should not be isolated from each other.

One difficulty with Foucault and other poststructuralists like Judith Butler is that they discuss "discourses" on "the body" but attend wholly to the socially constructed and theorized aspect of individual bodies without consideration of either the biological-neurological body or the way in which these flesh-and-blood bodies interact.[32] Thus in framing my project in terms of embodiment, I am not interested in restricting my treatment to a history of ideas or concepts about the body or about prayer, although the book may contribute to such a project. Nor am I concerned here with how prayer texts might be analyzed and systematized to reflect particular theological doctrines. My interest is in some sense more pragmatic and concerned with how bodies engage oral and written texts. My concern is in how, using an approach that integrates methods from both the humanities and the sciences, we can understand praying bodies to shape a particular kind of self and community by engaging oral and written texts that are invested, or come to be invested, with a revelatory status.

I use the term "liturgical body" to refer both to the individual biological body of the praying subject and to the communal, social body gathered together for the purposes of listening, praying, and engagement. The ambiguity between single body and collective body is intentional, because it is just the intersection that I hope to illuminate in discussing how communities take shape through the interaction of the individual "self" and

30. Nancy Scheper-Hughes and Margaret M. Lock, "The Mindful Body: A Prolegomenon to Future Work in Medical Anthropology," *Medical Anthropology Quarterly* n.s. 1, no. 1 (March 1987): 6–41.

31. The more recent work of Mark Johnson distinguishes five aspects of the body, including three aspects of the biological body as it interacts with its environment. Mark Johnson, *The Meaning of the Body: Aesthetics of Human Understanding* (Chicago: University of Chicago Press, 2007), 276–277.

32. See, for example, the critical evaluation of the work of Michel Foucault, and by implication other poststructuralists such as Judith Butler, by Terence Turner in "Bodies and Anti-Bodies: Flesh and Fetish in Contemporary Social Theory," in *Embodiment and Experience: The Existential Ground of Culture and Self*, ed. Thomas J. Csordas (New York: Cambridge University Press, 1994), 27–47.

a collective whole. I draw from a range of theoretical interlocutors to inform such an embodied approach, from anthropology to memory studies to ritual theory to neuroscience.

I.3 THE FORMATION OF SCRIPTURES AND DISCERNING REVELATION

A defining aspect of scripture is its revelatory character. Understanding the body in relation to text and its sacred character requires some discussion of the nature of scriptures during the Hellenistic-Roman era as well as relevant cultural institutions. Scripture is distinguished from other literature for any given community to the degree that the former is understood to have, ultimately, a divine origin.[33] Throughout the Hellenistic-Roman period, the Torah and the Prophets stood as the bipartite collection of scriptures, and their divine origin was implied.[34] The designation "Torah of Moses" was of course understood to represent the divine gift of the law to Moses at Sinai. The books of the Prophets were understood to contain collections of divine oracles pronounced to commissioned divine messengers. Yet even after the presumed end of prophecy claimed by Josephus and others, many other texts circulated that claimed revelatory status.[35] Some of these texts were discovered among the Dead Sea Scrolls. Some others are works that would enter the New Testament. Still others entered no canon.

One group of such texts, pseudepigraphic works written in the names of ancestral figures, proliferated. Hindy Najman has made a cogent case for rehabilitating our understanding of such attribution as a means of extending the discourse of a founding figure.[36] The sacred status and authority of the earlier work were extended to a later work written in the name of the prophet. Already in the book of Deuteronomy, Sinai is "seconded" by extending a Mosaic discourse that reenvisions the founding moment of divine lawgiving. The same might be said of works attributed to Enoch, Ezra, or Isaiah in various ways. The reworking and extension of earlier scripture that constitute such works can be understood as means of acquiring and extending

---

33. See the discussion in Lim, *The Formation of the Jewish Canon*, 4–15.

34. On the twofold character of Jewish scriptures during this era, see Barton, *Oracles of God*.

35. For a discussion of the presumed decline of prophecy in the Second Temple period, see Alex P. Jassen, *Mediating the Divine: Prophecy and Revelation in the Dead Sea Scrolls and Second Temple Judaism*, STDJ 68 (Leiden: Brill, 2007), 11–19.

36. Hindy Najman, *Seconding Sinai: The Development of Mosaic Discourse in Second Temple Judaism*, JSJSup 77 (Leiden: Brill, 2003).

the divine authority of the older work. While Najman's conceptualization has proven valuable in understanding the literary phenomenon of pseudepigraphy, the ultimate test of a text's authoritative character requires delineation of the social context in which a text is used. Because knowledge of the social context in which most of the pseudepigrapha were disseminated is absent, it is less clear as well for whom and how these works held authority in antiquity and thus to what degree they were understood as scripture.

Authority is not inherent in texts alone but is ultimately a social phenomenon rooted not simply in authorial attribution or textual claims but also in readership and communities that receive them.[37] In reflecting on whether or not there were texts considered sacred by the Qumran Yaḥad movement, Hanne Von Weissenberg and Elisa Uusimäki have offered a nuanced discussion of the dynamics of the "sacred" as a graded and relational category.[38] They evaluate Catherine Bell's depiction of four stages in the emergence of scripture: revelation, textualization, canonization, and scriptural interpretation. The late Second Temple evidence complicates this linear trajectory, because, as Von Weissenberg and Uusimäki demonstrate for the Yaḥad movement, the process of textualization does not result in the end of revelation. Sacral status, and thus authority, inheres in leadership figures in the movement, in particular the Teacher of Righteousness, the presumed founding figure of the movement, and the Maskil, a chief officer, who offers inspired interpretation of earlier scripture in new compositions. The Pesharim, connected to the Teacher, and the Hodayot, connected to the Maskil, contain explicit and implicit interpretations of scripture that in turn become new revelatory sites.[39]

37. The decisive role of community in authorizing text and its interpretation as a diachronic process is a point well made decades ago by James A. Sanders, *Canon and Community: A Guide to Canonical Criticism* (Philadelphia: Fortress, 1984).

38. Hanne von Weissenberg and Elisa Uusimäki, "Are There Sacred Texts in Qumran? The Concept of Sacred Text in Light of the Qumran Collection," in *Is There a Text in This Cave? Studies in the Textuality of the Dead Sea Scrolls in Honour of George J. Brooke*, ed. Ariel Feldman, Maria Cioată, and Charlotte Hempel, STDJ 119 (Leiden: Brill, 2017), 21–41.

39. Von Weissenberg and Uusimäki build on the insights of George Brooke, who has argued in a series of essays that the reworking and interpretive reuse of scripture plays a dual role in both increasing the authoritative status ("canonizing") of the scripture that is interpreted and in sacralizing ("authorizing") the new composition. See, for example, Brooke, "Between Authority and Canon: The Significance of Reworkng the Bible for Understanding the Canonical Process," in *Reworking the Bible: Apocryphal and Related Texts at Qumran*, ed. Esther G. Chazon, Devorah Dimant, and Ruth Anne Clements, STDJ 58 (Leiden: Brill, 2005), 85–104; and Brooke, "The Formation and Renewal of Scriptural Tradition," in *Biblical Traditions in Transmission: Essays in Honour of Michael A. Knibb*, ed. Charlotte Hempel and Judith M. Lieu, JSJSup 11 (Leiden: Brill, 2006), 39–59.

Such sacral authority lodged in interpreting mediators can be seen elsewhere in the Second Temple period. Two related aspects of the cultural
terrain of Hellenistic Judaism further inform the way in which revelation
and its mediation are depicted, whether by characters in narratives, like
Daniel, or by authorial figures, like Paul. The first is the shifting conception
of the prophetic. While some segments of Judaism understood prophecy
as a continuing phenomenon, such as the Yaḥad movement, others would
appropriate the language of prophecy, particularly in relation to the possession of divine spirit, for crafting a new understanding of the sapiential,
the priestly, and the messianic. Spirit language thus does various duties
in relation to the understandings of embodiment and textual production.

A second aspect of Hellenistic culture influencing Judean culture was
classical pedagogy, or *paideia*.[40] *Paideia*, like the Hebrew practice of *musar*,
involved not simply cognitive or memory work confined to the mind, but
also physical discipline as a means of character formation and educat-
ing the body in performance.[41] Such training took time and happened in
stages. The highest educational achievement in an ancient context was oral
mastery of the cultural repertoire. The "living voice" of the teacher was a
consummate authority that enabled the old to be transmitted through interpretive engagement, amplification, and augmentation.[42] Thus orality
and performativity played essential roles in revealing what could only be
imparted through a highly trained body. The figure of a leader or teacher
who embodies the tradition is crucial to understanding what I call "revelatory discernment" in extending scripture to emphasize the mediated and
processual aspect of this revelation.

The extension of the textual legacy of early Judaism is a traditioning
process, enabled by such teachers. The traditioning process happens in
the interstices between performances or enactments of the texts, in their

40. H. Gregory Snyder, *Teachers and Texts in the Ancient World: Philosophers, Jews and Christians* (London: Routledge, 2000). Cf. note 3 above. See, too, the recent col-
lection of essays on the topic, *Pedagogy in Ancient Judaism and Early Christianity*, ed.
Karina Martin Hogan, Matthew Goff, and Emma Wasserman, EJL 41 (Atlanta: SBL
Press, 2017).

41. Two essays provide insight into this: Karina Martin Hogan, "Would Philo Have
Recognized Qumran Musar as *Paideia*?" and Patrick Pouchelle, "*Kyropaideia* Versus
Paideia Kyriou: The Semantic Transformation of *Paideia* and Cognates in the Translated
Books of the Septuagint," both in *Pedagogy*, ed. Hogan, Goff, and Wasserman, 81–100;
101–134.

42. Loveday Alexander, "The Living Voice: Scepticism Towards the Written Word in
Early Christianity and in Graeco-Roman Texts," in *The Bible in Three Dimensions: Essays
in Celebration of Forty Years of Biblical Studies in the University of Sheffield*, ed. David
J. A. Clines, Stephen E. Fowl, and Stanley E. Porter, JSOTSup 87 (Sheffield: Sheffield
Academic Press, 1990), 221–247.

actual use in communal study sessions or in other such liturgical settings. Such use and extension of scripture sometimes occurred in new generic forms, such as psalm-like Thanksgiving Hymns from Qumran or the letters of Paul. Paul, trained in his ancestral Judean heritage, will frame his revelatory experience and his teaching partly in traditional terms, through retrieving and interpreting his Judean cultural repertoire, preeminently the Torah and the Prophets. His encounter with a risen Jesus who had suffered and died, "according to the scriptures," as an anointed one, as Christ, is an identification centrally formed by traditions of eschatological expectation and Jewish messianism themselves shaped within the cultural context of the Hellenistic-Roman period. The new, moreover, is formulated in terms of the cultural repertoire he knows in his own body that has itself experienced trauma and near-death suffering. The prayer he offers at the beginning of 2 Corinthians attests to that.

I.4 FROM LITERARY TEXT TO SCRIPTURE

How can we identify when a literary text has changed status, so to speak, and enters the realm of scripture, a text that is formative for a particular community? To illustrate the way in which cultural text is transformed into scripture through liturgical practices, I examine four early textual sites from the Hellenistic-Roman period: Daniel, Sirach, 2 Corinthians, and the Hodayot. I refer to them not as texts but as "sites" because they might better be considered as construction sites in process. Like any building constructed over time, the construction was not linear, so renovations, remodelings with additions or subtractions, might occur over the years, depending on the communities that used these texts. Yet the metaphor fails to the degree that texts did not stay in one place. They were liable to move. We need to factor in repurposing of old materials in new buildings, as well as mobile homes. Ben Sira seems to have included a separate traveling poem about Woman Wisdom known in a different version in the 11QPsalms scroll; moreover, in its peripatetic career the text moved from Jerusalem to Egypt to become Sirach.

In any case, the textual sites reflect a representative sample of the diversity of early Jewish "architecture" and its literature in the late Second Temple period, both ideologically and in terms of genre. I have chosen these also because there is more information about the circumstances and early communities linked to their composition than others, from Daniel's *maskilim* to Ben Sira's scribal students, from the Qumran Yaḥad to Paul's mixed gatherings in Corinth. While I focus on these particular textual sites because of the comparative wealth of information we have about their contexts, I also consider related early Jewish texts that might have gone through similar processes in the movement toward scripture.

The activity of praying served five purposes in transforming texts into scripture. First, prayer serves in the formation of the self by helping to constitute a strong central executive self, serving to bolster conscious agency in the world. Thus it has a transformative function as an essential practice that shapes consciousness in relation to an Other.[43] This universal, neurocognitive aspect of prayer is not unique to early Judaism. The second pertains to Jewish practice and belief as predominantly monotheistic, however one might want to qualify an understanding of monotheism in relation to angelic or other beings.[44] Prayers, and especially petitions, as communications to the divine with whom the pray-er is in relationship, are understood by those offering them to generate a response of some kind. While not all such prayers are answered, and indeed, God can be said not to listen to prayers in certain circumstances, prayer prompts revelation or divine action from the standpoint of those praying. This is a rather obvious point, but it has been overlooked as a means whereby texts gain sacred status when such revelation or divine action is recounted or becomes a part of the text.

Prayer that is "scripturalized" or otherwise engages the traditional cultural repertoire can be understood to have interrelated functions reflected in the third and fourth roles. A third function of prayer relates to the one who leads in prayer. The one who is understood to compose or to perform such prayer provides a communal model of an ideal prayer leader, one who has ingested and can reenact the tradition. Fourth, such scripturalized prayers in turn shape the community who witnesses them, or who joins in offering them. As we shall see, scripture is not reappropriated innocently, but is done to shape particular kinds of subjects and particular kinds of communities. The inclusion of such prayers in texts lends them a divine authority, typically mediated through community leaders, whether they are depicted in a narrative, like Daniel, or as the explicit "author," if not scribe, of a letter, like Paul.

A fifth function of prayer relates to its distinctively performative character. Prayers that are found imbedded in texts are there for a range of

---

43. Patrick McNamara has been among the most forceful proponents of this view; *The Neuroscience of Religious Experience* (New York: Cambridge University Press, 2009).
44. On this complex issue, see, for example, the collection of essays in *Early Jewish and Christian Monotheism*, ed. Loren T. Stuckenbruck and Wendy E. S. North (London: T. & T. Clark, 2004).

reasons. While they often were composed for a given narrative as part its warp and woof, it is also the case that prayers circulated independently. We see independent prayers inserted into cultural texts and prayers as excerpts from texts. Such prayers reflect different stages on the oral-written-oral continuum.[45] Prayers from texts could be learned and reoralized. The Song of Moses is one well-known example of such a moveable prayer. It was eventually collected with others that were imbedded in narrative texts as part of the Christian canticles used in worship. This phenomenon suggests the way in which worship and texts intersect and reinforce each other even *before* scripture is formed.[46]

Outline of the Book

The book is structured to show four different aspects of the liturgical body in relation to the formation of scripture as an open-ended project during this era. Chapter 1 evaluates the role of prayer in shaping the scribal self of Ben Sira. I draw on the neuroscientist Patrick McNamara's work on the decentering and reintegrative function of religious practices to explain the role of prayer and *paideia* in unifying a fragmented self-consciousness and transforming the self. The daily confessional prayer is understood by the sage to result in divinely given wisdom. This enables the scribe's teaching, which itself in turn becomes textualized in the book. The sage's pursuit of wisdom is central to his learning and teaching to the next generation of males. Ben Sira's teaching emphasizes activities that promote honor. His acquisition of wisdom permits him to teach and give voice to praise. While the teaching of the sage reflects a largely oral process, the prologue, with its stress on writtenness and interpretation of the Torah of Moses and the Prophets, provides a trajectory toward scripturalization as the collection moves from Jerusalem to Egypt and beyond.

Chapter 2 focuses on the confessional prayers in the books of Daniel and Baruch in relation to the Jeremiah tradition and textual production. The narrative context of the Babylonian Exile is crucial to understanding their formation. Like Ben Sira, the legendary sage Daniel is depicted as praying daily (Daniel 6), yet the composite book reflects at least two "bodies" being

---

45. On the concept of an orality-literacy continuum and interaction in a predominately oral culture, see Susan Niditch, *Oral World, Written Word*, LAI (Louisville, KY: John Knox Press, 1996), 99–107.

46. The likely dependence of the Christian canticles on Jewish traditions of interpretation is cogently argued in James L. Kugel, "Is There but One Song?," *Biblica* 63 (1982): 329–350.

formed: the pious dream interpreter serving in the royal court and Daniel the ascetic visionary. Visionary Daniel partakes in the first explicit engagement with the writings of a named prophet. The prayer with its interpretation of the scriptural repertoire models Daniel as a learned sage, but one who still cannot understand Jeremiah without angelic help to extend revelation. I argue on the basis of the manuscript evidence from Qumran that the long confessional prayer in Daniel 9 was a "moveable piece" that was included in the Daniel narrative in order to contest the role of confession in early Judaism. This is evident in its intertextual relationship with the books of Jeremiah and Baruch. Baruch can be understood as the first to institute the practice of corporate confession after the Exile. The scribe Baruch composes his prayer by discerning the fulfillment of Jeremiah's oracles. Whereas the textual legacy connected to Sirach is anthological and agglutinative, related closely to proverbial wisdom traditions from Israel's legacy, the narratives of Daniel and Baruch might be considered a never-ending story in exile. Daniel and Jeremiah-Baruch were thus much more open-ended than has often been thought.

In Chapter 3, I turn to Paul and the community in Corinth, in particular 2 Corinthians and two practices that result in communal formation through liturgical practices. One is the collection for Jerusalem, which is meant to forge a communal relationship between two far-flung ecclesial bodies. The second practice is lodged in the introductory blessing, with requests for reciprocal prayer in the face of shared suffering. In this letter, Paul is particularly concerned to establish his authority with the congregation, a status that is contested by other Judean teachers. Paul's self-fashioning as a suffering servant of the gospel models as well an implicit retrieval of Israel's scriptures. Cultural memory theory and trauma theory provide insights for understanding Paul's relationship to his past and present. Catherine Bell's theory about the ritualization of text helps to explain how this letter comes to serve as one of the foundation stones in a growing scriptural anthology of Paul's collected letters.

Chapter 4 focuses on the first-century collection of poetic Thanksgiving Hymns, or Hodayot, in 1QH^a. While these poems as a collection never entered a later "Bible," they nonetheless exhibit many of the dynamics seen in previous chapters, namely, a revelatory understanding of prayer considered instrumental in shaping the self, the interpretation of earlier scriptures in order to shape a particular kind of community, and the ritualization of the text through its connection to an inspired leader of a community. Several factors suggest the Hodayot's authoritative status for the Yaḥad movement. A first is its close connection to the Maskil, a learned figure who played multiple roles including as chief liturgical officer of the

Yaḥad. A second is the revelatory knowledge claimed in the hymns performed by the Maskil. A third is the evidence of the hymns' diachronic formation. The large size and state of the manuscript on which the youngest copy was inscribed suggests it was highly valued by the community. The quest for the ideal self and the shaping of community through prayer was and remains an ongoing project and site of revelation.

This book is by no means a complete taxonomy of scripture formation. The material evidence from antiquity is too fragmentary and incomplete to allow for that. It is nonetheless my hope that the ongoing life of scriptures intertwined with their use by individuals and communities in worship will serve as a new window into understanding Jewish life and letters "before the Bible."

CHAPTER 1

✧

Shaping the Scribal Self Through Prayer and *Paideia*

The Example of Ben Sira

The role of scribes in the production of the Bible has attracted consider-able scholarly attention in recent years. We assume that learned scribes were responsible for the composition and transmission of cultural texts. The characterization of scribes and their role in shaping biblical texts, whether the Hebrew Bible or the New Testament, is inferred by comparison with Babylonian, Assyrian, Egyptian, or Greco-Roman scribes. Yet we know very little about the lives of Israelite and Jewish scribes and their activities be-yond the marks they left on manuscripts. A notable exception comes from the book of Sirach, a wisdom collection originating in the second century BCE in which the scribe's day-to-day activities are described. I want to draw attention in this chapter not to Ben Sira's scribal hand, however, but to the scribal *body* that is evoked in this book. The activities of the "mindful body," to use the term of Scheper-Hughes and Lock discussed in the introduction, shape the identity of a scribal self. Ben Sira's body is a praying body. Ben Sira's body is also a disciplined teaching body.

In this chapter, I argue that the subjectivity resulting from the activity of daily prayer is intertwined with scribal teaching and ultimately the gen-eration of texts. Because the sage's teaching is represented as deriving from divine inspiration, the result of this textual production has been viewed as scripture by both Jewish and Christian communities. There are also clear signs in the book that the collection was edited and augmented over time by later sages who sought to emulate Ben Sira the scribe. Sirach was thus something of an open book in antiquity.

In order to make this argument, I consider first the portrayal of Ben Sira as one who engages in daily prayer. I then discuss the prayer practice from a neurocognitive perspective as an ongoing process of strengthening self-agency. Selfhood cannot be understood in biological terms alone, but must be coupled with an understanding of the cultural context in which the self is shaped. The most pronounced feature of Ben Sira's culture reflected in his teaching is honor and shame. These values can be seen especially in relation to instruction concerning women. In the final part of the chapter, I consider the way in which the formation of self is implicated in the formation of the text of Sirach. The book of Sirach must be understood as the ongoing enactment of Ben Sira's teaching, which includes not only prayer but the interpretation and extension of earlier scripture. This helps to explain how the formation of the book of Sirach, like other sapiential works of its era, was an open-ended production through the training of new sages.

1.1 PRAYER AND THE FORMATION OF THE SCRIBE

Let me begin, however, by introducing the pious sage encountered in Sirach.[1] The book depicts the sage as a creature of transformative daily habit. In the middle of a long passage that describes the scribe's occupation, we learn that the ideal sage followed a specific morning routine. While sipping a cup of coffee may be the first morning ritual for most in the twenty-first century, the ideal Judean scribe in the Hellenistic period is said to occupy his mouth in another way: "He sets his heart to rise early to seek the Lord who made him, and he petitions in the presence of the Most High; he will open his mouth in prayer and entreat concerning his sins" (Sir 39:5–6).[2] Ben Sira's daily prayer is not surprising given that daily prayer as an individual and communal practice appears to have been customary in many parts of Judea and the diaspora in the late Second Temple period.[3]

---

1. I use the Hebrew "Ben Sira" to refer to the persona of the author of the work, understood to be a scribe or sage. Although the work was initially composed in Hebrew, I refer to the textual product using the Greek "Sirach" in order to distinguish the constructed notion of author found in the book from the textual compilation.

2. In this chapter, I generally follow the NRSV translation except where noted because of textual complications.

3. Daniel K. Falk has argued that daily prayer in the morning and the evening came to be practiced by a variety of Jews in the late Second Temple period; *Daily Sabbath, and Festival Prayers in the Dead Sea Scrolls*, STDJ 27 (Leiden: Brill, 1998), 47. Daily prayer was also a diverse phenomenon without as yet universally fixed texts, as Jeremy

Yet the significance of daily prayer as a practice that shapes selfhood has been largely ignored.

Three aspects of this daily practice are notable here. First, he petitions in the presence of the Most High—that is, he names the God to whom he prays, and with that comes an immanent sense of the deity. Second, the sage opens his mouth, giving voice to prayer—it is not silent or contemplative prayer but an activity that requires breath and physical effort. Finally, he requests forgiveness of sins—he offers a confession because of an awareness of his own errant behavior. Thus, as he starts out each day, Ben Sira is intently focused on his relationship to his creator, whose imagined proximity is portrayed clearly, despite the epithet "Most High."

But what exactly does praying have to do with the scribal vocation? Sir 39:6–8 continues:

> If the great Lord wishes, he will be filled with a spirit of understanding; he will pour forth his words of wisdom and give thanks to the Lord in prayer. He will direct counsel and knowledge, and meditate on his hidden things. He will show forth the instruction of his training, and in the law of the Lord's covenant he will boast.

As this passage makes clear, the text depicts prayer as a spur to divine inspiration. Like the ur-sage King Solomon himself, if the deity desires it, he will receive a spirit of understanding, and as in the Wisdom of Solomon, another Greco-Roman wisdom book, prayer is understood as the key to acquiring it (cf. 1 Kgs 3; Wis 7:7). As a result, Ben Sira is said to "pour forth" wisdom, which he acknowledges with thanksgiving and praise. This singular account of the sage's daily activity thus discloses what James Crenshaw has observed about the book as a whole: "Ben Sira places prayer and praise at the very center of the intellectual endeavor."[4] The gift of inspiration is understood to amplify his own wisdom, enabling his teaching

---

Penner's recent book has argued cogently. There is no legal mandate for daily prayer in the Pentateuch. Penner has identified three different rationales for its practice: modeled on sacrificial times, grounded in scripture (especially Deut 6:7), and connected to the luminary cycles. See Penner, *Patterns of Daily Prayer in Second Temple Judaism*, STDJ 104 (Leiden: Brill, 2012), 208. The "Words of the Luminaries" (4Q504–506) found at Qumran provide the earliest extant communal set of daily prayers to be said during the course of a week. See Esther G. Chazon, "The Words of the Luminaries and Penitential Prayer in Second Temple Times," in *Seeking the Favor of God*, vol. 2, *The Development of Penitential Prayer in Second Temple Judaism*, ed. Mark J. Boda, Daniel K. Falk, and Rodney A. Werline, SBLEJL 22 (Atlanta: SBL Press, 2007), 177–186.

4. James L. Crenshaw, "The Restraint of Reason, the Humility of Prayer," in *The Echoes of Many Texts: Reflections on Jewish and Christian Traditions: Essays in Honor of Lou H. Silberman*, ed. William G. Dever and J. E. Wright, BJS 313 (Atlanta: Scholars Press, 1997), 81–97, at 93.

and underscoring the divine role at work in his efforts. Divine revelation, here described in terms of wisdom, is thus understood to be mediated by the person of the scribe.

Most commentators have assumed that the passage does not just describe an exemplary scribe and his activities but is a description of the author Ben Sira himself. While I would not collapse the authorial voice with a historical Ben Sira of Jerusalem too neatly, I assume the learned person who wrote this passage *lived* it.[5] This description represents the activities of a typical scribe of elevated social status, a member of the retainer class in service to elites, in the case of a scribe in Jerusalem; this would mean an elite comprising mainly priests.[6] The first part of the passage in which it appears mentions his corpus of study: the law, wisdom of the ancients, histories and famous sayings, prophecies and parables, proverbs and riddles. He learns through experience as well. The sage also serves among high-ranking officials and travels abroad to learn about other cultures as part of his profession. Such academic and political activities, however, do not fully constitute what was entailed in the scribe's job description because they do not include his personal worship regimen.

Although petition, confession, and praise not only are mentioned in Sir 39:5–8 but figure amply elsewhere, along with another well-known passage describing prophetic-like inspiration (Sir 24:31–33), little sustained attention has been paid to the role of worship in relation to the scribe's activities and the formation of the book.[7] I would argue, however, that the practice of daily prayer is the indispensable starting point in understanding the formation of the scribal self in Sirach along with the wisdom teaching, and ultimately the textual deposit that results from it. If the depiction of the sage in Sirach can be understood to represent the activities of learned Jewish scribes more generally in the Greco-Roman period,

5. Benjamin Wright has pointed in a helpful new direction concerning the book's authorship by cautioning against reading the autobiographical material in the book at face value. Rather, the first-person sections of the book must be assessed according to their rhetorical end of shaping an exemplary character worthy of emulation. See Wright, "Ben Sira on the Sage as Exemplar," in *Praise Israel for Wisdom and Instruction: Essays on Ben Sira and Wisdom, the Letter of Aristeas and the Septuagint*, JSJ 131 (Leiden: Brill, 2008), 165–178.

6. For a fuller discussion, see Richard A. Horsley and Patrick Tiller, "Ben Sira and the Sociology of the Second Temple," in *Second Temple Studies III: Studies in Politics, Class and Material Culture*, ed. Philip R. Davies and John M. Halligan, JSOTSup 340 (Sheffield: Sheffield Academic Press, 2002), 74–107.

7. For a review of scholarship on prayer in Sirach, see Werner Urbanz, *Gebet im Sirachbuch: Zur Terminologie von Klage und Lob in der griechischen Texttradition*, HBS 60 (Freiburg: Herder, 2009), 4–19. Cf. also Jan Liesen, *Full of Praise: An Exegetical Study of Sir 39, 12–35*, JSJSup 64 (Leiden: Brill, 1999).

then prayer is an important factor in the composition of scriptural texts. At the heart of this textual collection, then, is prayer and teaching (Heb. *musar*), or to put it in the Greek language into which this instruction will be translated, *paideia*.

What Does Prayer Do?

A skeptical modern reader may well ask at this point: how can prayer actually be understood to *do* anything? What does this account of Ben Sira's inspiration really mean? I should clarify that my purpose in this chapter is not to evaluate the ontological reality of a presumed divine response but rather to probe the effects of prayer on the one who offers it. These questions can be answered by assessing this account of the scribe's prayer from the perspective of "lived religion," as part of a matrix of cultural practices.[8]

I will argue that there are two answers to the questions concerning the efficacy of prayer practices. First, prayer shapes the sage. As a daily practice, it is a means of self-formation. Second, the prayer also functions rhetorically in the context of the book in that it becomes part of the wisdom teaching embedded in the collection. The book describes the sage praying, includes instruction on prayer, and contains actual prayers, hymns, and other liturgical material. These two aspects, prayer and teaching, are interrelated. I will discuss teaching at greater length below. The point to be made is that understanding the relationship of the person of the sage to the textual product is more than conceiving simply of a hand holding a pen and inscribing a papyrus or leather scroll. The formation of written text is intertwined with the formation of the scribal self and the social setting in which he is embedded, not to mention the inheritors of this traditional teaching. As we shall see, it is not possible to isolate definitively stages in the making of the book of Sirach, much less a single Hebrew "original text"; it is a diachronic process. We will start, however, on the formation of the scribal self as a pedagogical figure before addressing issues related to the formation of the book of Sirach.

---

8. The concept of "lived religion" derives from the work of Robert Orsi, David Hall, and others. It focuses on the practice of religion among individuals and communities within specific social contexts, rather than the more essentializing study of normative religious beliefs and practices. See the introductory essays in David D. Hall, ed., *Lived Religion in America: Toward a History of Practice* (Princeton, NJ: Princeton University Press, 1997).

1.2 THE SELF THROUGH NEUROLOGICAL LENSES

How can we understand the selfhood of the scribe? To put it more collo-
quially, what made Ben Sira tick? Understanding the nature of the self,
whether in antiquity or modernity, is not a new quest. Anthropologists,
historians, philosophers, psychologists, and most recently neuroscientists
have all sought to understand the nature of what provides a sense of self-
identity.[9] Consciousness of "self" is what gives an animate mass of bones,
flesh, nerves, and organs the ability to speak as an "I." One generally accepted theory of self posits two aspects of selfhood.[10] The first is a "min-
imal self," which is the immediate subject of sensory experience. The second
is the "narrative self," which presupposes memory, language, along with a
temporal sense, that is, the ability to think about the past and future and
move through the world as a strategic agent. Another way to construe these
two aspects is as the material self and the social self.[11] Although we may
take the sense of selfhood and "I"-ness for granted, consciousness of self is
understood as the result of a costly struggle from a biological standpoint.
The default state of the self is one of fragmentation: of conflicting desires,
impulses, and sensory inputs.[12]

Decentering the Self of the Scribe

The neuroscientist Patrick McNamara understands the problem of the divided or fragmented self as a central factor inhibiting the development of a

9. My discussion of the self is indebted to two pieces of scholarship that appeared
at about the same time: the prescient book of James L. Kugel, *In the Valley of the
Shadow: On the Foundations of Religious Belief (and Their Connection to a Certain, Fleeting
State of Mind)* (New York: Free Press, 2012), especially 43–88, and Carol Newsom's
pathbreaking analysis of moral agency, "Models of the Moral Self: Hebrew Bible and
Second Temple Judaism," *Journal of Biblical Literature* 131 (2012): 5–25.

10. A good brief overview is found in Shaun Gallagher, "Philosophical Conceptions
of the Self: Implications for Cognitive Science," *Trends in Cognitive Sciences* 4, no. 1
(2000): 14–21.

11. Antonio Damasio separates a proto-self and a core self as the "material me"
and the autobiographical self as the "social me"; *Self Comes to Mind: Constructing the
Conscious Brain* (New York: Pantheon, 2010), 22–23. This draws to mind the first two
aspects of the "mindful body" described by Scheper-Hughes and Lock, mentioned in
the introduction to this volume.

12. Rather than a static or stable entity, neuroscientists understand the self as a process that is related both to the structure of the brain and to the activity of consciousness. Todd E. Feinberg, *From Axons to Identity: Neurological Explorations of the Nature of
Identity* (New York: W. W. Norton, 2009), 204.

healthy sense of self with unified aims and goals.[13] The antidote for a fragmentary self with its default state is the strengthening of what he terms the executive self, or what can be understood as "conscious agency."[14] In his book *The Neuroscience of Religious Experience*, McNamara has argued that engaging in ritual or devotional practices, private or public, that involve religious narratives and ideals can provide a means of achieving a strong sense of self, of unified conscious agency and goal-directedness. The practice of prayer can serve such a purpose. Through a four-stage process he calls decentering, the self moves from a fragmented or unfocused state to a new and improved self that is informed by cultural and religious values and able to achieve goals. The four stages are the neurological means of achieving this end as the brain moves through a process of releasing control in order ultimately to gain more control.[15] Decentering results in clarity of mind and unity of purpose.

McNamara's representation of religion in his book is less refined than his scientific work, but the cognitive process of decentering and reintegration that he describes would seem to provide a fitting model for understanding the process of confession and praise and teaching that marks the sage's daily routine.[16] We will return to evaluate these practices in more detail, but first we need to take account of another aspect of the self and its formation that is not charted by McNamara.

13. The term "central executive self" was coined by Patrick McNamara to refer to the developable results of the executive cognitive functions of the brain; *Neuroscience of Religious Experience* (New York: Cambridge University Press, 2009), 156–166.

14. Newsom, "Models of the Moral Self," 6.

15. The process of decentering and its four stages are described in McNamara, *Neuroscience*, 44–58. The first is the state of impasse or the experience of a conflicted self that results in a suspension in agency. This can occur through religious practices, such as prayer or ascetical fasting, or be induced by substances like hallucinogenic drugs. Suffering or depression can also result in such a reduction in agency. It allows the brain to go "offline" in the sense that it suspends intentionality. Such "decoupling" of the self from agency, in the next stage, permits access to what he terms a "suppositional space." In the third stage, there is a search for "ideal" selves, which are considered as a possible solution to the conflicted or fragmented current self. This might be a god or supernatural agent. The ideal self is not consciously imagined and the search is constrained by the number of ideals contained in the individual's semantic memory. Mythic figures and supernatural agents can all factor in and serve to figure an ideal. The final stage is one of binding, in which the old self or identity is integrated with the new self into a kind of "new and improved" self.

16. McNamara's initial claim that "one of religion's major self-proclaimed aims is the salvation of the individual Self" is framed in Christian terms, though his broader treatment of transformation of self holds true for a range of religious traditions; *Neuroscience*, 1. He does not fully account for the role of decentering in the non-theistic tradition of Buddhism, for example, in which the self itself is considered a problematic feature of existence.

1.3 THE SELF AS A CULTURAL ACHIEVEMENT

In addition to its more strictly neurological aspect, the self is also a dynamic cultural achievement in that it is constituted in relation to specific social and historical contexts. As such, it is possible to refer to a "local theory of the person," as do ethnopsychologists in their quest to understand the self in diverse cultures. Modern Western notions of the self entail a sense of inwardness, freedom, and individuality with clear demarcations between self and other.[17] By contrast, to take one well-known example, the traditional Dinka people of southern Sudan have no modern conception of the "mind" or inwardness as a mediating experience of the self.[18] The self portrayed in Sirach falls somewhere in between. The scribal figure is both an individuated being and one constituted by the formative influence of his larger community.

The way in which the self is conceived in relation to the human body also differs because the body as a social construction varies considerably.[19] The idea of the modern Western self generally presumes that the individual skin-encased body contains the self with no remainder, though "local theories" might depart from that. The conceptions of the self in relation to the body in Greco-Roman antiquity exhibit a range of local conceptions.[20] For example, a self that envisions participation in common human and angelic worship and, arguably, even angelic transformation, such as we see in the Qumran Yaḥad movement, has a different construction than a Hellenized Alexandrian Judean citizen visiting synagogue each week to study the Torah of Moses in Greek. Specific beliefs and practices allow each particular self to take shape.

17. Charles Taylor, *Sources of the Self: The Making of Modern Identity* (Cambridge, MA: Harvard University Press, 1989).

18. The British anthropologist Godfrey Lienhardt conducted a study of the Dinka people and their culture in the mid-twentieth century, *Divinity and Experience: The Religion of the Dinka* (Oxford: Oxford University Press, 1961).

19. I refer here again to the differentiation of the second of the three senses of body as articulated in Nancy Scheper-Hughes and Margaret M. Lock, "The Mindful Body: A Prolegomenon to Future Work in Medical Anthropology," *Medical Anthropology Quarterly* n.s. 1., no. 1 (March 1987): 6–41.

20. Although understanding the self from the perspective of neuroscience is a new trend in scholarship, the literature on the self and body is now vast. One signal contribution is the collection of essays in *Religion and the Self in Antiquity*, ed. David Brakke, Michael L. Satlow, and Steven Weitzman (Bloomington: Indiana University Press, 2005). Two books that concern the ritual or liturgical shaping of the self are Gavin Flood, *The Ascetic Self: Subjectivity, Memory, and Tradition* (New York: Cambridge University Press, 2004) and Derek Krueger, *Liturgical Subjects: Christian Ritual, Biblical Narrative, and the Formation of the Self in Byzantium*, Divinations (Philadelphia: University of Pennsylvania Press, 2014).

The Indigenous Psychology of Ben Sira

In order to map the "local theory of person" in Sirach, we should begin with the area in the body that we might identify with conscious agency. Modern neurocognitive accounts locate the fragmented self of the divided consciousness and impaired agency in parts of the brain, yet neither Hebrew nor Greek has a particular word for "brain." The most important part of the body in terms of receiving, comprehending, and transmitting wisdom and cognition in ancient Israelite culture was the heart (Heb. *lev*, Gk. *kardia*). Ben Sira continues with this traditional view. The passage about the scribe's daily prayer, cited at the beginning, includes the phrase "He sets his *heart* to rise early" (Sir 39:5). The heart is the seat of volition, which enables the person to think and act virtuously.[21]

Thus we can see the conflicted nature of the default self, the starting point of McNamara's decentering process, described in language of the heart in Sirach. It appears in this admonition "Do not disobey the fear of the Lord; do not approach him with a divided heart" (Sir 1:28). A "divided heart" (or literally a "double heart") inhibits the possibility of exhibiting the fear of the Lord. Sin is thus understood in relation to an impaired heart.

Other aspects of the anthropology of Sirach in addition to the language of heart can be seen perhaps most clearly in Sirach 17, which includes an account of human creation.

> The Lord created a human being out of earth and he returned him into it again. He gave them days in number and a fixed time, and he gave them authority over the things upon it. He clothed them in a strength like himself, and in his image he made them. He placed the fear of him upon all flesh, even to have dominion over beasts and birds. (Sir 17:1–4)

The passage relies on wording and ideas from Genesis 1–3, but interprets and expands it. Humans are made in the divine image (Gen 1:26–27), and that involves the capacity for cognitive reflection: God endowed them with "deliberation and a tongue and eyes, ears and a *heart* for thinking" (Sir 17:6).[22] In Sir 17, humans are depicted as filled by God with understanding from their creation. Sirach has a more positive perspective on the ability of human beings to refrain from wrongdoing than we see, for example,

---

21. Leo G. Perdue, *The Sword and the Stylus: An Introduction to Wisdom in the Age of Empires* (Grand Rapids, MI: Eerdmans, 2008), 10.

22. This appears in the Greek I manuscript. I will discuss the complexities of the textual situation of Sirach below.

in the "local theory" of the Qumran Hodayot (Thanksgiving Hymns).[23] In Sirach, free moral agency is assumed. Elsewhere, it is stated explicitly: "If you choose, you can keep the commandments" (Sir 15:15). Discipline and training, however, are needed in order to observe them continually and ultimately to obtain wisdom.

Humanity and the Impulse to Worship

Another way in which humans are like God, according to Sirach, is that they are made to inspire fear in other living creatures. Humans in turn fear the Most High, because it is said, "He put the fear of him upon their *hearts*, to show them the majesty of his works. And they shall praise a name of holiness in order to recount the majesties of his works" (Sir 17:8–10). Fear of God is thus said to be the impetus for praise. Fear of the Lord reflects an attitude of deference rooted in worship of God as creator and sustainer of the cosmos.[24] A distinctive aspect of Sirach's "local theory of the person" is that the liturgical disposition is built into humanity from creation.[25] Human beings are here described as born with the purpose of praising God. Repentance and confession are also envisioned as a part of the process of restoration that enables praise (Sir 17:24–27). The passage in Sir 17 thus contains the image of the ideal self. Such an ideal represents the "aspirational self" that is identified in the third stage of McNamara's decentering process before the final process of integration and strengthening of conscious agency.

The Importance of Characterizing God in Self-Formation

In describing Ben Sira's daily prayer, we noted the significance of naming the deity as a means of identifying the divine character. We should thus consider here as well the nature of the God to whom the sage prays and its role in shaping the self. The Most High is a frequent expression for God,

23. On this contrast, see Newsom, "Models of the Moral Self," 14–24.

24. Leo G. Perdue, *Wisdom and Cult: A Critical Analysis of the Views of Cult in the Wisdom Literatures of Israel and the Ancient Near East*, SBLDS 30 (Missoula, MT: Scholars, 1977).

25. See the astute observations of Mika S. Pajunen, "The Praise of God and His Name as the Core of the Second Temple Liturgy," *Zeitschrift für die alttestamentliche Wissenschaft* 127 (2015): 475–488. Pajunen sees praise and blessing as "the very essence of the Second Temple liturgy" (486). I am less inclined to see Judaism and its liturgical practices during the Greco-Roman era as quite so monolithic.

and the fear of the Lord is an important attitude to hold in relation to him, but God is also cast as a divine pedagogue, a divine teacher like the sage himself, as in this passage:

> The compassion of human beings is for their neighbors, but the compassion of the Lord is for every living thing. He rebukes and trains and teaches them, and turns them back, as a shepherd his flock. (Sir 18:13–14)

The way in which a deity is named and characterized has effects on cognition and embodied state, according to recent studies. One neurocognitive study from Denmark found that those who believe God to be real and capable of reciprocating requests use brain areas, including the frontal lobe, related to social cognition and theory-of-mind processing when they pray. They are in effect imagining a personal God in relationship to them.[26] Naming and characterizing God also has notable effects over time in shaping the mindful body. A study involving nuns who altered their characterization of God in their prayers in the wake of Vatican II changes actually brought an improvement in health.[27]

Effectiveness at prayer is not instantaneous and in fact takes time and imagination to cultivate, but techniques can be taught to enhance efficacy. In her study of the role of prayer in shaping the cultural matrix of evangelical Christians, the anthropologist Tanya Luhrmann observed that some

---

26. This is not unsurprising, but the contrast with the control group was marked. The control group comprised atheists or non-theists and they did not have social cognition implicated. See Uffe Schjødt et al., "Highly Religious Participants Recruit Areas of Social Cognition in Personal Prayer," *Social Cognitive and Affective Neuroscience* 4 (2009): 199–207.

27. Another recent study by Anna Corwin assessed the differences in a group of nuns and the way in which pre– and post–Vatican II theological conceptions shaped their prayers and their sense of embodied self. Imagining and praying to a God as an authoritarian omnipresent judge, characteristic of their training in pre–Vatican II theology had quite different effects from the post–Vatican II shift to conceiving and invoking an indwelling, accompanying, gentle divine presence. This has changed the embodied emotions of the nuns and their self-understanding and their dispositions toward the world. One of the nuns, for example, who had suffered for decades from a chronic illness, for years understood the pain she experienced as part of the divine will, as part of punishment of a divine judge on creaturely humanity. But after a shift in Vatican II prayers, in which God was named and characterized as a loving creator, she came to have a different view of the amoebas that infected her body, seeing them as fellow and beloved creatures of God. The result, astonishingly, was a significant decrease in her experience of pain. Corwin concludes: "This transformation has afforded new subjectivities .... [It] has also influenced their experiences of the world, their experience of their bodies, and ultimately their ideologies and experiences of illness and chronic pain." See "Changing God, Changing Bodies: The Impact of New Prayer Practices on Elderly Catholic Nuns' Embodied Experience," *Ethos* 40 (2012): 390–410, at 406.

people are recognized as better at prayer than others.[28] In the movement she studied, some were acknowledged prayer experts who reported sensory experiences of God, of hearing the divine voice and feeling the divine touch. To be sure, the God imagined by contemporary American evangelicals has a different character from the God to whom Ben Sira prays, a familiar friend as opposed to a remote benefactor. That is the case because the modern American self-conception is culturally different from the ancient Judean self. Nonetheless, the practice of honing prayer through regular discipline and cultivating a relationship with the deity is a similar phenomenon. So too is the fact that, like an evangelical prayer specialist, the sage has become an expert and is able to teach others to pray.

To sum up the presentation of the ideal self in Sirach and the God to whom he yokes himself: the scribal figure is a sage who prays to a God Most High who inspires fear even as his immanent presence is imagined, a God who is a divine patriarch and pedagogue teaching through bodily disciplines. This God is most worthy of praise from a self who is free from sin. As we learn from contemporary anthropological studies, the ideal self and the God who is imagined are tightly linked to the embodied experience of prayer. In the book of Sirach, we can see that the practices that are inculcated through Ben Sira's instruction are designed to discipline this mindful body and its sometimes unruly parts.

The Communal Context for Self-Formation: Honor and Shame

Although the authorial voice of Ben Sira seems to emphasize the individual, the gathered community plays a large role in confirming or negating the identity of the sage. The self envisioned in Sirach is framed most broadly in terms of a patriarchal honor and shame value system that was common throughout the Mediterranean.[29] The system was deeply socially embedded

---

28. T. M. Luhrmann, *When God Talks Back: Understanding the American Evangelical Relationship with God* (New York: Vintage, 2012). Members of the Vineyard, the group she studied, imagined a God who is intensely personal and loving. Cultivating this image of God required techniques of prayer that are in fact quite common in ancient Christianity. Luhrmann observed, "I believe that the central but often implicit technology of evangelical prayer is an intense focus on mental imagery and other sensory experience. The focus is structured in specific ways and directed toward specific goals, but the techniques first and foremost heighten and deepen internal sensation: seeing, hearing, and touching above all" (161).

29. For the pervasiveness of honor and shame in Ben Sira, particularly as it relates to the construction of gender, see the cogent arguments of Claudia Camp, *Ben Sira and the Men Who Handle Books* (Sheffield: Sheffield Phoenix, 2013).

and enacted communally.[30] Thus while as a whole, Ben Sira's teaching contains practical advice on a range of topics—social conduct, friendship, domestic matters, and so on—the framework within which he works is most studiously aimed at avoiding shame and maximizing honor.

Shame, in Ben Sira's traditionally Judean value system, is brought about by sin. As discussed at the beginning of the chapter, the sage is eager to rid himself of sin each morning through confession so that he can ultimately praise God. The following passage locates shame arising in the context of the group:

> Do not exalt yourself, or you may fall and bring dishonor upon yourself. The Lord will reveal your secrets and overthrow you before the whole congregation, because you did not come in the fear of the Lord, and your heart was full of deceit. (Sir 1:30)

The heart is again mentioned as the site of cognition. In this case, arrogance, or self-exaltation, reveals an impaired heart, which prevents the fear of the Lord, the proper attitude that enables both worship and the acquisition of wisdom. Most significantly, the shame brought about by this impairment is made manifest in the community, in the gathering of people who are witness to it (cf. Sir 41:14–18). Shame is only fully evident in public, even though the emotion can be felt privately by an individual. Once sin is confessed, however, a reorientation can begin to occur.

The communal context for understanding the shaping of Ben Sira is one in which these values are performed before an assembly or congregation. A sage is honored through praise in the assembly. An example of this is found at the end of the passage, considered earlier in this chapter, that describes the ideal sage. The final goal of the sage who has offered daily prayer and confessed his sins is one that occurs not alone but in community. Sir 39:9–10 states:

> Many will praise his understanding, and it will never be blotted out; his memorial will not depart, and his name will live for generations of generations. Nations will narrate his wisdom, and an assembly will proclaim his praise.

---

30. On the cultural framework of honor-shame, see the seminal work of Bruce J. Malina, *The New Testament World: Insights from Cultural Anthropology*, rev. ed. (Louisville, KY: Westminster/John Knox, 1993), 28–62, and Philip F. Esler, *The First Christians and Their Social World* (London: Routledge, 1994). See also Halvor Moxnes, "Honor and Shame," *Biblical Theology Bulletin* 23 (1993): 167–176.

Praise and honor can be understood as closely correlated; praise is the vocal expression—and indeed, within a communal setting, the embodied performance—that recognizes the virtue of honor. Thus the honor-shame value system that pervades the Mediterranean region is connected in Ben Sira's case with the liturgical span of confession-praise. The self is a construct that is dependent not only on individual practices but also on its enactment in community, either for shame, with its attendant need for confession, or for honor and its ultimate reward, praise. Thus humans are like God to the extent that they might be deemed praiseworthy.

The Cognitive Reward of Praise and Honor

Scholars have long noted the prominence and importance of praise in Sirach, but certain people are said not to be able to offer genuine praise.[31] A telling passage occurs toward the beginning of the book: "Praise is unseemly on the lips of a sinner, for it has not been sent from the Lord" (Sir 15:9). From the perspective of Ben Sira, sin and praise are incompatible. Since human beings were born to praise the God who created them (Sir 17:8–10), sin detracts from their telos. Confession performs a purgative function that allows for the free expression of praise to God. To return to our earlier discussion of self-formation and neurocognition: if one is burdened by sin, this in effect is to have a less than unified consciousness. The awareness of something called sin points to an awareness on the part of the "current self" of the pray-er that something is less than ideal, something that impinges agency, preventing the attainment of goals. According to McNamara's model of decentering, this relates to the default fragmentary nature of the self. The means to achieving a strong self is through the daily regimen of prayer: petition, confession, and ultimately thanksgiving and praise. In the midst of this, and as a result of this clarity of mind enacted daily, instruction in wisdom occurs.

31. Dieter Lührmann, "Ein Weisheitspsalm aus Qumran (11QPsᵃ XVIII)," *Zeitschrift für die alttestamentliche Wissenschaft* 80 (1968): 87–97; Johannes Marböck, "Structure and Redaction History of the Book of Ben Sira: Review and Prospects," in *The Book of Ben Sira in Modern Research: Proceedings of the First International Ben Sira Conference 28–31 July 1996 Soesterberg, Netherlands*, ed. P. Beentjes, BZAW 255 (Berlin: De Gruyter, 1997), 61–80; Michael Reitemeyer, *Weisheitslehre als Gotteslob: Psalmentheologie im Buch Jesus Sirach*, BBB 127 (Berlin: Philo, 2000); Reitemeyer, "'With All Your Heart': Praise in the Book of Ben Sira," in *Ben Sira's God: Proceedings of the International Ben Sira Conference, Durham-Ushaw College 2001*, ed. Renate Egger Wenzel, ZAW 321 (Berlin: De Gruyter, 2002), 199–213.

More than simply the sage's own response to God, praise becomes a subject for teaching. The most prominent example of this lies in Sir 39:12–35. The passage appears soon after the characterization of the scribe's activities. The sage himself is assured of praise (Sir 39:9) with an enduring memory: "Nations will narrate his wisdom, and an assembly will proclaim his praise" (Sir 39:10). The third-person description of the sage gives way to first-person instruction, as the persona of the sage takes over and he exhorts the audience to praise. The teaching (Sir 39:12–15, 32–35) frames a sapiential hymn (Sir 39:16–31). Thus it not only constitutes instruction in the practice of praise but also contains a model hymn of praise.[32] The sage, furthermore, teaches students about the need for confession (Sir 4:26a, 5:7a, 18:21, 21:1, 34:30–31, 38:10).[33] The transformation that comes with confession of sin permits the "whole heart" to praise and bless: "And now with a whole heart and mouth sing hymns, and bless the name of the Lord" (Sir 39:35).

I have argued that the scribal self of Ben Sira is constructed through daily prayer, and in particular a daily confession that allows for him to strengthen conscious agency by praying to a God imagined as an ideal pedagogue. The self is constructed not only through the decentering activity of prayer but also through the ongoing project of pedagogy, of *paideia*. I want to turn to the cultural framing of the pedagogical project in Sirach as both an embodied fact of practice and performance and a gendered one in which the female identification of Wisdom is central to that project.

Self-Discipline and the Embodied Sage

The instruction found in Sirach includes much in the way of admonition, precepts about what the student should or should not do. But the larger pedagogical project involved more than simply adhering to rules. In antiquity, teaching frequently involved physical discipline.[34] The teacher's instruction also included precepts about bodily comportment. God himself was considered the ultimate discipliner-in-chief: "The one who seeks God

---

32. Liesen, *Full of Praise*, 281. Cf. also Matthew E. Gordley, *Teaching Through Song in Antiquity*, WUNT2.302 (Tübingen: Mohr Siebeck, 2011), 208–214.

33. Maurice Gilbert, "Prayer in the Book of Ben Sira," in *Prayer from Tobit to Qumran*, ed. R. Egger-Wenzel and J. Corley, ISDCL 1 (Berlin: De Gruyter, 2004), 117–135, at 129–130.

34. David M. Carr, *Writing on the Tablet of the Heart: Origins of Scripture and Literature* (New York: Oxford University Press, 2005), 182.

will accept his discipline [*paideia*] and those who rise early to seek him will find favor" (Sir 32:14).[35] A teacher might strike his student, but even more so, each student, and the teacher, must discipline his own body. In the traditional patriarchal perspective of Sirach, the typical body is the male body and students are addressed as "sons."

For Sirach, the honor/shame dichotomy is a gendered value system reflected in the teaching. While such patriarchy can be seen in other wisdom texts, the misogynistic perspective of the book has long been noted. Its climax can be found nowhere more clearly than in Sir 42:14: "Better a man's wickedness than a woman's goodness; it is a woman who brings shame and disgrace."[36] Claudia Camp has argued that the fear of loss of control over desires and impulses is at the heart of the sage's teaching about women, whether the "strange woman" (Sir 9:2–9) or his own wife and daughter (Sir 42:9–14). She writes that Ben Sira's teaching results from "felt anxiety—the personal experience of ambiguity and uncertainty of an attenuated self—which might have produced them."[37] Like McNamara's conflicted self in need of decentering, the sage is prey to continuing impulses that distract from his main goal of observing the law and acquiring wisdom.

While we have observed that from Ben Sira's perspective humans are seemingly capable of choosing to avoid sin, nonetheless the body parts almost seem to have a "heart" (or mind) of their own. This is evident in a number of passages, but perhaps most tellingly right before a prayer that serves as part of Ben Sira's instruction:

> Who will set a guard over my mouth, and an effective seal upon my lips, so that I may not fall because of them, and my tongue may not destroy me?
>
> O Lord, Father and Master of my life, do not abandon me to their designs, and do not let me fall because of them! Who will set whips over my thoughts, and the discipline of wisdom over my heart, so as not to spare me in my errors, and not overlook my sins? Otherwise my mistakes may be multiplied, and my sins may abound, and I may fall before my adversaries, and my enemy may rejoice over me. O Lord, Father and God of my life, do not give me haughty eyes,

35. See the discussion of Rodney A. Werline, "The Experience of God's *Paideia* in the Psalms of Solomon," *Experientia*, vol. 2, *Linking Text and Experience*, ed. Colleen Shantz and Rodney A. Werline, SBLEJL 35 (Atlanta: SBL, 2012), 17–44, especially 24–29.

36. Patrick W. Skehan and Alexander A. Di Lella, *The Wisdom of Ben Sira*, AB39 (New York: Doubleday, 1987), 483.

37. Camp, *Ben Sira and the Men*, 139.

and remove evil desire from me. Let neither gluttony nor lust overcome me, and do not give me over to shameless passion. (Sir 22:27–23:6)

According to this passage, prayer is an important step in restraining from sin, and the further antidote is to retrain the appetites. The instruction that follows the framing prayer relates to discipline of the tongue through control of speech (Sir 23:7–15) and then strong cautionary teaching about adultery (Sir 23:16–27). Such adjustment of the appetites is especially connected to the avoidance of women and the reorientation toward the idealized female figure Wisdom, who appears throughout the collection (Sir 1:1–8, 4:11–19, 6:18–31, 14:20–15:10, 24:1–34, 51:13–30). The passage with its concern about passion and wayward sexual appetites provides a preparation for one of the most well-known passages, in which the personified figure of Wisdom gives voice to her own self-praise (Sir 24:1–22). Prospective sages must sublimate their bodily passions and reorient their appetites toward Wisdom, who exhorts her students: "Come to me, you who desire me and eat your fill of my fruits . . . . Whoever obeys me will not be put to shame and those who work with me will not sin" (Sir 24:19, 22). In the words of Benjamin Wright: "For Ben Sira, then the true sage pursues Wisdom as a lover and finds her wherever she can be found."[38] In contrast to the shame-inducing erotic impulse arising from a wandering male eye (e.g., Sir 9:8, 25:21), Wisdom, the female principle, is acquired through the sage's oral teaching, that is, through the student's ears.[39] Mouths and ears thus require a different kind of teaching and training.

So far we have considered the role of habitual prayer in the formation of the sage and the way in which prayer is intertwined with the scribe's teaching, both thematically as part of the instruction of the student and in practice through the learning of prayer. We turn now to the question of how Ben Sira, the sage, is connected to a text, Sirach.

38. Benjamin G. Wright, "Torah and Sapiential Pedagogy in the Book of Ben Sira," in *Wisdom and Torah: The Reception of "Torah" in the Wisdom Literature of the Second Temple Period*, ed. Bernd U. Schipper and D. Andrew Teeter, JSJSup 163 (Leiden: Brill, 2013), 157–186, at 183.

39. Gazing at a woman who is not one's wife is associated with the risk of sexual entrapment. Thus women are associated with danger through their appearance. The eyes are untrustworthy in more ways than simply the risk of erotic glance, however. According to Sirach, dreams and visions, which are also associated with the eye, potentially present duplicitous or untrustworthy information (Sir 34:1–7).

1.4 BECOMING SIRACH: UNDERSTANDING THE FLUID MANUSCRIPTS

The textual tradition of Sirach as a whole is notoriously complex, and up to this point I have not discussed the textual issues related to the composition and transmission of the work. While originally written in Hebrew by a sage who left his name in a colophon connected to the collection, according to the prologue it was translated into Greek by his grandson.[40] The Greek text prepared by Joseph Ziegler contains more emendations and corrections than any other text of the Septuagint.[41] While approximately two-thirds of the book is available in Hebrew, aside from roughly four chapters of material found at Masada and in the 11Q Psalms scroll from Qumran, the Hebrew manuscripts from the Cairo Genizah are medieval, dated centuries after the putative second-century BCE time of Ben Sira.[42] There are many open questions about the relationship of the Hebrew, Greek, Syriac, Latin, and other languages into which manuscripts were translated.[43]

40. The colophon Yeshua ben Eleazar ben Sira appears in Sir 50:27 of the Greek and Syriac. The single Hebrew manuscript that preserves this passage, MS B, uses Simeon rather than Yeshua as his first name.

41. Joseph Ziegler laments the text's incomparable difficulty in the very first sentence of his foreword to *Sapientia Iesu Filii Sirach*, Septuaginta Vetus Testamentum Graecum Auctoritate Societas Litterarum Gottingensis Editum, vol. XII/2 (Göttingen: Vandenhoeck & Ruprecht, 1965).

42. Pancratius C. Beentjes, *The Book of Ben Sira in Hebrew: A Text Edition of All Extant Hebrew Manuscripts and A Synopsis of All Parallel Hebrew Ben Sira Texts* (Leiden: Brill, 1997). See also the discussion of Maurice Gilbert, who notes the problem of the many different readings between the 1973 critical edition of the Hebrew texts and that of Beentjes: "Methodological and Hermeneutical Trends in Modern Exegesis on the Book of Ben Sira," in *The Wisdom of Ben Sira: Studies on Tradition, Redaction, and Theology*, ed. Angelo Passaro and Giuseppe Bellia, DCLS 1 (Berlin: De Gruyter, 2008), 1–20. Benjamin G. Wright's study amply illustrated the difficulties of trying to reconstruct a Hebrew *Vorlage* of the Greek text; *No Small Difference: Sirach's Relationship to its Hebrew Parent Text*, SLDSCS 26 (Atlanta: Scholars Press, 1989), 232. In spite of Moshe Zvi Segal's careful and concerted attempt at reconstructing an original Hebrew, the quest would thus seem to be a futile one; see *Sefer Ben Sirah Hashalem*, 2nd ed. (Jerusalem: Bialik, 1958). A helpful website with digital photos, transliterations, and translations of the Hebrew text constructed by Gary Rendsburg and Jacob Binstein of Rutgers University is available at www.bensira.org.

43. The textual picture makes the Syriac tradition also an important witness. Cf. Eric Reymond's analysis of the Hebrew "ghost letters" on MS A, which indicates this MS was closer to the Syriac than to the Greek manuscripts; "New Hebrew Text of Ben Sira Chapter 1 in MS A (TS 12.863) (1)," *Revue de Qumran* 103, no. 26 (2014): 327–344. The ninth-century Slavonic translation by Methodius is another intriguing witness to early textual tradition as well. See the essay by Svetlina Nikolova, "The Composition and Structure of Ben Sira in the Oldest Slavonic Translation," in *The Bible in Slavic Tradition*, ed. A. Kulik, C. MacRobert, S. Nikolova, M. Taube, and C. Vakareliyska, SJ 9 (Leiden: Brill, 2016), 243–256.

How can we make sense of all the diverse textual witnesses? The traditional paradigm of textual criticism seeks after the original text or the earliest inferable text. Most recent scholarly readings of the book have sought to locate a historical Ben Sira as author in early second-century Judea and to relate the book's meaning to one specific local historical context, namely, the time of Ptolemaic or Seleucid domination before the period of Hasmonean independence.[44] But this is to belie another aspect of the book that is generally recognized—that the process of composition was evidently not all of a piece but, like other ancient Jewish texts, reflected a long process of editing and accumulation of older textual traditions.

While a scribal colophon appears in Sir 50:27 and again in Sir 50:29, we might ask whether it represents a single author, a scribal function, or something else.[45] In writing about a contemporaneous early text, Annette Reed asks: "To what degree does the unity within 1 Enoch reflect the production of its parts within a single socio-religious sphere, and to what degree is the appearance of unity created retrospectively by the act of collection?"[46] An important question is whether a Ben Sira of Jerusalem was responsible for a book with its current fifty-one-chapter girth that was later corrupted

44. See, for example, the commentary of P. Skehan and A. Di Lella in an eight-page section in the introduction on "Ben Sira and His Times," in *The Wisdom of Ben Sira*, AB 39 (New York: Doubleday, 1987), 8–16. A notable recent trend is to evaluate the work from a postcolonial perspective, in which Ben Sira's textual production is understood as a hybridized response to foreign empire; see, for example, R. Horsley's recent *Scribes, Visionaries, and the Politics of Second Temple Judea* (Louisville, KY: Westminster John Knox, 2007). Leo Perdue, *The Sword and the Stylus: An Introduction to Wisdom in the Age of Empires* (Grand Rapids, MI: Eerdmans, 2008), exemplifies such an approach. Reflective of that orientation is Perdue's summative comment about Sirach: "What is more, the movement of history has not culminated in the theocracy of Judah and awaits its final realization in the elimination of foreign groups from the sacred homeland." Perdue, *Wisdom Literature: A Theological History* (Louisville, KY: Westminster John Knox, 2007), 266. This is true as well for a recent study of the role of the temple in Ben Sira by J. Zsengellér, "Does Wisdom Come from the Temple," in *Studies in the Book of Ben Sira*, ed. G. Xeravits and J. Zsengellér, JSJSup 127 (Leiden: Brill, 2008), 135–149.

45. The colophon appears not just once: it is extant in a single Hebrew manuscript (MS B), which differs from the Greek, and in a second expanded version in Sir 50:29. The twelfth-century MS B also includes the following colophon at the end of the book: "The wisdom of Simon ben Yeshua ben Eleazar ben Sira. Blessed be the name of the Lord from now until eternity." Eva Mroczek, *The Literary Imagination in Jewish Antiquity* (New York: Oxford University Press, 2016), 92–93.

46. Annette Yoshiko Reed, "Interrogating 'Enochic Judaism': 1 Enoch as Evidence for Intellectual History, Social Reality, and Literary Tradition," in *Enoch and Qumran Origins: New Light on a Forgotten Connection*, ed. Gabriele Boccaccini (Grand Rapids, MI: Eerdmans, 2005), 336–344, at 341, as found in Anathea Portier-Young, *Apocalypse Against Empire: Theologies of Resistance in Early Judaism* (Grand Rapids, MI: Eerdmans, 2011), 305.

by various tradents, resulting in the diverse manuscript witnesses we find today, or whether, in fact, the notion of corruption, with its suggestion of a pristine authorial original, may itself be a problematic idea.[47] Eva Mroczek has argued along the latter lines, that the modern quest to discover an original text of Ben Sira in fact lies in conceptual tension with the very process of creating texts in antiquity. The Hebrew manuscripts evince no "book" consciousness but rather point to a process of tradition-making. It is only in the Greek prologue that the concept of "book" appears. She avers that Sirach, far from being intended as a closed edition, was meant to be expanded, for the work was composed as an "open book." In her words: "In addition to books that were conceptualized as 'open' by their authors, there were also books that were 'opened' by later readers who adapted the texts for their own needs."[48] While we can understand the use of a colophon as an innovation rooted in influence from the larger Hellenistic world in which Ben Sira of Jerusalem lived, the teaching and proverbial sayings in this work are nonetheless quite traditional, as has often been noted. This reconceptualization of the authorial process in relation to text and transmission offers an important corrective because it liberates us from anachronistic conceptions of printing, publishing, and closure often projected onto antiquity. Her articulation raises questions about these later "readers" and whether Sirach should be conceived in literary and philological terms alone.

Oral Teaching and Written Words

My point is to understand the formation of the written text not only through excavation of the literary strata but also by thinking about the way the text was used over time in social settings. In this final part of this chapter, I therefore want to highlight the continuing revision and amplification of this wisdom collection. The reason for this open-endedness, I would suggest, has to do with the enactment of the pedagogical process enjoined and exemplified by the figure of Ben Sira. Subsequent generations of students entrusted with this sapiential legacy sought to continue to give it life and meaning through both the adoption of the way of life

47. See the recent study by Jeremy Corley, who has tentatively argued for four different redactional stages of the book's composition: "Searching for Structure and Redaction in Ben Sira," in *The Wisdom of Ben Sira: Studies on Tradition, Redaction, and Theology*, ed. Angelo Passaro and Giuseppe Bellia, DCLS 1 (Berlin: De Gruyter, 2008), 21–48.

48. Mroczek, *Literary Imagination*, 107.

modeled by the sage and the adaptation of its text through continuing engagement.

The Shifting Shape of Wisdom Discourse

In order to make my case, it is helpful to recall the character of this textual collection. As is well known, Sirach does not stand alone as a wisdom work, but follows in a long tradition of such wisdom literature as Proverbs, Ecclesiastes, and Job, which are collections of *meshalim*, two-part poetic sayings. Each *mashal*, or proverb, serves as witness to the larger divine order at work in the world. A sage can accrue many such insights over a lifetime. Such sayings, which might reflect bits of observation about the natural order or advice about social behavior, were collected in order to teach the next generation how to live an ordered existence in accordance with the ordered divine creation.

This anthological temper, as James Kugel calls it, so characteristic of the wisdom tradition, took a decisive shift in Judaism of the Greco-Roman period.[49] Sirach, as well as the Wisdom of Solomon and other wisdom writings of the Greco-Roman era, reflect a new development related to the evolution of scripture. Sirach not only recognizes the accrual of ancestral lore, of wise sayings, as part of the wisdom tradition, but also accepts the Torah of the ancient sage Moses and the Prophets as sources of wisdom. We thus see the scripturalization of wisdom, and the sapientialization of scripture, a point made most overtly in Sirach 24. Through this interpretation of the scriptural repertoire, wisdom is made manifest; the pump is primed for more wisdom by the wisdom already inherent in the Torah. The study of these ancestral texts can themselves generate new wisdom.

Both the prologue penned by Ben Sira's grandson and the manuscript evidence from Qumran and the Cairo Genizah shed light on the ongoing transmission of this textual site as an open-ended project in both Hebrew and Greek. The prologue provides clear evidence not only for the work's translation but also for its journey from Jerusalem to the diaspora region of Egypt with its large Greek-speaking Judean population. The translator calls on those who, like his grandfather, are lovers of learning and learned in the scriptures to help others understand the cultural legacy through both speech and writing. If Ben Sira the sage was said to travel to gain wisdom

---

49. On the conception of the amassing of *meshalim* in the wisdom tradition more generally, see James L. Kugel, "Wisdom and the Anthological Temper," *Prooftexts* 17 (1997): 9–32.

as part of his vocation, here we see that the textual product Sirach could also travel in order to dispense wisdom for the benefit of others. *Paideia*, or teaching, is a big theme in the prologue, mentioned three times in its short span. Understanding the nature of *paideia* as involving both oral instruction by a live teacher and writing is important in order to map the process of textual formation.

The Living Voice of the Teacher and Emulating the Sages

Perhaps surprisingly for a scribe who presumably made his living with his pen, there are very few mentions of writing in the book. That is not to say books were not important to the author. The mention of the "book of the covenant of the Most High God" in Sir 24:23 identifies a written source. All of the sources of the sage's wisdom—wisdom of the ancients, prophecies, sayings, parables, and proverbs—could well have been learned orally from a teacher. Indeed, the scribe is said ultimately to pour forth words of instruction, rather than write them. But *instruction* was clearly meant to be primarily an oral phenomenon. Wisdom comes forth from the mouth of the Creator (Sir 24:3), and it comes pouring forth from the inspired mouth of the prophet-like sage (Sir 24:33), especially after the daily discipline of prayer (Sir 39:6).

The emphasis on the oral character of Ben Sira's teaching should not come as a surprise. In Greco-Roman antiquity, the most credible learning was offered in person, through the "living voice" of the teacher. Loveday Alexander has drawn attention to a common proverb circulating in antiquity that favored the living voice over written expression in instruction. It is mentioned by many ancient writers, from the physician Galen to Seneca, Quintilian, and Pliny, who aver that the living voice of an orator provides a more powerful means of communication than the written words of texts. The principle was current across a range of social classes and contexts, different philosophical schools and occupations: rhetoricians, doctors, craftsmen, teachers. She writes: "In the schools generally it serves as a reminder of the primacy of person-to-person oral instruction over the study (or the production) of manuals and handbooks."[50]

---

50. Loveday Alexander, "The Living Voice: Scepticism Towards the Written Word in Early Christianity and in Graeco-Roman Texts," in *The Bible in Three Dimensions: Essays in Celebration of Forty Years of Biblical Studies in the University of Sheffield*, ed. David J. A. Clines, Stephen E. Fowl, and Stanley E. Porter, JSOTSup 87 (Sheffield: Sheffield Academic Press, 1990), 236.

We can see this emphasis not only on the living voice but also on the live teacher who embodies learning in Sirach. To understand the formation of the textual collection in relation to prayer practices requires understanding how the text was used as a part of the curriculum for students. The sage who is described in both first-person and third-person passages in the book serves as the model for his students. The student is not expected simply to follow the sage's advice, provided so copiously in the collected anthology; the student is to emulate the figure of the ideal sage who is depicted in Sirach. Students must study the teacher's actions and emulate them in order to be shaped into a sage. Students are thus enjoined to enact wisdom through their behavior and to add to the wisdom collection. We began this chapter with the description of the sage and his daily habits in Sir 39:1–11 with his pattern of piety and *paideia*. Benjamin Wright argues that this construction occurs not only through such third-person description but also through the first-person speeches and the behavior of the scribe. As Wright concludes, "The ideal sage then is one who embodies Wisdom, and the student also can embody Wisdom only inasmuch as he regards the sage as the exemplar to be emulated."[51] Such emulation, I would argue, can be seen within the expanse of the extant manuscripts of Sirach.

Instruction nonetheless certainly involved texts. At the earliest, most elementary level of learning, students memorized texts, but at the highest levels of education, the truly learned person no longer relied on them.[52] The interpretation and extension of the cultural repertoire were signs of the learned person's mastery. While in antiquity there were scribes of lesser education who served primarily to produce documentary texts, the kinds of scribal sage whom Ben Sira was training were to be learned adepts of the cultural repertoire.

The "living" dimension of this performance suggests, moreover, organic growth and dynamism in that which is passed on, even when this is crystallized in written form. Thus the tradition is considered vitally malleable, and subject to continuing expansion and revision. In Alexander's words: "The effects of this attitude can be seen clearly in the written texts, where alongside the insistence on received tradition is the assurance of continual addition, selection and correction in line with the author's own experience of 'what is useful.'"[53]

---

51. Wright, "Ben Sira on the Sage as Exemplar," 181.
52. On the stages of education in the Hellenistic period, see Raffaella Cribiore, *Gymnastics of the Mind: Greek Education in Hellenistic and Roman Egypt* (Princeton, NJ: Princeton University Press, 2001), 160–264.
53. Alexander, "The Living Voice," 235. More recent scholarship on the interface of orality and writing in Greco-Roman antiquity, particularly in New Testament studies and rabbinics, has only reinforced the point about the priority of the oral world that

The Ongoing Cycle of Prayer and Pedagogy

But it is the enactment of the repertoire on the way to becoming a sage that is of significance to us, the way in which, as the prologue states, "those who love learning might make even greater progress in living according to the law." There are different ways budding sages might enact this wisdom. The most elementary means of demonstrating wisdom is in the appropriation and application of proverbs to daily life. This involves discernment on the part of the student into any given social situation. Should one offer the advice "A stitch in time saves nine" or "Look before you leap"?[54] The choice involves the wise judgment of the sage. The oral-written nexus could happen in different ways, but if we assume that proverbial material emerged in an oral context, a student who has memorized it with the help of written text might give voice to it once again. This is what Susan Niditch has described as the reoralization of the material as it is used in a life setting.[55]

The curriculum of the sage also included the ingestion and interpretation of the cultural repertoire. Like the learned Greek rhetor who had mastered the corpus of Homer, so too the textual body of Moses and the prophets must be consumed and thoroughly digested so that they become a natural part of the sage. Another way in which wisdom might be performed thus involves its augmentation. Consider this piece of instruction found in Sirach: "When a man of understanding hears a wise saying, he will praise it and add to it" (Sir 21:15).[56] A budding sage, to prove himself a

Alexander made in her seminal article twenty-five years ago. See the excellent study by H. Gregory Snyder, *Teachers and Texts in the Ancient World: Philosophers, Jews and Christians* (London: Routledge, 2000). Recent interest in orality in New Testament studies was spurred by Werner Kelber's 1983 work (recently reissued), *The Oral and the Written Gospel: The Hermeneutics of Speaking and Writing in the Synoptic Tradition, Mark, Paul, and Q* (Bloomington: Indiana University Press, 1997). See also *Jesus in Memory: Traditions in Oral and Scribal Perspectives*, ed. Werner H. Kelber and S. Byrskog (Waco, TX: Baylor University Press, 2009). For Israelite literature, Susan Niditch's work has been equally seminal; *Oral World and Written Word*, LAI (Louisville, KY: John Knox Press, 1996). In rabbinics, see Steven D. Fraade, "Literary Composition and Oral Performance in the Early Midrashim," *Oral Tradition* 14 (1999): 33–51; Martin S. Jaffee, *Torah in the Mouth: Writing and Oral Tradition in Palestinian Judaism, 200 BCE– 400 CE* (New York: Oxford University Press, 2001); and Elizabeth Shanks Alexander, *Transmitting Mishnah: The Shaping Influence of Oral Tradition* (Cambridge: Cambridge University Press, 2006).

54. See the insightful comments of Amy Plantinga-Pauw, *Proverbs and Ecclesiastes: A Theological Commentary on the Bible* (Louisville, KY: Westminster John Knox, 2015), 117.

55. On the concept of reoralization, see Niditch, *Oral World, Written Word*, 39–77.

56. I am grateful to Dr. Tzemah Yoreh for drawing my attention to this verse.

man of wisdom, must also add to the collection of sayings by reflecting on wisdom he already knows, interpreting and amplifying it. There are many examples of such subtle adjustments and amplifications in Sirach. One example appears in part of a larger passage (Sir 6:18–31) concerned with the instruction that the student should yoke himself to Wisdom: "Put your feet into her fetters, and your neck into her collar" (Sir 6:24). The following proverb makes allusion to Deut 6:5, a verse that would be included in the Shema: "Come to her with all your soul, and keep her ways with all your might" (Sir 6:26). Serving Woman Wisdom is here a substitute for loving God. Elsewhere the allusion to Deut 6:5 is connected to the commandment to honor parents (Sir 7:27–30).[57] The way in which scripture is alluded to and augmented suggests both a deep ingestion of scripture and a thoughtfully engaged interpretation of it.

Interpreting and Extending Scripture

Like the model sage Ben Sira, the more accomplished sage was expected not only to memorize sayings and modify or amplify them as necessary but also to study prior scripture and interpret it. The following instruction articulates this principle: "Reflect on the statutes of the Lord, and meditate at all times on his commandments. It is he who will give insight to your mind, and your desire for wisdom will be granted" (Sir 6:37).[58] This verse asks the student to reflect on the law. Through this process, divine inspiration will ensure and provide insight and wisdom into scripture. The more well-known passage already discussed, Sirach 24, correlates such wisdom with the "book of the covenant of the most High."

The augmentation of the wisdom corpus was rooted both in updating in terms of contemporary cultural understanding and in ongoing interpretation of scripture. An example of each tendency can be found in the way in which one of the two principal Greek manuscripts, GII, expands upon the other, GI, in Sir 17:1–25, a poem on creation and a passage we have already discussed.

---

57. For a nuanced discussion of these verses in Sirach in the context of the development of the Shema, see Elizabeth Shanks Alexander, "Women's Exemption from Shema and Tefillin and How These Rituals Came to be Viewed as Torah Study," *Journal for the Study of Judaism in the Persian, Hellenistic, and Roman Periods* 42 (2011): 531–579, especially 544–545.

58. Cf. Hebrew Ms A, which offers a different version: "And reflect on the fear of the Most High and meditate on his commandments always. And He will give your heart understanding and make you wise which is what you wanted."

3 He clothed them in a strength like himself,
    and in his image he made them.
4 He placed the fear of him upon all flesh,
    even to have dominion over beasts and birds.
5 *They received use of the five faculties of the Lord,*
    but, apportioning a sixth, he gave to them the gift of mind,
    and the seventh, reason, the interpreter of his faculties.
6 Deliberation and a tongue and eyes,
    ears and a heart for thinking he gave them.
7 With knowledge of understanding he filled them,
    and good things and bad he showed to them. (Sir 17:3–7)

The passage reflects on the puzzle of what exactly it means for humanity to be made in the divine image. While GI has identified five faculties that constitute such likeness, GII (italicized) adds two more. Whether or not the hand that added it was Stoic, as one scholar has argued, it is clear that the anthropological perspective has taken a decided shift.[59]

Within the same chapter, we also see the way in which scripture continues to be mined for ways in which it might shed light on the wisdom already articulated:

12 A perpetual covenant he established with them,
    and his judgments he showed to them.
13 Majesty of glory their eyes saw,
    and the glory of his voice their ear heard.
14 And he said to them, "Be on guard against all wrong,"
    and he commanded each of them concerning his fellow.
15 Their ways are before him always;
    they will not be hidden from his eyes.
16 *Their ways from youth are upon evil things,*
    and they were not strong enough to make their hearts of flesh
    rather than of stone. (Sir 17:12–16)

The italicized additions of GII can be understood as a means of clarifying an ambiguity imbedded in the earlier poem. Is this poem about all humanity, and thus universal, or is it about Israel and its special relationship to God? The first half of the passage in Sir 17:1–10 would

---

59. Rudolf Smend cites Grotius to this effect; *Die Weisheit Jesus Sirach Erklärt* (Berlin: Reimer, 1906), 150.

seem to be an interpretation of the creation accounts of Genesis and thus refer to all humanity, not Israel in particular. The mention of the "perpetual covenant" in Sir 17:12a seems to relate in particular to Israel and the observance of the sabbath after Sinai in Exod 31:16. But of course the "eternal covenant" is also found in the priestly account to refer to the Noahic covenant with all flesh in Gen 9:16 as well as the Abrahamic covenant in Gen 17:19. The allusions to God's transformation of Israel's heart of stone into hearts of flesh are clearly to Ezek 11:19 and Ezek 36:26, thus further clarifying that the passage shifts in verse 12 to make reference to Israel.[60]

We can also see this interpretive process of augmentation occurring in the larger framework of the textual collection itself over time. We saw in Sir 39 that the ideal sage is supposed to petition for sins, study, interpret, and teach, and then offer thanks and praise. So too in the larger shaping of the textual collection, the anthological impulse to collect wisdom from various places is reflected in the addition of material.[61] After a collection (Sir 1– 39) that contains the sapiential instruction "poured forth" from the ideal sage and interspersed with prayers and hymns, there follows a recounting of praiseworthy ancestors, from Enoch to the high priest Simeon (Sir 44–50), that further reflects the ingestion and interpretation with allusive references to the Torah and Prophets. The scribal colophon in Sirach, which is normally found at the end of a text, is augmented in both Greek and Hebrew manuscripts by an autobiographical piece in which the authorial voice of Ben Sira describes his search for Wisdom (Sir 51:1–12). The passage is also found at the end of 11Q5, the great psalms scroll from Qumran, so it occurs in Hebrew as something of a traveling text, known from another collection. The Cairo Genizah Hebrew text B appends yet another prayer of thanksgiving at 51:12. The examples of amplification and interpretive additions I have adduced confirm the words of Maurice Gilbert: "So many hands have touched the book of Ben Sira. For centuries it remained

---

60. As Greg Goering observes about other such clarifications in this longer passage: "Like the nations, Israel contains its own share of wickedness (v 20). Yet, despite her wickedness, GII's insertion of v 21 proposes, the Lord continues to care for Israel and spares her. The hortatory address in Sir 17.25–32, calling for a return to YHWH, then, should be read as addressed to Israel, not human beings in general, at least from the viewpoint of GII." See *Wisdom's Root Revealed: Ben Sira and the Election of Israel*, JSJSup 139 (Leiden: Brill, 2009), 196–197.

61. Rodney Werline makes this point about the larger pattern well, though with more confidence in the notion of a single author than I have here argued. Werline, *Penitential Prayer in Second Temple Judaism: The Development of a Religious Institution*, SBLEJL 13 (Atlanta: Scholars Press, 1998), 85–86.

open to modifications, not always casual, but very often intentional, generally made by unknown authors."[62]

CONCLUSION

According to the sage's self-presentation, the discipline of prayer permits his central activities of teaching and learning in the pursuit of wisdom and his own observance of the commandments. This is evident in the first instance through his daily routine. Petition and confession of sins are understood to prime the pump of sapiential disclosure for the sage. Confession of sins and praise of the deity are two liturgical poles within the sage's daily prayer. Confession and praise are inculcated through both practice and teaching. Not only do they serve to decenter the sage, allowing him to identify an ideal on which to focus and orient action, but in small compass they articulate a larger pattern manifest in the production of the book itself, as a collection of learning aimed at training the next generation of sages. Yet it is in what lies between the prayer for confession and the act of praise, in terms of embodied action, that the life pursuit and transformation of the sage occurs. His account of confession and its effects constitute a reorientation of his consciousness. It permits a deeper meditation on both exoteric ("law of the Lord's covenant") and esoteric ("hidden things") divine teaching. The embodied wisdom that is textualized in Sirach is aimed at the cultivation of male sages and the training of their appetites. Certainly not all those who heard the teachings of Sirach were disposed or able to become learned scribes. Yet it seems clear that some who did emulate the pattern of Ben Sira would become scribes who transmit and augment the written corpus of Sirach. Once the sapiential self is honed and the acquisition of wisdom achieved, they too, like the God they fear and the sage they emulate, might draw from the great sea of wisdom and contribute to it as well by pouring forth their own wisdom in the form of augmentation. The formation of the scribal self through prayer is thus centrally implicated in

62. Gilbert, "Methodological and Hermeneutical Trends," 13. Cf. also the assessment of Jean-Sébastien Rey, who cautions against finding "the" Hebrew text of Ben Sira. He suggests another alternative : "Elle consiste à prendre en consideration l'ensemble des témoins pour eux même comme autant de variantes, de relectures, de recompositions du texte." See Rey, "La transmission des sentence proverbiales dans les différents témoins hébreux du livre du Siracide," in *Corpus anciens et bases de données,* ed. Marie-Sol Ortola, *Analyse linguistique et interculturelle des énoncés sapientiels et de leur transmission de l'Orient à l'Occident et de l'Occident à l'Orient* 2 (2012): 27–39, at 37.

the generation of sapiential wisdom, scribal teaching, and ultimately, the scribe's textual product that results from it.

The figure of Ben Sira, as a scribal sage, represents an important feature of the literary corpus and cultural life in the Greco-Roman period, particularly in its alignment between the Torah of Moses and the interpretive practices of the sage. But the wisdom tradition is not the only place where we can see the entwinement of prayer practices and the production of scripture. We turn now from the transmission of sapiential instruction to prophetic literature and its extension.

CHAPTER 2

⌘

Confessing in Exile

The Reception and Composition of Jeremiah in (Daniel) and Baruch

In Chapter 1, I argued that the scribal self in Ben Sira was shaped centrally by prayer. Confession and praise formed two compass points in the liturgical response of Ben Sira. Between the two, wisdom was received, and *paideia* was inculcated in the implied audience of the next generation of student sages. Yet there was not just one ideal scribal self delineated in Sirach. In this chapter, we shift our center of focus from the formation of the scribal self to the formation of text in relation to liturgical practice.

The development of prayer practices and the transmission and composition of scripture happened in tandem. By looking at the traditions associated with Daniel we can see that the very process of creating the texts is intertwined with those of the developing practices of prayer. The story of Daniel's gradual composition integrally involves issues of worship and the practice of prayer in early Judaism. I argue that the formation of the book of Daniel is narratively entangled with the formation of the prophetic book of Jeremiah and the lesser known "apocryphal" book of Baruch. These works are set in the diaspora during the exilic period. They are intertwined over the role of confessional prayer as a means of ending the post-exilic situation of diaspora.

How does the book of Jeremiah end? For many, the answer is clear. Contemporary biblical commentators end their own books with MT Jer 52, the "historical appendix" that describes Nebuchadnezzar's siege against

Jerusalem, the destruction of the Temple, and the exile of the king and population to Babylon. That episode would seem to bring to an end the story of the nation-state of Israel in the land. But in the Greco-Roman period, centuries before the Leningrad Codex had crystallized as the unquestionable basis of the Hebrew Bible, that "sense of an ending" was very much an open question.[1] While the nation-state may have ended, the covenant people endured. As communities tried to make sense of the institutional disruption and population dispersion first created by the exile, multiple works related to the narrative world of Jeremiah were composed and circulated. We know from the Qumran caves that the earliest manuscript evidence for the prophetic text of Jeremiah reveals texts in flux at least as late as the second century BCE. In addition to texts that correspond in some degree to the later MT Jeremiah and LXX Jeremiah, we find the so-called Apocryphon of Jeremiah texts, the *Epistle of Jeremiah* (found in Greek in 7Q), and the textual traditions in which Baruch plays a lead role, Baruch, 2 Baruch, 3 Baruch, and *Paraleipomena Ieremiou*.[2] The narrative setting of these works is in the critical era of the exile and its immediate aftermath. They deploy this narrative setting in order to reshape conceptions of that history and by doing so, to contest theological, social, and political issues in the present.

My focus in this chapter is on Daniel and Baruch, two texts engaging the Jeremiah tradition that emerged when the Jeremiah tradition was still fluid. Daniel and Baruch contain different views concerning prophecy, not to mention differing views of the diaspora population and its relation to Jerusalem. The practice of confessional prayer in relation to prophecy is the crux upon which we can most clearly see two contrasting perspectives on revelation and restoration. I would argue that "Baruch" was written in order to engage and extend a form of the text of Jeremiah, and to figure Baruch as the learned sage and liturgical maestro who institutes the practice of efficacious confession to bring about the return from exile. For Baruch, the institution of prophecy is dead; yet the oracular legacy of the prophet lives on. The scribal sage claims the mantle of leadership of Jewish communities both in diaspora and in Jerusalem through his role as authoritative interpreter of the Torah and Prophets. Implicitly, Baruch serves as a counter-discourse to such second-century texts as Daniel and ApocJeremiah C, in

---

1. My allusion is to Frank Kermode's well-known book, *The Sense of an Ending: Studies in the Theory of Fiction* (New York: Oxford University Press, 1967).

2. This is not to mention works in which the figure of Jeremiah emerges alongside interpretive motifs like the fate of the Temple implements in 2 Macc 1–8 or the isolated mention of a Jeremianic oracle in CD 8:20.

which angelic revelation and prophecy were considered to be a continuing means for discovering divine reality. This argument should not be entirely surprising in light of rabbinic claims to the cessation of prophecy in the Persian period, but I want to draw attention to the rhetorical means by which this extension of prophetic scripture is accomplished. The ongoing practice of confession and the integration of scripturalized confessions in evolving textual traditions were decisive factors in how the text of what we might call "Jeremiah-Baruch" was reshaped and claimed authority for itself as scripture in the era "before the Bible." In order to substantiate this argument, we will first consider the phenomenon of confessional prayer more generally before turning to a brief treatment of Daniel 9 and finally a more extended consideration of Baruch in relation to both Daniel and Jeremiah.

2.1 DANIEL AND BARUCH WITHIN THE CONTOURS AND PRACTICE OF CONFESSIONAL PRAYER

The prayers in Daniel 9:4–19 and Baruch 1:15–3:8 are part of a larger body of confessional prayers evident in the Persian and Greco-Roman eras.[3] The trauma of the Babylonian Exile played a crucial role in stimulating the development of a confessional prayer tradition in the Persian period. Such confessions, cast in the first person plural even when offered by an individual, are characterized by their extended and repeated confession of sin in the context of reviewing the history of Israel and including a petition for forgiveness.[4] Confessions can be contrasted with laments, for example, which do not admit culpability for the negative situation of the lamenter.

---

3. While the number and identification of confessional prayers included in the list varies, the following prayers are usually included: Ezra 9:5–15; Neh 1:4–11, 9:6–37; Dan 9:4–19; Bar 1:15–3:8; Prayer of Azariah; Tob 3:1–6; 3 Macc 2:1–10; 4Q393 (Communal Confession); and 4Q504 2 v-vi (Words of the Heavenly Lights). Related texts include Solomon's prayer of dedication at the Temple, 1 Kgs 8:22–53, and the later Prayer of Manasseh. Rodney Alan Werline was the first to offer a monograph-length treatment, *Penitential Prayer in Second Temple Judaism: The Development of a Religious Institution*, SBLEJL 13 (Atlanta: Scholars Press, 1998). For a concise summary of scholarship on confessional prayers, see Mark Boda, "Confession as Theological Expression," in *Seeking the Favor of God*, vol. 1, *The Origins of Penitential Prayer in Second Temple Judaism*, ed. Mark Boda, Daniel K. Falk, and Rodney A. Werline, SBLEJL 21 (Atlanta: SBL, 2006), 21–45. Cf. also Daniel Falk's clear exposition, "Scriptural Inspiration for Penitential Prayer," in *Seeking the Favor*, vol. 2, *Development of Penitential Prayer in Second Temple Judaism*, ed. Mark J. Boda and Rodney A. Werline, SBLEJL 22 (Atlanta: SBL, 2007).

4. I use the term "confessional prayer" rather than "penitential prayer" because I understand penitence as a process aimed at restoration or reconciliation that involves acts in addition to recitation of prayer. "Confessional prayer" thus can be understood potentially as a part of a larger penitential sequence of practices.

Early scholarship on confessional prayers in the Bible was informed by Claus Westermann's form-critical and theological assessment that laments were gradually displaced by confessional prayers as a result of the exilic experience and as an attempt to justify God's righteousness in that light.[5] A renewed phase of scholarship has focused in particular on the tradition-history of the confessional prayers of the post-exilic period, assessing, among other elements, their compositional use of scripture.[6] The prayers admit guilt for wrongdoing in a corporate confession and recognize divine righteousness for punishment, using in particular wording from Leviticus 26 and Deuteronomy 28 that was thought to ensure the reversal of the covenant curses of Deuteronomy. Most of the confessional prayers thus seek to put an end to negative conditions resulting from the exile, or implicitly in a later era to the situation of diaspora. Yet no confessional prayer, whether found as part of a narrative work or circulating separately like the Qumran liturgical prayers 4Q393 or 4Q504–506, is identical to another one.

Of the confessional prayers that populate the landscape of Jewish practice during the Greco-Roman era, the two prayers of Daniel and Baruch have been understood to have a particularly close relationship. They share elements of language.[7] Both are also related to the developing Jeremiah

5. Claus Westermann, "Struktur und Geschichte der Klage im Alten Testament," *Zeitschrift für die alttestamentliche Wissenschaft* 66 (1954): 44–80. On the scholarly genealogy of research into this topic, see the discussion of Samuel Balentine, "'I Was Ready to Be Sought Out by Those Who Did Not Ask,'" in *Seeking the Favor*, vol. 1, ed. Boda, Falk, and Werline, 1–20, at 2–10.

6. The initial work of Rodney Werline and Mark Boda stimulated the constitution of an SBL Penitential Prayer Group that resulted in the publication of *Seeking the Favor of God*, three volumes of collected essays on its origins and evolution. Vols. 1 and 2 are cited in note 3; vol. 3 is *The Impact of Penitential Prayer Beyond Second Temple Judaism*, ed. Mark J. Boda, Daniel K. Falk, and Rodney A. Werline, SBLEJL 23 (Atlanta: SBL, 2009).

7. While some commentators have understood the relationship as one of literary dependence, with Daniel serving as the model for Baruch (cf. Odil Steck, Reinhard Kratz, and Ingo Kottsieper, *Das Buch Baruch. Der Brief des Jeremie, Zusätze zu Ester und Daniel* [Göttingen: Vanderhoeck & Ruprecht, 1998], 39), others express less certainty. The suggestion that they both may have been independently adapted from an earlier work comes from Anthony Saldarini, "The Book of Baruch: Introduction, Commentary, and Reflections," *Introduction to Prophetic Literature, the Book of Isaiah, the Book of Jeremiah, the Book of Baruch, the Letter of Jeremiah, the Book of Lamentations, the Book of Ezekiel*, ed. Leander E. Keck, NIB 6 (Nashville, TN: Abingdon Press, 2001), 931; see also Carey A. Moore, *Daniel, Esther, Jeremiah: The Additions*, AB 44 (New York: Doubleday, 1977), 260. The answer to their inexact similarity is likely to be owing to the oral ingestion and transmission of texts, particularly related to prayer practice among elite literate scribes responsible for composing cultural texts. Scribes would rely on memory rather than exact replication of the cultural repertoire. Although there is not space in this chapter to explore their relationship in detail and the role of confession in the larger narrative of Daniel, Daniel serves as a pointed contrast to Baruch in contesting the efficacy of confession as I have discussed elsewhere.

tradition in their respective narrative contexts. Another common aspect is that although both works were compiled in the second century BCE, they are set in Babylon in the early years of the exile.[8] They are thus part of the cohort of compositions that suggest the notion of an "enduring exile," indicating a period of continuing distress even after the return of people to the land and the rebuilding of the Temple in 515 BCE.[9] This common narrative setting during the exile, moreover, sets them apart from the three confessional prayers of Ezra-Nehemiah, which are set after the return under the Persians.

Yet it is the *differences* between the prayers in Daniel and Baruch that are particularly revealing. The contents and the way in which the confessional prayers in Daniel and Baruch appear in their respective stories shape distinctive counternarratives, in no small part because of the way they relate to Jeremiah and his oracles. In the book of Daniel, Jeremiah appears only in the ninth chapter and Daniel's relationship to Jeremiah is external to the confession itself. Baruch weaves Jeremianic language into the composition of his confession. In this and in its narrative introduction, "Baruch" self-consciously links itself to the Jeremianic corpus.

2.2 DANIEL, JEREMIAH, AND THE ANGELIC ORACLE

To consider first the case of Daniel, the use of Jeremiah in Daniel 9 is both explicit and thematic. Daniel "perceives in the scrolls the number of years that, according to the word of the Lord to Jeremiah must be fulfilled for the devastation of Jerusalem: seventy years" (Dan 9:2). While this verse

---

8. The setting of the book as a whole (Daniel 1) is in the immediate aftermath of Nebuchadnezzar's destruction. The narrative setting of Daniel 9 is in the time of "Darius son of Ahasuerus," who should be understood as a fictitious character. See John J. Collins, *Daniel: A Commentary on the Book of Daniel*, Hermeneia (Minneapolis: Fortress, 1993), 348.

9. Ernest W. Nicholson noticed this (*Deuteronomy and Tradition* [Oxford: Blackwell, 1967]), but Michael A. Knibb was the first to discuss this phenomenon at length; "The Exile in the Intertestamental Period," *Heythrop Journal* 17 (1976): 253–272. Aside from Daniel 9, he considers 1 En 89–90, 1 En 93:1–10, 1 En 91:11–17, Ep Jer, Ass. Mos., Jub. 1:9–18, CD, Tob 14:4–7, 4 Ezra, and 2 Baruch. Cf. Donald E. Gowan, "The Exile in Jewish Apocalyptic," *Scripture in History and Theology: Essays in Honor of J. Coert Rylaarsdam*, ed. A. W. Merrill and T. W. Overholt, PTMS 17 (Pittsburgh, PA: Pickwick, 1977), 205–223. Of more recent vintage is James M. Scott, "Exile and Self-Understanding of Diaspora Jews in the Greco-Roman Period," in *Exile: Old Testament, Jewish and Christian Conceptions*, ed. J. M. Scott, JSJSup 56 (Leiden: Brill, 1997), 173–218. On the origins of the metaphorical conceptualization of the exile, see Martien Halvorson-Taylor, *Enduring Exile: The Metaphorization of Exile in the Hebrew Bible*, VTSup 141 (Leiden: Brill, 2010).

and the chapter as a whole have attracted inordinate attention because of the seventy-years prophecy, a small textual detail that often goes unremarked is the plural of *sepher*. This itself might be construed as a plurality of scrolls of Jeremianic prophecy.[10] Despite this mention of writings, the use of Jeremiah in Daniel does not derive from the *language* of Jeremiah beyond the seventy-years concept.[11] It is only on that basis that scholars have connected it to specific passages (Jer 25:11–12; Jer 29:10).[12] More significant from our perspective is the unfolding of the story in relation to prayer. After looking in the prophetic scrolls, Daniel turns to his ancestral God and seeks an answer through prayer and supplication accompanied by self-abasement of the body with fasting, sackcloth, and ashes.

The confession that Daniel then offers shows clear signs of being redacted into its current narrative context. Many have noted these seams.[13] Unlike the rest of Daniel, the prayer itself contains Deuteronomic and other

10. André LaCocque offers a different view: "C'est là un témoignage important de la canonisation progressive des livres qui formeront deux siècles plus tard la Bible hébraïque." *Le Livre de Daniel* (Neuchâtel: Delachaux et Niestlé, 1976), 134. Collins understands the reference to books to refer presumably to the corpus of "prophets" more broadly; *Daniel*, 348.

11. Knibb, "The Exile," 254. He admits one possible exception, that the word לְהָשִׁיב in Dan 9:25 is a reminiscence of Jer 29:10.

12. This stands in contrast to 2 Chr 36:19–21, which combines wording from Lev 26:34–35 and Jer 25:9–12. The lack of Jeremianic language also calls into question Michael Fishbane's references to "mantological exegesis" or even "divine exegesis" to refer to a presumed divine scrutiny of a finalized biblical text. Fishbane writes, "Prophetic words are no longer predominantly living speech, but rather inscribed and inscrutable data whose true meanings are an esoteric mystery revealed by God to a special adept and his pious circle"; *Biblical Interpretation in Ancient Israel* (Oxford: Clarendon, 1985), 484. The chapter in which Jassen treats Daniel is entitled "Revelatory Exegesis in Second Temple Literary Traditions"; *Mediating the Divine: Prophecy and Revelation in the Dead Sea Scrolls and Second Temple Judaism*, STDJ 68 (Leiden: Brill, 2007), 213–240. For his discussion of Daniel 9, see 214–221. On Fishbane's "mantological exegesis," see *Biblical Interpretation*, 487–495. For a critical assessment of Fishbane's use of this phrase, see Matthias Henze, "The Use of Scripture in the Book of Daniel," in *A Companion to Biblical Interpretation in Early Judaism*, ed. Matthias Henze (Grand Rapids, MI: Eerdmans, 2012), 279–307. Similarly problematic is Alex Jassen's characterization of the seventy-years prophecy interpretation in Daniel 9 as "revelatory exegesis." This is especially misleading in the second instance of Dan 9:24–27 in which he refers to "Gabriel's method" for discerning meaning "through careful exegesis of the prophetic scriptural writing." This implies a close and careful interpretation of scriptural wording when in fact Gabriel is simply described as being sent.

13. Dan 9:4b and the conclusion in Dan 9:21 duplicate the substance of 9:3 and 9:20. Sharon Pace, *Daniel* (Macon, GA: Smyth and Helwys, 2008), 288–289. This was noted already in the late nineteenth century by August F. von Gall, *Die Einheitlichkeit des Buches Daniel* (Giessen: Ricker, 1895), 123–126. Anathea Portier-Young views the seams as rhetorically purposeful, "as a stylistic device aiming to highlight Daniel's act of prayer"; *Apocalypse Against Empire: Theologies of Resistance in Early Judaism* (Grand Rapids, MI: Eerdmans, 2011), 250.

traditional phraseology composed in smooth Hebrew free of Aramaisms. Its distinctive character is apparent in that the divine name YHWH appears six times within the prayer as a mark of the traditional covenant relationship between God and Israel, while the tetragrammaton occurs nowhere else in the book outside of Daniel 9. Dan 9:7, 11, 20 are the only places in which "Israel" as a name for the people appears in the book. While there are linguistic links between the prayer and its context, these do not extend beyond Daniel 9, thus suggesting that this was part of an authorial tweaking process in order to situate and integrate the traditional prayer.[14]

While the prayer mentions the people of Judah (but does not refer to the northern region of Israel or Samaria) in Dan 9:7, the real concern as reflected in the historical prospect (Dan 9:4–14) and the petition (Dan 9:16–19) is on Jerusalem and restoring the sanctuary (Dan 9:7, 16, 17, 18, 19, 20). Another distinctive and related feature of this prayer and its petition is that the character of the Temple rises almost to that of personification. Daniel petitions God to "let your face shine upon your desolated sanctuary" (Dan 9:17b).[15] The use of wording from the priestly blessing of Num 6:24–26 is in itself not unique. This formula is regularly redeployed and adapted in prayers that request divine salvation (cf. Pss 31:16; 67:1; 80:3, 7, 19; 119:135) or blessing (1QS 2:2–4, 1QSb).[16] Yet God's beaming face and the divine blessing are elsewhere trained only on people, and nowhere else on the Jerusalem Temple itself.

Moreover, in relation to the narrative, the confessional content of the prayer is not what motivates the divine response. When the angel arrives on the scene, Gabriel tells Daniel that the divine *davar* was set in motion at the very beginning of his supplications (Dan 9:23) at the time of the evening sacrifice, establishing in this instance a temporal correlation with the Temple. This new revelation then unlocks the real meaning and explanation of the Jeremianic writings, with its extension of the time of exile to 490 years. In sum, Daniel's lesson is that prophetic texts such as Jeremiah require additional and mediated revelation to reveal their deeper meaning.

---

14. John Collins notes the following verbal correspondences between the prayer and its context: ליכשׂהל in vv. 13 and 22; forms of בוש and לכשׂ in vv. 13 and 25; a form of סמשׁ in v. 17 and 27 in connection with the temple, an oath העבשׁ in v. 11 is poured out ךתת, in verses 24 and 27 the same roots recur though in a different form; "supplications" תחונגים appears only in Daniel 9 in the prayer and framework (9:3, 17, 18, 23), and finally, the word for "sin" אטח appears in 9:20, 24, and only elsewhere in Dan 4:24; Collins, *Daniel*, 348.

15. The Old Greek reads here "holy mountain" for "sanctuary" and also "for the sake of your servants, Lord."

16. Fishbane, *Biblical Interpretation*, 329–334; Bilhah Nitzan, *Qumran Prayer and Religious Poetry*, trans. Jonathan Chipman, STDJ 12 (Leiden: Brill, 1994), 145–172.

Acts of prayer and abasement can spur such a response, but the confession itself will not effect the end of exile, nor alter the divine eschatological plan. Thus for Daniel, the "end of Jeremiah" lies not in the events of deportation but stretches far beyond that book's historical horizon.

2.3 CONFESSING WITH BARUCH IN BABYLON AND JERUSALEM

In conceiving the relationship between the prayer in Daniel 9, Baruch, Jeremiah, and other texts, it is also helpful to consider the cogent definition of "living tradition" offered by Alasdair Macintyre as "a historically extended, socially embodied argument, and an argument precisely in part about the goods which constitute the tradition."[17] Part of the "socially embodied argument" we can see in Baruch lies in the self-conscious construction of an ideal scribal sage and author of scripture, a role promoted at the expense of the active office of the prophet in relation to Judean communities both in the land and diaspora. The book of Baruch as it appears in modern Bibles comprises five chapters that are intent on shaping a view of a society and its future rather different from that of Daniel and his fellow *maskilim*. The narrative introduction (Bar 1:1–16) provides the frame for contextualizing the long prayer in 1:15–3:8, a poem extolling wisdom as Torah in 3:9–4:4 that resonates with Ben Sira 24 and Job 28, and a poem of consolation to and about Zion that anticipates the return from exile (4:5–5:9) in language drawn in part from 2 Isaiah.[18] There is no scholarly consensus on the date of Baruch's composition, though most settle for the Hellenistic period, with the second century BCE being a favored dating, thus making it roughly contemporaneous with the book of Daniel.[19]

---

17. Alasdair Macintyre, *After Virtue* (Notre Dame, IN: University of Notre Dame Press, 1981), 222.

18. The issue of the "unity" of Baruch will not concern us here. Some scholars view Baruch as the product of a single author (Jonathan A. Goldstein, Odil Steck). Others see it as a redacted compilation of constituent sources (Anthony Saldarini, Antonius H. J. Gunneweg, Carey Moore). I find the latter view more compelling. Steck's creative suggestion that the book relates to different parts of Jeremiah 29 is intriguing (Bar 1:15–3:8 to Jer 29:5–7; Bar 3:9–4:4 to Jer 29:8–9; Bar 4:5–5:9 to Jer 29:10–14 (*Das apokryphe Baruchbuch: Studien zur Rezeption und Konzentration "kanonischer" Überlieferung*, FRLANT 160 [Göttingen: Vandenhoeck & Ruprecht, 1993],10); however, the difficulty with it is that Jer 29 suggests that the return will happen only after seventy years, and Baruch depicts the end of exile as imminent (cf. Bar 4:25, 36–37; 5:4).

19. For a comprehensive treatment of scholarship on this issue over the past two hundred years, see David G. Burke, *The Poetry of Baruch: Reconstruction and Analysis of the Original Hebrew Text of Baruch 3:9–5:9*, SBLSCS 10 (Chico, CA: Scholars Press, 1982), 26–29.

While Daniel's use of Jeremiah is limited to a reference to his "books" and to the literal reference to the seventy-years prophecy that must be interpreted by the angelic mediator, Baruch's use of Jeremiah is pervasive, if cloaked and subtle. The relationship of Baruch to Jeremiah can be considered from three aspects. The first two relate to the intertextual relationship with Jeremianic language. The third is related to the manuscript tradition of Jeremiah and Baruch. Baruch's engagement with the Jeremianic tradition appears most clearly in the introduction (Bar 1:1–14) and in the second half of the prayer (Bar 2:19–3:8), which displays no overlap with the prayer in Daniel 9.

Contextualizing the Narrative Introduction of Baruch 1:1–14

The narrative introduction of Baruch presents the book as a whole as explicit teaching, with an emphasis on the written authority of the scroll and Baruch as its author. Baruch is connected with five generations of figures known in connection with their levitical origins and scribal culture.[20] The idea of written communication between the diaspora and Jerusalem is a motif familiar from Jeremiah's letter sent "from Jerusalem to the remaining elders among the exiles" (Jer 29:1–3/LXX 36:1–3). Yet, whereas Jeremiah's prophetic word goes from center to periphery, Baruch's instructive scroll moves in the opposite direction. Moreover, Baruch's work is longer than a letter and includes liturgical instruction for use at the Temple itself, advocating particular prayer practices of confession and ritual mourning. Baruch is said to have read "the words of this book" to Jeconiah, king of Judah, and to all the people in Babylon by the river Soud (Bar 1:3–4).[21]

20. Kipp Davis, "Prophets of Exile: 4Q *Apocryphon of Jeremiah C*, Apocryphal Baruch, and the Efficacy of the Second Temple," *Journal for the Study of Judaism* 2013: 497–529, at 502 n. 14. Cf. also the longer discussions of Moshe Weinfeld, *Deuteronomy and the Deuteronomic School* (Oxford: Clarendon Press, 1971), 244–319, and Leo G. Perdue, "Baruch Among the Sages," in *Uprooting and Planting: Essays on Jeremiah for Leslie Allen*, ed. John Goldingay, LHT/OTS 459 (Edinburgh: T. & T. Clark, 2007), 260–290, at 275–276.

21. It is now clear from the history of traditions parallel in 4QApocrJer C^d (4Q389 1 7) that the Greek Σουδ (1:4) is a misspelling of the Hebrew סור owing to the common confusion between the Hebrew letters *resh* and *dalet*. See Lutz Doering, *Ancient Jewish Letters and the Beginning of Christian Epistolography*, WUNT 298 (Tübingen: Mohr Siebeck, 2012), 159. This was originally proposed in an unpublished paper presented at the IOQS 1992 by Devorah Dimant, "The Apocryphon of Jeremiah," 20 n. 18 (the published version did not discuss 4Q389a); as cited in George Brooke, "Parabiblical Prophetic Narratives," in *The Dead Sea Scrolls After Fifty Years: A Comprehensive Assessment*, vol. 1, ed. J. VanderKam and P. W. Flint (Leiden: Brill, 1998–1999), 271–301, at 283 n. 53.

He then sends the scroll to the high priest and people in Jerusalem with instructions to pray for Nebuchadnezzar (1:11) and to pray for the exiles (1:13). Baruch introduces the prayer by designating the time and place for its recitation as well as making it a communal obligation: "And you shall read aloud this book that we are sending you to make your confession in the house of the Lord on the days of the festivals and at appointed times" (1:14).

The introduction to Baruch shows connections not only to Jeremiah but also to the so-called 4Q ApocrJer C manuscripts, particularly 4QApocrJer C^d (4Q389 1).[22] Indeed, the unique appearance of the "river Sour" in both texts ties them together through tradition-history.[23] There is not space to detail the possible interconnections among these manuscripts.[24] Devorah Dimant has recently argued that there are similarities in three details between Baruch 1:1–4 and 4Q389 1: (1) there is a gathering where something is read in public, (2) attendees are Israelites living on the river Sour, and (3) the date of the assembly is recorded. On that basis, she concludes, "it may be assumed plausibly that Baruch was also involved in the episode related in the *Apocryphon of Jeremiah C, although his name is not preserved*" (emphasis mine).[25] I would argue the reverse.[26] The differences between them suggest they are not part of a harmonious whole. The date of the

---

22. For the editio princeps, see Devorah Dimant, *Qumran Cave 4.XXI: Parabiblical Texts, Part 4: Pseudo-Prophetic Texts*, DJD 30 (Oxford: Clarendon Press, 2001), 91–260. The manuscripts do not contain any overlap with each other, thus raising the question of whether they are one work or not.

23. The Greek translator's confusion of the Hebrew *resh* with *dalet* is evident in the Septuagint's rendering of this elsewhere unmentioned river as "Soud" (Bar 1:4); Devorah Dimant, "From the Book of Jeremiah to the Qumranic *Apocryphon of Jeremiah*," *Dead Sea Discoveries* 20 (2013): 452–471, at 465. As Dimant points out, following Steck, the Syriac Peshitta reflects knowledge of the form "Sour," thus supporting the idea that the Syriac knew the Hebrew recension of Baruch (465 n. 56).

24. Cf. Lutz Doering, "Jeremia in Babylonien und Ägypten: Mündliche und schriftliche Toraparänese für Exil und Diaspora nach 4QApocryphon of Jeremiah C," in *Frühjudentum und Neues Testament im Horizont Biblischer Theologie: Mit einem Anhang zum Corpus Judaeo-Hellenisticum Novi Testamenti*, ed. W. Kraus and K. W. Niebuhr (Tübingen: Mohr Siebeck, 2003), 50–79. Cf., most recently, Dimant, "From the Book of Jeremiah"; Davis, "Prophets of Exile." Davis also thinks *Jeremiah Apocryphon C* "shows a striking similarity" with the prologue of Baruch (502), but he ignores the salient fact that Jeremiah is never mentioned in Baruch!

25. Dimant, "From the Book of Jeremiah," 468.

26. See as well the argument of Kipp Davis suggesting that Egypt and Babylon within the 4Q Apocryphon of Jeremiah C materials represent two different symbolic geographic places with correspondingly different perspectives on the presumed unfolding of the 490-year scheme: "Torah-Performance and History in the *Golah*: Rewritten Bible or 'Re-presentational' Authority in the *Apocryphon of Jeremiah C*," in *Celebrating the Dead Sea Scrolls: A Canadian Collection*, ed. P. Flint, J. Duhaime, and K. Baek, EJL 30 (Atlanta: SBL Press, 2011), 467–495.

assembly is different in the two: 4Q389 1 is set in the thirty-sixth year of exile (531 BCE), whereas Baruch is set in the fifth year after the destruction (586 BCE). Another difference that is left unaddressed is the role of Baruch and Jeremiah in each. Given the fact that Jeremiah is never mentioned in the text of Baruch, and Baruch does not appear in the extant ApocrJer C manuscripts, a more cogent argument is that the text (or texts) were written as counternarratives in order to isolate and distinguish the activities of the scribe from those of the prophet. For example, 4Q385ᵃ depicts Jeremiah as refusing to intercede on the people's behalf, but lamenting instead, and actively working as a prophet pronouncing oracles concerning idolatry to the exiles in Egypt. This stands in contrast to Baruch, who is centrally concerned with intercessory prayer, even instructing the population in Jerusalem to pray for the exiles (Bar 1:13).[27] The distinctive characterization of Baruch and Jeremiah can be further substantiated by looking at the confessional prayer.

The Distinctiveness of Baruch 1:15–3:8

Like Daniel and all other confessional prayers, Bar 1:15–3:8 is thickly allusive to scripture. The prayer itself begins as the explicit instruction from Baruch about the appropriate words to say, starting with an acknowledgment of divine righteousness and the guilt of the inhabitants of Judah and Jerusalem (1:15–2:10). The second part (2:11–19) is signaled by the transitional "and now" (*we-atah*), a common feature of confessional prayers. It acknowledges divine power in the Exodus and offers a threefold confession (2:12; cf. 1 Kgs 8:47) and a petition for deliverance from the situation of exile. The third part of the prayer (2:20–35) recalls divine oracles that have been fulfilled in the process of the exile and destruction of the Temple. The final part of the prayer (3:1–8) shifts rhetorically to give voice to the current generation, the descendants of those who have gone into exile.[28]

---

27. For later texts that put Jeremiah in Babylon, see Paraleipomena Jer 4:5, Apoc of Baruch 10:33, Seder Olam 26, and JTSanhedrin 1:19a.

28. Moore argued for four different parts to the prayer, each of which may have constituted an independent prayer (Bar 1:15–2:5; 2:6–10; 2:11–35; 3:1–8), and each with its own distinctive geographical setting; *Daniel: Additions*, 291–294. Such over-specification has received rightful criticism on form-critical grounds. See the discussion by Odil Steck, who argues for the coherence of the prayer as a piece, *Das apokryphe Baruchbuch*, 93–94.

Though innocent, they nonetheless must confess the sins of their ancestors.[29]

Scholars have long recognized the verbal parallels between the prayers in Daniel 9:4–20 and Baruch 1:14–3:8. Odil Steck is representative in assuming that Baruch was dependent on Daniel 9, and his dating of Baruch to the time of the high priest Alcimus thus hinges on the twin assumptions of a Maccabean date for the final form of MT Daniel and of Baruch's direct literary dependence on Daniel 9.[30] Yet the manuscript evidence from Qumran relating to Daniel 9 that might support this argument, published after Steck wrote his commentary, is ambiguous.[31] Even many scholars who do not date the work so precisely assume this unilateral dependence in order to figure relative dating.[32] Even in the overlapping sections, however, variations that reflect adaptation of a possible shared source reveal their distinctive rhetorical strategies. A close comparison of the two reveals that the common phrases are almost always adapted and amplified, but both Daniel and Baruch show such amplifications and deletions.[33] To take just one example:

Pray also for us to the Lord our God, for we have sinned against the Lord our God, and to this day the anger of the Lord and his wrath have not turned away from us. (Bar 2:13)

O Lord, in view of all your righteous acts, let your anger and wrath, we pray, turn away from your city Jerusalem, your holy mountain; because of our sins and the

29. The ancestors are mentioned three times in this section (Bar 3:5, 7, 8). Michael D. Matlock, *Rediscovering the Traditions of Prose Prayers in Early Jewish Literature*, LSTS 81 (New York: Bloomsbury, 2012), 109–110.

30. Steck, *Das apokryphe Baruchbuch*, 88–92.

31. Eight extant manuscripts have been identified with the canonical book of Daniel. 4Q116 is the only manuscript that suggests any overlap with the prayer of Daniel 9. It is written in a cruder script than other manuscripts relating to Daniel. Its much smaller size than the other manuscripts (8 cm) seems to suggest it may have circulated independently, perhaps as a private copy. Eugene Ulrich, who edited the Daniel scrolls, allows for the manuscript as either an excerpt from Daniel or a prayer that was used as the source for Daniel 9: "The early date of the scroll makes one wonder whether it is a copy derived from the full Book of Daniel or rather a copy of an originally separate prayer which was then incorporated into chapter 9." "The Text of Daniel in the Qumran Scrolls," in *The Book of Daniel: Composition and Reception*, vol. 2, ed. John J. Collins, Peter W. Flint, and Cameron VanEpps (Leiden: Koninklijke Brill NV, 2001) 582. See also the brief discussion in Collins, *Daniel*, 347–348.

32. Matlock, *Rediscovering the Traditions of Prose Prayers*, 51; Edward J. Wright, *Baruch Ben Neriah: From Biblical Scribe to Apocalyptic Seer* (Columbia: University of South Carolina Press, 2003), 52, 142; Rodney A. Werline, *Penitential Prayer*, 65–108; Bernard N. Wambacq, "Les prières de Baruch (I 15–ii 19) et de Daniel (ix 5–19)," *Biblica* 40 (1959): 463–475.

33. See the systematic treatment of André Kabasele Mukenge, *L'unité littéraire du livre de Baruch*, EB 38 (Paris: Librairie Gabalda, 1998), 176–202.

iniquities of our ancestors, Jerusalem and your people have become a disgrace among all our neighbors. (Dan 9:16)

The ideas and wording are quite similar at points, but even where similar wording occurs in a given verse, it occurs in different formulations. The comparison in this case reveals Daniel's special concern with the sanctity of Jerusalem, which we have already discussed. Moreover, in some of the presumed parallel passages, Daniel resembles other confessional prayers or scriptural wording more closely than Baruch's phraseology.[34] In the end, it is impossible to determine clear literary dependence in either direction.[35]

Aside from the question of the relative direction of intertextuality, some scholars have taken the use of earlier texts more broadly in the book as a sign of the composer's lack of creativity, such as Carey Moore's evaluation: "A mosaic of older biblical passages, I Baruch has virtually no new or original religious ideas."[36] His negative assessment about the prayer's content ignores the way in which it serves to characterize the figure of Baruch as a learned sage. Baruch is depicted as a liturgical teacher who has mastery over the corpus of Torah and Prophets such that he can compose a textually dense confessional prayer that is appropriate to the situation. Like a jazz musician whose ability to improvise on melodies, harmonies, or time signatures reveals his skill, so too the unique character of scripturalization in Baruch's prayer depicts him as consummately knowledgeable about the scriptural repertoire such that he can adapt and interpret it. Baruch thus embodies the living tradition.

In any case, the parallels between the two prayers do not extend beyond Baruch 2:19. Their respective petitions are almost entirely different (Dan 9:16–19; Bar 2:11–3:8). The influence of Jeremiah is apparent most clearly in the petition of the prayer.

34. The great majority have considered Baruch to be literarily dependent on Daniel. For a concise discussion of the issues related to literary dependence in one direction or another or common source, see Moore, *Additions*, 291–293. A more recent evaluation of scholarship can be found in Kabasele Mukenge, *L'unité littéraire*, 160–175. A minority of scholars have considered the two as both dependent on a common written source. See the discussion in J. T. Marshall, "The Book of Baruch," *Hastings' Dictionary of the Bible*, I:251–254.

35. Some scholars express more doubt about tracing dependence. Anthony Saldarini suggests that both the prayers of Daniel 9 and Baruch may be dependent on an earlier work; "Book of Baruch," 931.

36. Moore, *Additions*, 259.

Baruch's Prayer and the Reception of Jeremiah

A unique feature of Baruch's prayer, absent from all other confessional prayers, is that it contains four citation formulas that include language introducing Mosaic or prophetic oracles, in Bar 2:2–3, 2:20–23, 2:24b, and 2:29–35.[37] Two reflect indirect discourse (Bar 2:2–3, 2:24b); two offer quotes of "divine speech" (Bar 2:20–23, 2:29–35). As we have mentioned, the issue of the continuity of prophecy in the Greco-Roman period was clearly a contested one in the centuries leading up to the turn of the Common Era.[38] For those who trusted only in the prophets of old, the discernment of oracles and their fulfillment was crucial in making the prophecy continue to bear fruit.[39] According to the Deuteronomic perspective, the assurance of true prophecy was found only ultimately in their fulfillment. The one who recognizes and pronounces such fulfillment, it would thus seem, is boosted in authoritative status.[40]

The way in which the prayer composed by Baruch both discerns the fulfillment of prophetic oracles and creates its own, while never naming the great prophet, thus reveals some rhetorical verve. The first oracle in Bar 2:20–23 is introduced as divine speech declared "by your servants the prophets" and introduced by the divine oracle formula "Thus says the

37. André Kabasele Mukenge, "Les citations interne en *Ba.* 1, 15–3, 8. Un procédé rédactionnel et actualisant," *Le Muséon* 108 (1995): 211–237, at 212.

38. In the Qumran scrolls, the fact that there was legislation against false prophecy (CD 6:1–2) and they kept a list of false prophets (4Q389) suggests the issue was quite a live one. As George Brooke has observed: "[Thus] the compositions that speak of false prophets strongly suggest the view that it was still possible to operate as a true prophet"; "Prophecy and Prophets in the Dead Sea Scrolls: Looking Backwards and Forwards," in *Prophets, Prophecy, and Prophetic Texts in the Dead Sea Scrolls*, ed. M. H. Floyd and R. D. Haak, LHB/OTS 427 (New York: T. & T. Clark, 2006), 151–165, at 159. Among other texts, he discusses 4Q375 1 I: 4, 6; CD 6:1–2, 1QH^a 12:16, and portions of the Temple Scroll. This can be seen in polemic about certain kinds of revelation and its mediators. Ben Sira famously expresses his mistrust of dreams (Sir 34:1–7; cf. Jer 29:8). In effect, for Ben Sira and his kind, the only good prophet was a dead prophet, to be honored and engaged for his written legacy. The role of scholars and worthies in the present was to interpret the collection of oracles accurately from the past, waiting for them to be realized (Sir 39:1–2).

39. As we will detail in the next chapter, Ben Sira exemplifies the sage who is concerned with prophecies and their interpretation (Sir 39:2). Sirach includes a petition about prophetic fulfillment in his own long confessional prayer: "Bear witness to those whom you created in the beginning and fulfill the prophecies spoken in your name. Reward those who wait for you and let your prophets be found trustworthy" (Sir 36:20b–21; cf. Tobit 14:4–5).

40. On the respective roles of Ben Sira as a *hakham* and Daniel's "apocalyptic scribalism" as constituting two rival discourses for claiming knowledge, see Carol A. Newsom, *The Self as Symbolic Space: Constructing Identity and Community at Qumran*, STDJ 52 (Leiden: Brill, 2004), 39–50.

Lord." The oracle calls on the exiles to serve the king of Babylon in language that recalls Jer 27:12 (LXX Jer 34:12). It includes a near-citation of first-person divine speech from Jeremiah's Temple sermon (Bar 2:23//Jer 7:34). The prayer affirms that the oracle has been fulfilled in its devastation of Jerusalem and the desolation of the land in its entirety. As Reinhard Kratz characterizes the importance of this first oracle: "Diese hier zitierte Ankündigung ist nichts weniger als der Boden auf dem die Verfasserschaft von Bar steht, denkt, und Israel lehrt. Sie bildet aber in jeder Hinsicht auch schon die Grundlage für das unmittlebar Folgende."[41] And what follows is another oracle.

The second oracle is in Bar 2:29–35:

> And you have done to us, O Lord, our God, according to all your fairness and according to all your great compassion as you spoke by the hand of your servant Moyses in the day where you commanded him to write your law before the sons of Israel, saying, "If you do not obey my voice, surely this great, voluminous buzzing will turn into a small one among the nations, there where I will scatter them. For I knew that they would not obey me, because the people are stiff-necked. And they will return to their heart in the land of their exile, and they will know that I am the Lord their God. And I will give them a heart and hearing ears, and they will praise me in the land of their exile, and they will remember my name, and they will turn away from their hard back and from their wicked deeds, because they will remember the way of their fathers who sinned before the Lord. And I will return them to the land, which I swore to their fathers, to Abraam and to Isaak and to Iakob, and they will rule over it, and I will multiply them, and they will not diminish. I will establish with them an everlasting covenant, that I be god to them and they be a people to me, and I will not disturb again my people Israel from the land that I have given them.[42]

The oracle is identified specifically as part of the Mosaic Torah, but significantly, in recalling the divine command to Moses to write the law in the presence of the Israelites, the passage summons the Deuteronomic *recasting* of the law (cf. Deut 27:3, 8) rather than the gift of the law in Exodus in which Moses is alone with God on Sinai when he writes on the tablets (Exod 34:27–28). This emphasis on writing is not incidental; this serves to enhance Baruch, the writer, as Mosaic heir. The oracle recognizes the

---

41. Steck, Kratz, and Kottsieper, *Das Buch Baruch*, 43–44.
42. All English citations from Baruch are from Albert Pietersma and Benjamin G. Wright, *A New English Translation of the Septuagint* (New York: Oxford University Press, 2007).

fulfillment of the prophecy of destruction related to disobedience concerning the Mosaic law (Bar 2:29), and it includes wording from oracles of hope that foresee the repentance of the people in exile, the end of the diaspora, and the creation of an everlasting covenant (Jer 32:40/LXX 39:40) with the promise that the people will remain in the land forever. The inclusion of these two "prophetic" oracles in the prayer is important rhetorically in relation to the status of Baruch. As the exilic leader cast as the author of the prayer, Baruch is the one understood as identifying and discerning both the prophetic oracles that have been fulfilled and those still imminently awaiting fulfillment. At the same time, the wording of these oracular prophecies represents a creative conflation of authoritative language, both from the "prophets"—again, Jeremiah is not mentioned—and from the prophecy of Mosaic Torah. "Baruch" is thus also writing his own prophetic oracles!

The final section of Baruch's prayer (Bar 3:1–8) shifts focus to the current generation.[43] It requests forgiveness for the sins of the ancestors, mentioned three times in the section (Bar 3:5, 7, 8).[44] The claim is that God has transformed the current generation, which is free of sin:

> Do not remember the injustices of our ancestors; rather, remember your hand and your name in this season. For you are the Lord, our God, and we will praise you, O Lord. For because of this you have given your fear in our heart in order that we call upon your name, and we will praise you in our exile, for we have put away from our heart all the injustice of our fathers who sinned before you. Look, we are today in our exile, there where you have scattered us for a reproach and for a curse and for a penalty according to all the injustices of our fathers who departed from the Lord our God.

The final two verses of the confession are significant for two reasons. While they are not framed as a prophetic oracle, they signal a fulfillment of a prophecy from Jer 32:40 (LXX 39:40) in which a new covenant brings with it the promise that God would put the fear of him in their hearts. Yet that

---

43. Moore argued for four different parts to the prayer, each of which may have constituted an independent prayer (Bar 1:15–2:5; 2:6–10; 2:11–35; 3:1–8), each with its own distinctive geographical setting; *Additions*, 291–294. Such overspecification has received rightful criticism on form-critical grounds. Cf. the discussion by Steck, who argues for the coherence of the prayer as a piece; *Das apokryphe Baruchbuch*, 93–94. Bar 3:1–8 is the least cohesive part of the prayer both because of the shift to the current generation and the fact that God is here alone in Baruch addressed as Almighty (παντοκράτωρ).

44. Matlock, *Rediscovering the Traditions of Prose Prayers*, 109–110.

oracle is also interpreted. In Jer 32:40, God states, "I will put the fear of me in their hearts so they will not turn from me." The covenant is also interpreted in such a way that the internalized fear of God is the factor that permits them to invoke God in prayer.[45] The very ability to confess sins thus reflects the fulfillment of a Jeremianic prophecy. Bar 3:7 explicitly describes the purpose of the transformational fear as the ability to pray and offer praise. The oracle as rewritten by Baruch with its interpretive explanation also proclaims its fulfillment through the very prayer that Baruch, the scribe, has composed for the people to pray. What is more, in this confessional prayer Baruch has effaced the name of his great master. The close of the prayer thus serves a central rhetorical aim of the book as a whole: to elevate the status of Baruch as an interpreter of Torah and the Prophets par excellence, at the expense of the role of the active prophetic office.[46]

To summarize the characterization of Baruch: he is a creative and innovative composer of confessional prayer. Such a scripturalized prayer depicts the one who composes it as a learned adept, one who knows scripture so well that he can produce this kind of piece. It is not prayer that has been learned by rote. Whereas Daniel models through his prayer an exemplary ideal that his audience might achieve, Baruch becomes an explicit liturgical maestro who teaches not only his community in Babylon but also his compatriots in Jerusalem—implicitly, even the Temple establishment—how to pray. In doing so, Baruch also provides an etiology of confessional prayer practice. This was the "first" such confession offered, five years into the exile (Bar 1:2), as a means for bringing an end to the exile and for reconstituting the people both in Babylon and Judah.

Unlike Daniel's confessional prayer and acts of bodily affliction, which are portrayed as a spontaneous response to his inquiry into Jeremiah's

---

45. The connection between seeking God in exile and the ability to pray is found also in the Words of the Heavenly Luminaries:

> You have remembered Your covenant whereby You brought us forth from Egypt while the nations looked on. You have not abandoned us among the nations; rather, You have shown covenant mercies to Your people Israel in all [the] lands to which You have exiled them. You have again placed it on their hearts to return to You, to obey Your voice [according] to all that You have commanded through Your servant Moses. [In]deed, You have poured out Your holy spirit upon us, [br]inging Your blessings to us. **You have caused us to seek You in our time of tribulation, [that we might po]ur out a prayer when** Your chastening was upon us . . . (4Q504 [4QDibHam-a] 18:10–18).

Targum Jonathan to Jer 32:40 reflects a similar reading that the "fear in the heart" enables prayer or worship.

46. And for that matter, the sacrificial role of the priests, which is never mentioned in Baruch.

writings, the prayer in Baruch reaches beyond the narrative itself, to claim a normative and regular ritual status in the lives of Jewish communities in Babylon and the land. Finally, as author of this prayer, Baruch is not simply scribe and tradent, but also creative author of prophetic oracles as part of prayer. Baruch thus implicitly subverts the role and function of Jeremiah, leaving for dead the ancestral prophet, but leaving alive and powerful in both Judea and the diaspora context of Babylon the authoritative figure of a sage and heir not simply of Jeremiah but also of Moses. This liturgical maestro implicitly wears the mantle of kings David (1 Chr 29, 11QPs^a 27) and Solomon (1 Kgs 8) as well, making him a figure who determines the circumstances and timing of prayer at the Temple.

Becoming Jeremiah: The Ritualization of Baruch and the Composition of Jeremiah

To return to our initial question, "How does the book of Jeremiah end?," for some in the Greco-Roman period it ended with Baruch's writing. We have traced the internal rhetorical factors involved in Baruch's compositional use of Jeremiah and its extension through a narrative set in the early exilic period and the composition of a confessional prayer infused with creative oracular fulfilment. In Bar 1:14 he issues the liturgical directive: "And you shall read aloud this scroll that we are sending you, to make your confession in the house of the Lord on the days of the festivals and at appointed seasons." A rhetorical sleight of hand is thereby lodged in this text. When performed as directed in and by the narrative, the prayer and indeed the entire book gain authority as scripture alongside and through the agency of its pseudonymous scribal author. This amounts to what the anthropologist Catherine Bell has referred to as the "textualization of ritual" and the simultaneous "ritualization of text."[47]

Moreover, there is also evidence external to Baruch that connects it to the developing text of Jeremiah. The transmission of Baruch's tricky book cannot be severed from the transmission of the writing(s) of Jeremiah. While scholars have debated the unity of Baruch, there is nonetheless a consensus that the narrative introduction and the prayer were composed in

---

47. Catherine Bell, "The Ritualization of Text and the Textualization of Ritual in the Codification of Taoist Liturgy," *History of Religions* 27, no. 4 (1988): 366–392. She also discussed the concept in her signal *Ritual Theory, Ritual Practice* (New York: Oxford University Press, 2009).

Hebrew.[48] Henry St. John Thackeray was the first to make the argument for a Hebrew form of Jeremiah that was appended by the book of Baruch.[49] He argued that there were two translators of Jeremiah into Greek, one responsible for Jer 1:1–29:8, the second for the rest of Jeremiah (LXX).[50] Based on the manuscript evidence from Qumran, Eugene Ulrich and Emmanuel Tov have argued for the existence of two "editions" of Jeremiah in the Greco-Roman period, one resembling the wording and order of the MT, the other closer to the Septuagint version of Jeremiah.[51] He has also argued, following Thackeray but with his own philological logic, that the second translator of Jeremiah revised the translation toward the Hebrew.[52] While there has been some criticism of Tov's criteria and argument for a revision, his argument for a Hebrew *Vorlage* of the Old Greek translation of Jeremiah that included Bar 1:1–3:8 is cogent and has been broadly accepted.[53]

48. J. J. Kneucker includes a retroverted Hebrew translation along with commentary in *Das Buch Baruch* (Leipzig: Brackhaus, 1879). Cf. also the remarks of Henry St. John Thackeray, *The Septuagint and Jewish Worship: A Study of Origins, The Schweich Lectures 1920* (London: British Academy, 1921), 86, who also points to marginal notes on Baruch in Origen's Syro-Hexaplar that state "not in the Hebrew" and which have been ignored or explained away by subsequent scholars. Emanuel Tov, *The Book of Baruch* (Missoula, MT: Scholars Press, 1975).

49. Thackeray, *The Septuagint and Jewish Worship*, 28–36.

50. Thackeray used the marked shift in distribution of the prophetic formula "thus says the Lord" as a decisive factor, though there were other lexical discrepancies used as well. The first translator used "τάδε λέγει κύριος" while the second translator favored the formula "οὕτως εἶπεν κύριος"; *The Septuagint and Jewish Worship*, 30–31. "That translator β was the weaker scholar of the two appears from some curious examples of what may be called 'imitation Hebrew' or the employment of words or phrases of which the only link with the Hebrew is a resemblance in sound, while they entirely fail to reproduce the sense"; *The Septuagint and Jewish Worship*, 32. Georg Fischer has made the argument for a single Greek translator; Fischer and A. Vonach, "Tendencies in the LXX Version of Jeremiah," in *Der Prophet wie Mose: Studien zum Jeremiabuch* (Wiesbaden: Harrassowitz, 2011), 64–72, at 71. Consider also the comment of Albert Pietersma: "Slowly but surely the conclusion is being forced upon me that the Greek translation of Jeremiah is the most complex book in the biblical Greek corpus." "Jeremiah and the Land of Azazel," in *Studies in the Hebrew Bible, Qumran, and Septuagint: Presented to Eugene Ulrich*, ed. Peter Flint, Emanuel Tov, and James VanderKam, VTSup 101 (Leiden: Brill, 2006), 403–413, at 403.

51. Emanuel Tov, *Textual Criticism of the Hebrew Bible, Qumran, Septuagint* (Minneapolis, MN: Fortress, 2012), 141–142.

52. This was the work of Tov's Harvard dissertation, *The Septuagint Translation of Jeremiah and Baruch: A Discussion of an Early Revision of the LXX of Jeremiah 29–52 and Baruch 1:1–3:8*, HSM 8 (Missoula, MT: Scholars Press, 1976), especially 111–133.

53. For a critique of Tov's theory concerning the revision toward a Hebrew text, see Hermann-Josef Stipp, "Offene Fragen zu Übersetzungskritik des antiken griechischen Jeremiabuches," *Journal of Northwest Semitic Languages* 17 (1991): 117–128. Cf. also Albert Pietersma, "From Greek Isaiah to Greek Jeremiah," in *Isaiah in Context: Studies in Honour of Arie van der Kooij on the Occasion of His Sixty-Fifth Birthday*, ed. Michaël van der Meer et al., VTSup 138 (Leiden: Brill, 2010), 359–387. Pietersma offers a critique of Tov's method in that he pays attention only to the differences and similarities

Pierre-Maurice Bogaert has also discussed the role of Baruch in the Septuagint ordering of Jeremiah. Jeremiah's prophecy to Baruch comes near the end of the collection in the Septuagint (LXX 51:32–35 = MT 45:1–5). Bogaert and others have interpreted this sequence as a kind of commissioning of Baruch as Jeremiah's prophetic successor.[54] If we can assume a compilation of Jeremiah already in the Greco-Roman period that resembles the Septuagint ordering and that Baruch was included in this sequence, then Jer 51 LXX served as a transitional chapter to connect the Jeremiah tradition to the natural successor of Jeremiah, Baruch. Baruch in his own book is thus implicitly writing as an extension of the Jeremiah legacy, and would in fact be considered as such by many early tradents, at least in Christian circles. What we now consider "Baruch" was consistently cited as part of Jeremiah in the Latin Church Fathers at least through the eighth century.[55] Thus Baruch "himself" in effect writes new scripture. Moreover, this scripture is considered both prophecy *and liturgy* through its inclusion of prayer, whether this work was ever performed as instructed or not.

CONCLUSION

The Talmud distinguishes two types of men who preserve tradition. The first is one who has learned by rote and can recite from memory the texts of all preserved tradition, thus making him effectively an "oral book." The second kind is one who not only receives what is handed down, with its inherent contradictions, but creates with this something new. According to

between the two "bi-sections" and does not pay attention to the differences and similarities within each section. He thus presupposes his bi-section, and that forces data without a sufficient control (362).

54. Pierre-Maurice Bogaert, "Le personage de Baruch et l'histoire du livre de Jérémie: Aux origines du livre deutérocanonique de Baruch," in *International Congress on New Testament Studies*, ed. Elizabeth A. Livingstone (Berlin: Akademie, 1982), 73–81; Martin Kessler, "Jeremiah Chapters 26–45 Reconsidered," *Journal of Near Eastern Studies* 27 (1968): 81–88, at 86; Jack R. Lundbom, "Baruch, Seraiah, and Expanded Colophons in the Book of Jeremiah," *Journal for the Study of the Old Testament* 36 (1986): 89–114, at 100–101.

55. Pierre-Maurice Bogaert, "Le Nom de Baruch dans la littérature pseudépigraphique: l'apocalypse syriaque et le livre deutérocanonique," in *La littérature juive entre Tenach et Mischna: quelques problèmes*, ed. Willem C. van Unnik (Leiden: Brill, 1974), 56–72, at 63. The citation of Bar 3:9–38 was particularly frequent in sacramentaries because it was used in the Roman liturgy on the Saturday before Pentecost and as part of the Easter Vigil. The Greek Church Fathers offer a more complicated picture (64–66). The *Apostolic Constitutions* 5:20 offers evidence that Baruch (named as such) was part of Jewish liturgy, perhaps as part of the Ninth of Av service; see the discussion in Thackeray, *The Septuagint and Jewish Worship*, 107–109.

Gershom Scholem, the "truly learned man is the one who is bound to tradition through his inquiries."[56] We can understand the depictions of both Daniel and Baruch as truly learned men, those who know and create for the present while inquiring of the past and wrestling from it a new word. We have considered the way in which they engage the Jeremianic tradition nonetheless, in quite different ways that reflect and create their own intramural tension.

The appearance of the confession in the book of Daniel articulates one side of this intra-Judean debate. Here, using the "goods" of the tradition, the book contests the very efficacy of the practice of corporate confession. The posture of prayer and humble gestures are in fact potent, but not for ensuring the end of the exile nor the ingathering of the people from the diaspora. Daniel's quest for understanding through Jeremiah's writings and humble prayer posture prompts an angelic revelation. Since the petition does not mention a return of the population but focuses on the purification of the Temple in Jerusalem, it would seem to be at peace with a continuing diaspora so long as access to a restored cult is maintained. The confession of sin cannot change the providential plan of God, which works according to its own logic. Divine time and the ultimate restoration of the Temple and Jerusalem after their desolation remain a mystery sealed in the book even at the end of Daniel—in need, perhaps, of further angelic elucidation. In Daniel, Jeremiah appears as the locus of ancestral tradition enshrined as a textual product. Yet we learn that sola scriptura is insufficient without the aid of additional angelic interpretation spurred by prayer and acts of self-abasement. The role of Jeremiah in Daniel 9 is thus strikingly different from the way it is used in Baruch. The prayer itself does not include oracles, as does Baruch's prayer. Rather, it assumes that revelation is an ongoing phenomenon.

Baruch, by contrast, uses Jeremiah surreptitiously. Baruch's pious homily in the fundamentals of confession was self-authorized because through its composition he effectively effaced his great predecessor Jeremiah, referring only to the legacy of "the prophets." He is the "first" from a narrative perspective in "writing" five years after the exile to actualize the petition described in Solomon's own prayer (1 Kgs 8:46–50), in which the people are promised forgiveness for sincere confession. Baruch affirms the role of ongoing traditional confession not only for the diaspora population but also for those in Jerusalem. The legacy of prophecy is overwritten through the

56. Gershom Scholem, *The Messianic Idea in Judaism and Other Essays on Jewish Spirituality* (New York: Schocken, 1971), 297.

ritualization of text. Baruch can thus be understood as producing an etiology of the practice of corporate confession in the diaspora and Jerusalem that is linked with festival observance at the Temple. Even more striking is the production of an extended scripture that left its legacy without ever fully undermining Jeremiah's own written legacy of oracles in Jeremiah-Baruch-Jeremiah. In that sense, the text of Baruch can be understood both to receive and compose "Jeremiah" with the sense of a new ending that overcomes exile itself.

We have now considered in Chapter 1 a sapiential, instructional text and in this chapter a pair of narrative texts that can be understood as diachronically intertwined owing to their concern for practices of confession. In order to demonstrate that the entwinement of liturgical practices with texts is a broad phenomenon in this era, we next turn to a new genre that emerges most prominently in the first century of the common era as a form of scripture, the epistolary genre, with a letter of Paul to the Corinthians serving as chief exemplar.

CHAPTER 3

✧

The Eucharistic Body of Paul and
the Ritualization of 2 Corinthians

From the apostle Paul's perspective, the chief burden in the Corinthian correspondence is how to shape a cohesive community from a fractious congregation. He is convinced this can happen only by securing their allegiance to him as the most authoritative teacher and leader "in Christ." Cementing the Corinthians' commitment required not one but multiple letters that were delivered by his co-workers. I want to argue in this chapter that 2 Corinthians played a distinctive role not only in shaping community cohesion but in securing the letter's own status as scripture. The letter calls attention to itself as a medium crucial to the ongoing communication of the gospel, with the apostle Paul squarely in the middle, portrayed as the embodied mediator of its message shared with others. It was not a single letter but continuing and open-ended performances of this correspondence that shaped not only the Corinthians but other early communities as they circulated. They elevated Paul as the legitimate teacher in absentia.

The first two chapters have considered the practice of prayer in the ongoing formation of self and scripture. In Sirach, we saw how the formation of the scribal self through daily prayer is intertwined with wisdom teaching in an ongoing cycle of instruction. Our examination of the long prayer in Baruch demonstrates how the efficacy of confessional prayer practices might be contested across the texts of Daniel, Jeremiah, and Baruch in an ongoing performance of textual production.

In this Pauline epistle, we evaluate the way in which scripture developed in relation to community formation by assessing the role of two practices that are instituted through the letter: the collection of money for the saints in Jerusalem and the prayer of the congregation on Paul's behalf found in the introductory blessing. A third practice implicit in the text is its performance as a collection of ecclesial traditions. This occurs at first through a trusted emissary and eventually, once the Corinthian correspondence is edited and collected with other Pauline epistles, by a host of other ecclesial groups. I will argue that the performative enactment of this textual collection played a key role in establishing Paul's credibility as a consoling sufferer "in Christ." Such revelatory authority effected through his own suffering body permitted not just the shaping of the eucharistic body of the Corinthian community but an ongoing corpus of letters connected to the Pauline figure.

3.1 THE COLLECTION FOR JERUSALEM AND GROUP COHESION

The Collection as Benefaction

In 1 Cor 16:1–4, Paul gives concise instructions for a regular collection of funds for the "saints in Jerusalem." He wants the Corinthian congregation to follow the same practice he had outlined for the Galatians. Once a week, the day after the Sabbath, each member is to put aside extra funds, so that the money will be available when Paul or someone else comes to collect it. The collection of funds, mentioned in other Pauline epistles (cf. Gal 2:10; Rom 15:25–27), is a recurrent theme in his correspondence. As indicated in 1 Cor 16, it is not an occasional practice but frequent and regularized, thus what may be regarded in contemporary terms as a ritual practice. The description of the collection in 2 Cor 8–9 is unique, however. The exhortation for funds is made at considerably more length and included not just once but in two seemingly separate addresses to the congregation, suggesting its importance for the rhetorical aims of this letter. Scholarly assessments have typically emphasized either theological or ideological factors as the reason for Paul's institution of the collection.[1] Various explanations have been given, including eschatological expectations rooted in prophetic scripture, with the expectation connected to those Gentiles who were oriented

---

1. Cf. Frank Matera's evaluation: "Although these chapters are an appeal for money, they also provide a theology of grace, namely, the graciousness of the God revealed in Jesus Christ, which allows and empowers people to be generous to each other." See Matera, *2 Corinthians: A Commentary*, New Testament Library Series (Louisville, KY: Westminster John Knox Press, 2003), 211.

toward Jerusalem.[2] Without denying that these factors may have played a role, what else might be said about the social significance of the collection?

Clues may be found in the language employed. 1 Cor 16:1–4 makes explicit that the collection is a monetary one, with its use of the term *logeia* (1 Cor 16:1), which refers to a collection of money or taxes. By contrast, and tellingly, money is nowhere mentioned in 2 Corinthians.[3] Addressing the congregation in Corinth, Paul introduces his appeal by reporting to them the divine *charis* that has inspired the churches in Macedonia in their own giving:

> We want you to know, brothers, about the gift [*charis*] of God that has been given to the churches of Macedonia, for during a severe ordeal of affliction, their overflowing joy and their extreme poverty have overflowed in a wealth of generosity on their part. For, as I can testify, they gave according to their ability, and even beyond their ability, with great earnestness entreating us that they might share in the gift [*charis*] and fellowship [*koinōnia*] of this service to the saints. (2 Cor 8:1–4)

The word used most frequently to describe the collection in 2 Corinthians is *charis*, ten times in total.[4] The role of the "gift" (*charis*) that permeates this account of the collection for Jerusalem suggests the larger Greco-Roman social context of benefaction or euergetism, the practice of public gifts. Benefaction originated in the polity of Greek city-states, in which elite families performed a kind of voluntary service on behalf of the various civic institutions.[5] This took a variety of forms, including the construction and renovation of public buildings.[6] Such benefactors were typically called

2. See Scot McKnight, "Collection for the Saints," in *Dictionary of Paul and His Letters*, ed. Gerald F. Hawthorne and Ralph P. Martin (Downers Grove, IL: InterVarsity Press, 1993), 143–147. Cf. the more extensive discussion of David J. Downs, *The Offering of the Gentiles*, WUNT 2.248 (Tübingen: Mohr Siebeck, 2008), 3–9. As Terence L. Donaldson has pointed out, the likely connection to the prophetic vision of Gentiles streaming to Jerusalem is less likely given that those prophetic texts are not cited by Paul in connection with the collection; *Paul and the Gentiles: Remapping the Apostle's Convictional World* (Philadelphia: Augsburg Fortress, 1997), 194.

3. Other terms are *diakonia* (2 Cor 8:4; 9:1, 12, 13), *koinōnia* (2 Cor 8:4, 9:13), *eulogia* (2 Cor 9:5, 9:6), and *leitourgia* (2 Cor 9:12). Mitzi Minor, *2 Corinthians* (Macon, GA: Smyth & Helwys, 2009), 177.

4. 2 Cor 8:1, 4, 6, 7, 9, 16, 19; 9:8, 14, 15. The NRSV and other translations mask this recurrence of *charis* though variable translations.

5. On the classical Greek origins of euergetism, see most recently Marc Domingo Gygax, *Benefaction and Rewards in the Ancient Greek City: The Origins of Euergetism* (New York: Cambridge University Press, 2016).

6. The classic study of benefaction is Paul Veyne, *Bread and Circuses: Historical Sociology and Political Pluralism*, trans. Brian Pearce (London: Penguin, 1992) (translation of *Le Pain et le cirque* [Paris: Seuil, 1976]). Another influential study is Philippe Gauthier,

euergetai in the honorary decrees and subsequent inscriptions describing their gifts. In Roman society, the ultimate benefactor was the emperor himself.

Reciprocity lay at the heart of benefaction. In other words, gifts in Roman antiquity were given with clear strings attached. The expectation of return was not simply of a monetary kind but also of what Pierre Bourdieu has termed cultural capital, an amassing of social status.[7] In the words of John Barclay, "The key element of the return was public honor: public announcements and decrees, front seats at public events, wreaths, statues, and crucially, all of this inscribed on stone or metal to be a permanent, public record of the gratitude of the city."[8] Gifts were thus not given without the expectation of something in return. Civic honor and glory were the currency of repayment, concretized in memorialization, honorary inscriptions, or statues of the benefactor. The telos of such public benefaction was not, however, simply to elevate the role of the donor. Such prominent displays were intended to motivate competitors, so that other elite benefactors would be drawn to support civic projects as well. The point of such elite gifts in antiquity was to create social ties, a network of associations and bonds that allowed for the continuation of elite civic life.[9]

Rekeying the Benefaction in Egalitarian Terms

Social ties and community cohesion lie at the heart of 2 Cor 8–9 as well. But the passages about the collection in 2 Corinthians, while using the language common to Greco-Roman benefaction, rekey its significance in egalitarian ways in order to reflect the values that Paul wishes to see in his communities. The distinctive emphasis evident in the two appeals made

Les cités grecques et leur bienfaiteurs (IVe–Ier avant J.-C.): Contribution à l'histoire des institutions, Suppléments du bulletin de correspondence hellénique 12 (Athènes: École Française d'Athènes, 1985).

7. The concept of cultural capital is perhaps best known from his seminal book, Pierre Bourdieu, *Distinction: A Social Critique of the Judgement of Taste* (Cambridge, MA: Harvard University Press, 1984) originally published in French as *La Distinction: Critique Sociale du Jugement* (Paris: Éditions de Minuit, 1979).

8. John M. G. Barclay, *Paul and the Gift* (Grand Rapids, MI: Eerdmans, 2015), 33. Such elite competitive rivalry exists in contemporary society. The Giving Pledge was initiated by Warren Buffett and Bill and Melinda Gates to encourage billionaires to donate the majority of their wealth to efforts that address society's biggest issues throughout the world, from education to efforts to combat poverty to health care. Yet the motivations and global reach are quite dissimilar.

9. Barclay, *Paul and the Gift*, 51.

in 2 Cor 8–9 is clear from the respective scripture quoted in each one. The first appeal in 2 Cor 8:1–24 emphasizes the "horizontal" aspects of the collection, that is, the interpersonal and intergroup dimensions of the gift. The second appeal in 2 Cor 9:1–14 highlights the service rendered to God through the collection, thus the "vertical" aspect.

To return our focus to the first of Paul's appeals excerpted above, the collection described in 2 Corinthians begins (and, as we shall see, ends) with divine *charis*. The benefactor is not the emperor, however; rather, the generating donor is understood to be God, for whom there is also the expectation of reciprocal return. Paul seeks the Corinthians' participation by comparing them to another regional group, the Macedonians: "We want you to know, brothers, the grace of God given to the churches of Macedonia, how that in much affliction by reason of adversity, the welling up of their joy and their extreme poverty have flowed out in the wealth of their generosity" (2 Cor 8:1–2). Though very poor, they are motivated to give, even beyond their means. Their gift out of their poverty is likened to that of Jesus himself, who in his gift (*charis*) became poor so that all would become rich. Paul here points to the Macedonians' extreme joy even in the face of affliction. The language of joy and affliction, as we shall see below in our discussion of the introductory prayer, plays a role in Paul's own perspective on life transformed in Christ. The analogy of the Macedonians' gift to that of Jesus thus removes the discussion from strictly monetary giving to a symbolic gift.[10]

The poor in Roman society were generally regarded as morally bereft and unworthy of attention and honor, but the rationale behind the collection in 2 Corinthians upends that valuation. Moreover, there is a desire to even the scales, with a "fair balance" (*isotes*) between those who have abundant wealth and those who are in need of the desired outcome. Some have seen in the use of *isotes* a model of Greco-Roman friendship and believe that Greco-Roman associations provide a helpful heuristic model for understanding the Pauline communities.[11] But the fact that Paul quotes Jewish

---

10. Although the exact meaning of Christ's wealth/poverty is not made explicit, Margaret E. Thrall rightly points to its symbolic character as referring to the incarnation or some aspect of the messianic mission; *2 Corinthians 1–7: A Critical and Exegetical Commentary on the Second Letter to the Corinthians*, vol. 1, International Critical Commentary Series (Edinburgh: T. & T. Clark, 1994).

11. Richard S. Ascough provides an overview of more recent work in "What Are They Now Saying About Christ Groups and Associations?," *Currents in Biblical Research* 13, no. 2 (2015): 207–244. Benedikt Eckhardt has rightly cautioned against the scholarly tendency to assume a monolithic and uniform associational culture from Spain to Syria at the expense of identifying local variations; "The Eighteen Associations of Corinth," *Greek, Roman and Byzantine Studies* 56 (2016): 646–662.

scripture (Exod 16:18) that recalls the Israelites' divinely mandated collection of only enough manna sufficient for that day's needs suggests that a distinctively Judean ethos lies behind the distribution, even though the collection draws from predominantly Gentile congregations.[12] Moreover, associations were predominantly local institutions in which any collections that might be raised would go to the common fund of the local group, so on this point a comparison is not helpful.[13]

In the first appeal Paul stresses the equality that will result from the redistribution of funds; thus the collection can be regarded as a subversion of the values represented by Greco-Roman euergetism. Indeed, the collection has been characterized as a postcolonial act of resistance to the practice of benefaction.[14] It also simply reflects a different valuation of wealth. While Greek-speaking Judean elites did not entirely eschew the practice of benefaction and its rivalry for honor, Judeans had a deeply rooted practice of charity for the poor that restrained such displays.[15]

12. Judeans, whether in the diaspora or the homeland, also participated in benefaction, though it was adapted in various ways, for example, to avoid overt conflicts with Jewish law that prohibited statues as idolatrous, or to avoid excessively honoring benefactors at the risk of deification. See Tessa Rajak, "Benefactors in the Greco-Jewish Diaspora," in *Geschichte-Tradition-Reflexion: Festschrift für Martin Hengel zum 70. Geburtstag*, vol. 1, ed. Hubert Cancik et al. (Tübingen: Mohr, 1996), 305–319.

13. Richard Ascough identifies some translocal associations that maintained contact with their home cities. This is of course, different from the interethnic model of Gentile-Judean relationship and specifically the financial commitment identified in Paul's letters. Ascough, "Translocal Relationships Among Voluntary Associations and Early Christianity," *Journal of Early Christian Studies* 5 (1997): 223–241.

14. Harry O. Maier, *Picturing Paul in Empire: Imperial Image, Text, and Persuasion in Colossians, Ephesians, and the Pastoral Epistles* (London: Bloomsbury, 2013), 59. Cf. also Steve Friesen, "Paul and Economics: The Jerusalem Collection as an Alternative to Patronage," in *Paul Unbound: Other Perspectives on the Apostle*, ed. Mark P. Given (Peabody, MA: Hendrickson, 2010), 27–54. The prism of postcolonialism has provided a means of understanding the significance of the collection; see Sze-kar Wan, "Collection for the Saints as Anticolonial Act: Implications of Paul's Ethnic Reconstruction," in *Paul and Politics: Ekklesia, Israel, Imperium, Interpretation*, ed. Richard A. Horsley (Harrisburg, PA: Trinity Press International, 2000), 191–215.

15. Martin Goodman, *The Ruling Class of Judaea: The Origins of the Jewish Revolt Against Rome A.D. 66–70* (Cambridge: Cambridge University Press, 1987), 125–133. For a discussion of Jewish ambivalence toward the practice of euergetism by Josephus, see Seth Schwartz, *Were the Jews a Mediterranean Society: Reciprocity and Solidarity in Ancient Judaism* (Princeton, NJ: Princeton University Press, 2010), 80–109. Counter to his argument, see the witness of Philo, who affirms the Roman emperor as benefactor and sees a tempered euergetism as consistent with the practices of Judaism; Steven Weitzman, "Mediterranean Exchanges: A Response to Seth Schwartz, 'Were the Jews a Mediterranean Society?'" *Jewish Quarterly Review* 102 (2012): 491–512.

The Financial Collection as a Costly Display
of Group Commitment

Before considering the character of the second appeal in 2 Cor 9, we should attend to another, more basic question. In a broader society in which ethnicity and kinship were fundamental to providing the strongest bonds of affiliation, what would motivate a group of non-Judeans to give to Judeans, and furthermore not simply in their own city or region but far away in Jerusalem?

To answer that is to address a larger question about human bonding and community formation over time. Recent research in the social sciences provides insights into how humans evolved to include large-scale non-kinship-based communities that allow for altruistic behavior within them. What evolutionary benefits are conferred that promote the formation of such cooperative groups? A growing consensus sees religion as having an instrumental role in creating such prosocial groups. Communities grounded in allegiance to "big gods" that govern morality and are considered powerful over cosmic forces exhibit distinctively strong forms of community cohesion.[16] As we noted at the outset, the gift (*charis*) is understood ultimately to derive from God. The framework for understanding this donation is thus a theistic one, motivated by an understanding of divine prerogatives.

The great cost of the gift to the Macedonians is a feature that Paul emphasizes. One aspect of this work on prosocial religions has focused in particular on the extravagance of some religious practices that is a common feature of many religious communities.[17] Such practices or rituals can involve physical and psychological pain but also time, energy, and material costs. The collection of funds from the Macedonians and the Corinthians for the saints in Jerusalem can be understood as a costly display of commitment to group beliefs and values. A chief social outcome of such practices is to enhance credibility among the rest of the community. Whereas statements of belief are not testable—that is, people can lie about whether they believe that Jesus is the promised Messiah, or about some other theological

---

16. The research on "prosocial religions" synthesizes work from various quarters in the social sciences. A recent overview essay, "The Cultural Evolution of Prosocial Religions" by Ara Norenzayan et al., followed by twenty-seven responses from fifty-one scholars, fills an entire issue of the journal *Behavioral and Brain Sciences* 39 (2016): 1–65.

17. An illustrative contemporary example is Mormon missionary service on the part of young men, which is a great investment of time and money. I should clarify that the term "prosocial" does not in fact mean that there are only positive results from such communal practices. Noxious sects and other maladapted "antisocial" groups also feature costly rituals and other practices that contribute to group cohesion.

dogma—actions that express the shared values of the group communicate information that is hard to fake.

From a sociological perspective, one advantage of group cooperation and cohesion is the elimination of those who are not fully committed to the project but who may gain benefits from membership in the group.[18] To the degree that all members participate in such practices, the cohesion and solidarity of the group are strengthened, along with demarcating lines between those inside the group and those outside the community. Members of such groups who show commitment to shared values through such practices are also more likely to be trusted in cooperative efforts of various kinds.[19] Too, the longevity of religious communities is related to the amount of costly signal commitment to the group.[20]

A number of studies have concluded that such behavior enhances group cohesion by galvanizing group solidarity. While contemporary inquiry recognizes that such psychological and social mechanisms can be found in secular societies as well, research makes clear that metaphysical grounding and sacred values are a particularly potent means of forging cohesive and long-lived community.

While the collection is designed to benefit the "in-group" and thus show parochial concern for those who follow Christ, whether Judean followers in Jerusalem or those of different ethnicities throughout the Mediterranean region, there is also an element of competition afoot. Paul's pointed reference to the Macedonians as voluntarily giving beyond their means, even though they are poor, is designed to induce the Corinthians to rivalry with other congregations through a commitment to their greater cause. Unlike in competitions among rival Greek

18. Such members are referred to in the literature as "free riders."

19. Rachel E. Watson-Jones and Cristine H. Legare, "The Social Functions of Group Rituals," *Current Direction in Psychological Science* 25 (2016): 42–46. Watson-Jones and Legare operate with a very simple definition of ritual as "socially stipulated group conventions" (42).

20. The anthropologist Richard Sosis conducted a comparative study of nineteenth-century utopian societies, quantifying most aspects of their communal life. For religious communes, the greater the sacrifices demanded of participants, the longer the group stayed together and the higher the group cohesion and commitment. This contrasted considerably with the secular communities, which had comparatively much shorter life spans. See Sosis, "Religion and Intragroup Cooperation: Preliminary Results of a Comparative Analysis of Utopian Communities," *Cross-Cultural Research* 34 (2000): 70–87; Richard Sosis and Candace S. Alcorta, "Signaling, Solidarity, and the Sacred: The Evolution of Religious Behavior," *Evolutionary Anthropology* 12 (2003): 264–274. The work has been corroborated by Joseph Henrich, "The Evolution of Costly Displays, Cooperation, and Religion: Credibility Enhancing Displays and Their Implications for Cultural Evolution," *Evolution and Human Behavior* 30 (2009): 244–260.

benefactors, they will not be awarded public honors for themselves, but a group benefit is envisioned.

The Collection as Vertical Movement and Eucharistic Liturgy

Up to this point, we have considered the communal, "horizontal" dimension of the collection and its role in producing group cohesion. The second appeal draws more attention to the "vertical" results of the collection in that the thanksgivings that ultimately result from the collection are aimed at the new, divine benefactor. Attention to the language and rhetoric of the chapters again reveals their aims.

Two conceptual metaphors govern this second description of the collection. The first is the collection as a harvest. Paul quotes a proverbial saying from LXX Psalm 111:9 that connects an agricultural image of the farmer who sows seed with giving to the poor as resulting in a harvest of righteousness (2 Cor 9:6–10). The image correlates well with language throughout the description of the collection that envisions overflowing abundance, from the verb *perisseuō*, resulting from Paul's request.

The second metaphor understands the collection as a cultic offering, a kind of sacrificial act that manifests praise and thanksgiving to the deity. The language deployed conjures associations with sacrificial contexts. Paul urges the audience to "carry out" their participation in the offering (2 Cor 8:11) using a verb, *epiteleō*, employed frequently for the performance of sacred rites or religious duties.[21]

The final lines of these two chapters bear extra scrutiny because they are particularly dense with such cultic, liturgical language:

> You will be enriched in every way for your great generosity, which will produce thanksgiving [*eucharistian*] to God through us; for the service of this liturgy [*diakonia tēs leitourgias tautēs*] not only supplies the needs of the saints but also overflows with many thanksgivings [*eucharistiōv*] to God. Through the testing of this ministry you glorify God by your obedience to the confession of the gospel of Christ and by the generosity of your sharing [*koinōnias*] with them and with all others, while they long for you and pray for you because of the surpassing grace [*charin*] of God that he has given you. Thanks [*charis*] be to God for his indescribable gift [*anekdiēgētōs dorēa*]! (2 Cor 9:11–15)

21. Downs, *The Offering of the Gentiles*, 135, and see his discussion more broadly at 131–146.

The "payoff" envisioned for the collection is twofold: the recipients in Jerusalem will "long for" and "pray for" the Corinthians, acts that also further enhance cohesion (*koinōnia*), but their efforts will ultimately produce thanksgivings directed to God. In 2 Cor 9:12 he also uses the phrase "the service of this liturgy." This clearly has a cultic ring. While in classical Greek usage *leitourgia* could refer broadly to public service, by the Hellenistic and imperial period it was used specifically for religious or cultic activities.[22] It is essential to note the involvement of the letters' addressees in the collection. In 2 Corinthians generally, *diakonia* refers to Paul's apostolic service toward the Corinthian congregation (2 Cor 3:7ff., 4:1, 5:18, 6:3ff.). In 2 Cor 8–9, however, the *diakonia* is extended to the co-participation of the Corinthians themselves in the activities constituting the larger community.[23]

Paul ends with an exclamation that circles around to the very beginning of the first appeal, in which God's *charis* is seen as the source of all: "Thanks be to God for his indescribable gift!" Others have noticed the cultic tenor of the final exclamation, including Margaret Thrall: "Since in the last few verses Paul has been speaking of prayer, of thanksgiving, and of glorifying God, it is not surprising that he should conclude with a climactic and liturgical-sounding expression."[24]

The performative dimension of this passage is significant, moreover, for understanding its potential for community formation through ritual practice. The term *anekdiēgētos*, translated as "indescribable" or "ineffable," is a *hapax legomenon* in the New Testament, but it is known from hymnic contexts in early Judaism in which the inability of humans to fully capture God's praise is proclaimed before just such a listing of God's gifts or deeds is made.[25] The phrase "for his indescribable gift" preceded a litany of "aretalogical lists of divine gifts." Hans Dieter Betz argues that 2 Cor 9:15, which concludes the appeal, is actually a liturgical beginning.[26] Betz takes into account the oral context in which the letters were

---

22. Downs, *The Offering of the Gentiles*, 144.

23. Eve-Marie Becker, *Letter Hermeneutics in 2 Corinthians: Studies in "Literarkritik" and Communication Theory* (London: T. & T. Clark International, 2004), 106.

24. Thrall, *2 Corinthians*, 594.

25. Hans Dieter Betz, *2 Corinthians 8 and 9* (Philadelphia: Fortress, 1985), 127. See further Reinhard Deichgräber, *Gotteshymnus und und Christushymnus in der frühen Christenheit: Untersuchungen zur Form, Sprache und Stil der frühchristlichen Hymnen*, SUNT 5 (Göttingen: Vandenhoeck & Ruprecht, 1967), 43.

26. Betz understands 2 Cor 8–9 as two separate letters. He built on a long tradition of scholarship. Already in the eighteenth century, Johann Semler noted the disjunction in 2 Cor 9; see the discussion in Betz, *2 Corinthians 8 and 9*, 3–4.

delivered in antiquity. As we will consider at greater length below, letters were not simply read in a monolithic rendition; rather, the reader interacted with the audience. In this case, Betz suggests the phrase would have served as a prompt for the congregation to include their own recitations about divine "gifts":

> Thus the first line of the prayer turns the worshippers into active participants. By reciting the first line of the prayer, Paul assumed the role of liturgist leading the congregation in prayer, which they were encouraged to continue on their own. His prayer had become their own, and hence their answer to all the things he had said in the letter. Thus the letter set in motion a thanksgiving service in the Achaian churches.[27]

Paul, of course, was writing letters because he was not able to be with the congregation in person, so in point of fact Titus or another co-sender would have been interacting with the group. But Betz is likely right that they would have heard "Paul's" voice and his place in instituting this practice, with its intended results: a proclamation of *charis* to God. While two additional aspects of Betz's larger argument are debatable, namely, that 2 Cor 8 and 9 constituted separate and individual letters and that the gathering of the assembly that received it was one of worship, his construal of the interactive social setting in which letters were received, as well as their circulation among more than one congregation, provides an essential dimension to our discussion, to which we shall return.

In sum, Paul's collection for the saints in Jerusalem can thus be seen as instituting a practice that not only demonstrates a costly display of commitment to the *ekklesia* but works to enhance the cohesion of the "eucharistic" body that is being exhorted to provide mutual support. Paul's role in the collection is threefold: Paul is understood to *institute* it through these exhortations; Paul *mediates* it by enlisting co-workers while retaining claim to authorship of the collection; and Paul as mediator ultimately *ritualizes* the practice, to use once again the term of Catherine Bell, through the dissemination of the correspondence. Before attending to this process of ritualization, we need to attend to the important role played by Paul as a conduit of blessing for the congregations he addresses.

27. Betz, *2 Corinthians 8 and 9*, 128.

3.2 BLESSING AS A SOURCE OF CONSOLATION AND APOSTOLIC AUTHORITY

A second practice that shapes the Corinthian community has been largely overlooked. Most commentators on 2 Corinthians consider the opening blessing in 2 Cor 1:3–11 primarily from a rhetorical or theological perspective, as a prelude that introduces the major themes that Paul will develop in the "body" of the letter, like the thanksgiving periods in Paul's other letters. Thus the opening blessing is considered as somewhat ancillary to the letter's purpose, which is instructing the congregation and solving their problems and conflicts. Frank Matera's summary is typical: "The opening benediction focuses the attention of the Corinthians on God, the Father of mercy and the God of all consolation, the God who raises the dead and rescues his apostle. In light of this understanding of God, Paul will now explain the nature of his apostolic ministry in terms of suffering, weakness, and affliction."[28]

I would argue that it is not Paul's *explanation* of his role as afflicted sufferer so much as the implied embodied *performance* of that role that is crucial to understanding the transformation of the letter into scripture within the community. While we meet Paul in the words of this letter, it is only the actions of Paul as the one who bears the marks of Christ on his body, and the empathic response of the congregation to that suffering figure, that permit the transformation from text to scripture. Thus while there is thematic linkage between the blessing and the rest of the letter, as Matera suggests, he neglects the importance of the performative character implicit in the letter form itself, and the blessing in particular as an element that would have shaped the gathering of the congregations who listened and were called to responsive action.[29]

2 Corinthians, moreover, offers a distinctive twist on this customary opening because it contains a traditional Jewish blessing instead.[30] This shifts the focus of prayer from his thanksgiving for the congregation ultimately to thanksgiving for Paul himself.[31] Indeed, the congregation

---

28. Matera, *2 Corinthians*, 44. Mitzi Minor observes its character as a "Jewish-like blessing of God" but without discussion of the form nor further exploration beyond the boundaries of the letter itself; *2 Corinthians*, 27.

29. Gordon P. Wiles, *Paul's Intercessory Prayers: The Significance of the Intercessory Prayer Passages in the Letters of St. Paul* (New York: Cambridge University Press, 1974), 229.

30. There are two other examples of introductory blessings in the New Testament: Eph 1:3–12 and 1 Peter 1:3–5. Deichgräber, *Gotteshymnus*, 64.

31. Paul Schubert, writing well before the Qumran discovery revealed many contemporaneous liturgical blessings, referred to this as a "strangely consistent structural

itself is understood to play an essential role in relationship to Paul's suffering:

> Blessed be the God and Father of our Lord Jesus Christ, the Father of mercies and the God *of all consolation, who consoles us in all our affliction,* so that we may be able to console those who are in any affliction with the consolation with which we ourselves are consoled by God. For just as the sufferings of Christ are abundant for us, so also our consolation is abundant through Christ.
>
> If we are being afflicted, it is for your consolation and salvation; if we are being consoled, it is for your consolation, which you experience when you patiently endure the same sufferings that we are also suffering. Our hope for you is unshaken; for we know that as you share in our sufferings, so also you share in our consolation.
>
> We do not want you to be unaware, brothers and sisters, of the affliction we experienced in Asia; for we were so utterly, unbearably crushed that we despaired of life itself. Indeed, we felt that we had received the sentence of death so that we would rely not on ourselves but on *God who raises the dead.* He who rescued us from so deadly a peril will continue to rescue us; on him we have set our hope that he will rescue us again, as you also join in helping us by your prayers, so that many will give thanks on our behalf for the blessing granted us through the entreaties of many. (2 Cor 1:3–11)

The blessing is structured in two parts. 2 Cor 1:3–7 describes a chain of consolation: God consoles Paul ("us") in our affliction, which in turns allows Paul to console others.[32] A crucial link in the chain of divine consolation

inversion" of an introductory thanksgiving; *The Form and Function of the Pauline Thanksgivings,* BZAW 20 (Berlin: A. Töpelmann, 1939), 50.

32. For a discussion of Jewish blessings and their evolution during the Second Temple period, see Esther G. Chazon, "Liturgy Before and After the Temple's Destruction: Change or Continuity?," in *Was 70 CE a Watershed in Jewish History? On Jews and Judaism Before and After the Destruction of the Second Temple,* ed. Daniel R. Schwartz and Zeev Weiss, AJEC78 (Leiden: Brill, 2012), 371–392, at 377–381. Her observation that during the Second Temple period blessings came to be used as openings and closings in liturgical prayer for regular communal prayer has implications for understanding Paul's use of the blessing in a letter that would presumably be read both initially and certainly in an ongoing way in community gatherings for worship. Cf. also Nitzan, *Qumran Prayer,* 72–78, and Eileen Schuller, "Some Observations on Blessings of God in Texts from Qumran," in *Of Scribes and Scrolls: Studies on the Hebrew Bible, Intertestamental Judaism and Christian Origins Presented to John Strugnell on the Occasion of His Sixtieth Birthday,* ed. Harold W. Attridge, John J. Collins, and Thomas H. Tobin, Resources in Religion 5 (Lanham, MD: University Press of America, 1990), 133–143.

is understood as the mediating sufferings of Christ, which are available abundantly to Paul. Whereas suffering is the condition understood to unite them all, afflictions are particular situations that cause suffering to individuals or communities.[33] The afflictions endured by Paul, described here but also elsewhere in the Pauline correspondence, are said to be all for their sake.

The second half of the blessing in 2 Cor 1:8–11 thus particularizes Paul's suffering in the account of his affliction and consolation. He offers an opaque description of his own near-death experience in Asia, during which he was "despairing of life itself." His survival gives him a heightened recognition of his dependence on "God who raises the dead."[34] His physical state is described in the linguistic register of affliction, consolation, and suffering (*thlipsis, parakalein*, and *pathema*). Paul understands Christ's own bodily suffering and that of the Corinthians because he himself bears the scars, both physical and psychic, of bodily trauma. He is an afflicted sufferer on behalf of the gospel he embraces, with its promise of consolation.

The end of the blessing transitions to Paul's extended reflection on his own affliction and the role of the saints of Achaia in participating in his restoration. Thus the blessing as a whole can be considered an "inverted thanksgiving" that reverses the usual direction of Paul's introductory prayers.[35] Uniquely in 2 Corinthians, the focus here is not on expressing to God Paul's thanksgiving for the congregation, but on the thanksgiving that the congregation will ultimately render on behalf of Paul's own suffering and restoration. We will return to consider Paul as a consoling sufferer below, but first consider how the message of consolation draws on cultural roots in Corinth and beyond.

---

33. On this distinction, see Peter Thomas O'Brien, *Introductory Thanksgivings in the Letters of Paul*, NTSup 49 (Leiden: Brill, 1977), 247–248.

34. Matera rightly identifies this second participial phrase as an indication that the blessing continues through verse 11: "Paul's description of God as the one who raises the dead is the climax of his benediction, and this understanding of God underlies all that he writes in 2 Corinthians." *2 Corinthians*, 44. Thrall, citing Windisch and other earlier commentators, suggests the phrase "comes in all probability from the Jewish synagogue liturgy, since it occurs in the Eighteen Benedictions"; *2 Corinthians*, 119. There is no evidence, however, for a fixed Jewish Amidah before the rabbinic era. As we have discussed in previous chapters, while there is evidence of daily prayer from the Dead Sea Scrolls (e.g., 4Q504–506, "The Words of the Heavenly Lights"), there is no evidence for a fixed statutory Amidah in the first century.

35. Paul Schubert was apparently the first to comment on this structural inversion; *Form and Function*, 50. Cf. Thrall, *2 Corinthians*, 126.

The Cultural Context of Consolation

How are we to understand the purpose of this inverted thanksgiving in relation to the congregation and Paul? The form of the prayer is a traditional
Jewish blessing, and the content is also deeply rooted in Judean cultural
memory. We have seen how Paul has rekeyed the conception of Roman benefaction in order to convey his ideal of an egalitarian collection that would
strengthen communal cohesion. In a similar way, the blessing both draws
on and reworks the Judean cultural heritage in the face of other Greco-
Roman cultural imprints to shape the communities the letter addresses.

Most striking from a rhetorical perspective is the repeated use of "comfort" language in this blessing. The homologous terms παρακαλέω and
παράκλησις, with the root meaning of "comfort" or "console," occur in the
highest concentration among all New Testament books in the first five
verses of the blessing, 2 Cor 1:3–7.[36] The use of this verb in its semantic
sense of consolation also recurs in 2 Cor 7:5–13 when Paul describes
the visit of his co-worker Titus. How is such focus on consolation to be
understood?

The Greco-Roman cultural context no doubt informs the depiction of
grief and consolation more broadly in 1–2 Corinthians, and it is especially
resonant in 2 Cor 7:5–13. The Corinthians knew about suffering and affliction. As Laura Nasrallah writes, Corinth was "a city used as a sign of grief
and destruction in the Roman period."[37] The Greek city suffered a trauma-
tizing utter destruction at the hands of the Roman army under Mummius
in 146 BCE. The imprint of trauma could be seen in the topography, in the
monumentalizing of traumatic events such as the fountains of Peirene and
Glauke, which commemorated mythic elements of loss and death. Although
Corinth was rebuilt by the Romans in 44 BCE, Nasrallah argues that the
legacy of death and grief maintained its hold on the cultural psyche. The

36. The cognate noun and verb *paraklesis* and *parkaleo* occur with great density, six
times in 2 Cor 1:3–7 and a total of eleven times in 2 Corinthians as a whole; Thrall,
2 Corinthians, 102. This stands in contrast to the occurrence of *paraklesis* seven
times total in the other recognized Pauline epistles. The word recurs in 2 Cor 7:5–16,
where it appears three times with the meaning "comfort." The common Greek usage
includes a semantic range of "to call to," "beseech," "exhort," and "console"; Otto
Schmitz, "παρακαλέω/παράκλησις," *Theological Dictionary of the New Testament*, ed.
Gerhard Kittel and Gerhard Friedrich, trans. Geoffrey W. Bromiley (Grand Rapids,
MI: Eerdmans, 1968), 5:773–779. Schmitz rightly understands the blessing to have
the semantic sense of consolation.
37. Laura Salah Nasrallah, "Grief in Corinth: The Roman City and Paul's Corinthian
Correspondence," in *Contested Spaces: Houses and Temples in Roman Antiquity and
the New Testament*, ed. David L. Balch and Annette Weissenrieder (Tübingen: Mohr
Siebeck, 2012), 109–140, at 137.

new Corinth of the Roman period was populated largely by ex-slaves who knew their own grief. They also encountered the old inheritance of pain and grief that was embedded and evoked again through their encounter with such memorializing features of the landscape.[38]

The emotions of pain and grief are likewise inscribed in 2 Corinthians. Many scholars have sought to understand the rhetoric of consolation in light of the ancient Greco-Roman genre of consolation letters.[39] Paul's account of his encounter with his emissary Titus in Macedonia in 2 Cor 7:5–17 contains the highest density of affective language in the letter. Titus brings news of the Corinthians' reaction to the "letter of tears" that Paul wrote, which caused pain and an emotional tumult (2 Cor 2:1–4). An excerpt provides a sense of this:

> But God, who consoles the downcast, consoled us by the arrival of Titus, and not only by his coming, but also by the consolation with which he was consoled about you, as he told us of your longing, your mourning, your zeal for me, so that I rejoiced still more. For even if I made you sorry with my letter, I do not regret it (though I did regret it, for I see that I grieved you with that letter, though only briefly). Now I rejoice, not because you were grieved, but because your grief led to repentance; for you felt a godly grief, so that you were not harmed in any way by us. For godly grief produces a repentance that leads to salvation and brings no regret, but worldly grief produces death. (2 Cor 7:6–10)

The passage contains an intensity of affective concern created by the repeated use of a number of words—"affliction," "comfort," "suffering," "pain/grief," "grace/gift"—as well as the rhetorical use of hyperbolic expressions.[40] Lawrence Welborn assumes that Paul is aware of the writings of the Epicureans, Stoics, and other popular philosophers of his time. Paul's distinctive perspective on the positive role of pain stands in opposition to the Stoic perspective, in which the emotions were to be suppressed. In his attempt to make sense of the intense evocation of emotions, Welborn has argued that the passage in 2 Cor 7 is designed as

38. Nasrallah, "Grief in Corinth," 124.

39. Stanley K. Stowers, *Letter Writing in Greco-Roman Antiquity* (Louisville, KY: Westminster John Knox, 1986), 142–144; also Frank W. Hughes, "Rhetoric of Reconciliation: 2 Corinthians 1.1–2.13 and 7.5–8.24," in *Persuasive Artistry: Studies in New Testament Rhetoric in Honor of George A. Kennedy*, ed. Duane F. Watson, Library of New Testament Studies 50 (Sheffield: JSOT Press, 1991), 336–350.

40. Lawrence L. Welborn, "Paul and Pain: Paul's Emotional Therapy in 2 Corinthians 1.1–2.13; 7.5–16 in the Context of Ancient Psychagogic Literature," *New Testament Studies* 57 (2011): 547–570, at 558.

part of a therapeutic exercise, in which the emotional response generated is meant to transform the audience.[41] "All in all, it is difficult to imagine that there is another letter from antiquity so obsessive in its concern for the emotions, so vulnerable in its disclosure of the author's emotional state, or so solicitous in its practice of what should be called 'emotional therapy.'"[42] Two starkly contrasting emotions in particular should be noted: grief (lupē), here frequently translated to be understood as "pain/grief," which is experienced by the Corinthians because of Paul's pain-inducing letter, and Paul's own experience of joy (chairō), which occurs as the result of learning about the godly grief occasioned by his letter. Worldly grief has caused separation between Paul and the congregation. Paul's joy comes at the evidence of their "godly grief," which causes them to repent of their mistakes.

Exile and Consolation in the Judean Context

The pagan surroundings of Corinth were by no means the only determinant of Paul's rhetoric. In his well-known essay "Collective Memory and Cultural Identity," Jan Assmann discusses the importance of pivotal historical events in shaping community memory:

> Cultural memory has its fixed point; its horizon does not change with the passing time. These fixed points are fateful events of the past whose memory is maintained through cultural formation (texts, rites, monuments) and institutional communication (recitation, practice, observance). We call these "figures of memory." The entire Jewish calendar is based on figures of memory.[43]

Assmann's identification of a "fixed point" is essential in understanding the role of the exile and restoration in constituting Judean liturgical and cultural life as well as the cultural memory that underlies Paul's blessing. While 2 Cor 1:3–11 and 2 Cor 7:5–13 share the theme of consolation, there are two points of essential difference between them in terms of understanding their role in forming community. The first is that in the blessing of 2 Cor

41. Welborn, "Paul and Pain." See too Welborn, "Paul's Appeal to the Emotions in 2 Corinthians 1.1–2.13; 7.5–16," *Journal for the Study of the New Testament* 82 (2001): 31–60.
42. Welborn, "Paul and Pain," 559.
43. Jan Assmann, "Collective Memory and Cultural Identity," *New German Critique* 65 (1995): 125–133 at 129; originally published in *Kultur und Gedächtnis*, ed. Jan Assmann and Tonio Hölscher (Frankfurt am Main: Suhrkamp, 1988), 9–19.

1:3–11, the mention of grief and joy, a prominent part of the account of Paul's meeting with Titus in 2 Cor 7, is strikingly absent. More important than grief and joy in the initial blessing are the suffering, affliction, and consolation that are depicted as a source of communal bonding. Suffering and affliction are not to be stifled or denied, as in Stoic philosophy, but to be endured as a productively generative experience that is assured of divine consolation. The second point of difference is the central role of Paul in the blessing as its endpoint and focus as afflicted sufferer.

A number of scholars have cogently argued that the language of comfort in 2 Cor 1:3–11 derives from Second Isaiah (sometimes referred to as "the book of Consolation").[44] Written in the wake of the Achaemenid ruler Cyrus's conquest of Babylon, the chapters of Second Isaiah are full of hope at the imminent restoration of the people and a seeming end to the exile. The break with the brutal suffering and punishment of the past is sharp in Isa 40:1 as the prophetic leaders of the exiles are exhorted to "comfort, comfort my people, says your God." The motif of comfort is woven in a prominent way throughout the second half of the book (Isa 49:13; 51:3, 12, 19; 52:9; 54:11; 57:18; 61:2; 66:13). In these passages, consolation is distinctively derived from a divine source, as in the Pauline blessing, rather than from fellow humans, as is the case in Greco-Roman letters of consolation.

The consolation language we have pointed to in Second Isaiah, which comes from the Persian period, cannot be understood in isolation from the larger tradition associated with the traumatic memory of the Babylonian exile that left a deep imprint on the prophetic corpus. Second Isaiah is dependent as an intertextual response on both Jeremiah and Lamentations.[45]

---

44. See most recently Reimund Bieringer, "The Comforted Comforter: The Meaning of παρακαλέω or παράκλησις Terminology in 2 Corinthians," *HTS Teologiese Studies/Theological Studies* 67, no. 1 (2011), doi: 10.4102/hts.v67i1.969; Jonathan Kaplan, "Comfort, O Comfort, Corinth: Grief and Comfort in 2 Corinthians 7:5–13a," *Harvard Theological Review* 104, no. 4 (2011): 433–445. The distribution of the language of παρακαλέω with the sense of "comfort" is limited to 2 Cor 1–7, thus lending support to the partition theory of the composition of 2 Corinthians. Cf. the work of Otfried Hofius, who sees the particular influence of Pss 71(70), 86(85), and 94(93) on the blessing because of their emphasis on God as the source of the consolation; "Der Gott allen Trostes: παράκλησις und παρακαλέω in 2 Kor 1, 3–7," in *Paulusstudien*, ed. Otfried Hofius, WUNT 51 (Tübingen: Mohr Siebeck, 1989), 244–254.

45. On this relationship, see Norman K. Gottwald, *Studies in the Book of Lamentations*, SBT 14 (London: SCM, Press, 1954), 44–46; Patricia Tull-Willey, *Remember the Former Things: The Recollection of Previous Texts in Second Isaiah*, SBLDS 161 (Atlanta: Scholars Press, 1997), 125–132; Benjamin Sommer, *A Prophet Reads Scripture: Allusion in Isa 40–66* (Stanford, CA: Stanford University Press, 1998), 127–130; Carol A. Newsom, "A Response to Norman K. Gottwald, 'Social Class and Ideology in Isaiah 40–55: An Eagletonian Reading,'" *Semeia* 59 (1992): 73–78.

This consolation language is part of a deeper exilic-affliction-consolation pattern in the prophetic tradition.

The Exile as Corporate Experience of Death

The depiction of exile as akin to death in the prophetic corpus must be elaborated. Exile is a kind of death, and restoration is a coming back to life. In his book *Resurrection and the Restoration of Israel*, Jon Levenson has observed, "The sources in the Hebrew Bible . . . have a definition of death and of life broader than ours. That is why they can see exile, for example, as death, and repatriation as life . . . . [I]n part this is because the ancient Israelites . . . did not conceive of death and life as purely and exclusively biological phenomena. These things were, rather, *social* in character."[46] To be alive meant to be "flourishing within a continuing kin group that dwelt in a productive and secure relation to the land."[47] Thus as a social phenomenon, to be bereaved of children or to be in exile in diaspora was necessarily to experience a kind of death. To be comforted, whether by fellow Israelites or by God, was implicitly to accept "the decree of God" as the ultimate source of life. The social aspect of affliction as potentially an alienation akin to death might also shed light on Paul's understanding of his own role as a sufferer who does not physically die but is socially alienated through his traumatic experiences, as described in his "hardship catalogues." His bearing the death of Jesus, however, requires some additional discussion below.

The book of Jeremiah arises from the experience of exile, and its poetic passages are thick with bereavement, lament, and loss. A well-known example comes from Jeremiah 31:15, which includes a lament of the eponymous matriarch Rachel:

> Thus says the LORD:
> A voice is heard in Ramah,
>> lamentation and bitter weeping.
> Rachel is weeping for her children;
>> she refuses to be comforted for her children,
>> because they are no more.

---

46. Jon D. Levenson, *Resurrection and the Restoration of Israel: The Ultimate Victory of the God of Life* (New Haven, CT: Yale University Press, 2008), 154–155.
47. Levenson, *Resurrection*, 155.

Jerusalem's devastation is here represented by Rachel as the mother of the children of Israel who have been killed or exiled. Like Jacob, her husband, mourning the presumed death of Joseph (Gen 37:34–35), she refuses consolation, "because they are no more." There is no future without children. Yet in the oracle God promises restoration and a return of the children to their land. Jeremiah provides hope for some future measure of comfort in a divine oracle: "With weeping they shall come, and with consolations I will lead them back, . . . for I have become a father to Israel" (Jer 31:9).

Lamentations offers a similar figure, though in that work the city of Jerusalem is personified as a grieving mother who has lost her children, the population of Judah, through exile and suffering. Lamentations is even grimmer because the woman is inconsolable yet has no one to comfort her in her grief. The fact that she has "no comfort" serves as a communal refrain (Lam 1:2, 9, 16, 21; 2:13).[48] Most significant in this figuration of both Rachel and Zion is that the individual figure is closely enmeshed with the corporate identity of the people, whether it be linked to the population of a city or to the broader population of exiles in geographic diaspora.

Emerging along with this conceptualization of exile as trauma and as individual figures embodying its pain is the idea of an afflicted righteous person who is vindicated and consoled in suffering, in near-death situations. The so-called Suffering Servant passages first identified in Second Isaiah are also relevant to our discussion of Paul's depiction in 2 Cor 1:3–11. The historical identification of the suffering servant with Moses, Jeremiah, or the Isaianic prophet in exile misses the point of its purposeful and versatile adaptive possibilities. The notion of an afflicted servant rooted in the textual depiction of this Isaianic figure is taken up in quite diverse works in later Second Temple literature, notably in the book of Daniel, the Wisdom of Solomon, and the Qumran Hodayot, not to mention, of course, the New Testament gospels in their depiction of Jesus.[49]

In discussing this corporate-individual relationship, Alan Mintz observes: "The solution undertaken by the authors of Lamentations was to transfer to the collective the attributes of individual experience and to view the nation as a whole in the aspect of a single individual: simply put: personification. The nation is represented as an abandoned woman, or,

---

48. Kaplan, "Comfort, O Comfort," 441.

49. On the role of cult performance in relating the death of Jesus to the figure of the suffering righteous one of Jewish tradition, see Ellen Bradshaw Aitken, *Jesus' Death in Early Christian Memory: The Poetics of the Passion*, NTOA 53 (Göttingen: Vandenhoeck & Ruprecht, 2004).

in a more complex instance, as a persecuted man."[50] This brings us closer, then, to understanding the way in which Paul's language of consolation can be seen both in connection to himself as an individual and in relation to the corporate community of which he was a part—both his own Judean identity and his newly forming congregations with their ethnically mixed makeup, seen through the prism of Israel's scriptures.

The consolation language of Second Isaiah thus comes in dialogical response to the affliction and suffering of exile as expressed in Jeremiah and Lamentations. The prophetic tradition contains a deep pattern of loss, destruction, and lament, born of exile, and of consolation and comfort, born of post-exilic restoration as contained in Second Isaiah.

The Continuing Enactment of Exile in Second Temple Judaism

With particular frequency the term *naham* (in the Hebrew literature), *paraklesis* (in the Greek), or its cognates continued to be used to describe the response of God to the trauma of exile, both in relation to the remembered history of the Babylonian exile and in terms of the ongoing reality of foreign domination and diaspora of the Jewish people that characterized life well into the first century and the time of Paul. The memory of the first destruction of Jerusalem and the Babylonian exile had left a deep scar that continued to reveal itself in both literature and practices in the post-exilic period, from the Persian to the Hellenistic and Roman eras. Most broadly, we can see the exile itself considered as a continuing state that had never been overcome.[51] This is evident in a wide range of late Second Temple literature (Daniel 9, Baruch, 1 Enoch, T Levi 16–17; Assumption of Moses 3; Jub 1:7–18, Tobit 13–14, CD 1:5–11).[52]

This language entered into a growing body of Jewish prayers and associated scriptural practices in the Second Temple period. The memory was reinforced, moreover, by practices of lamentation over the first destruction.

---

50. Alan Mintz, *Hurban: Responses to Catastrophe in Hebrew Literature* (New York: Columbia University Press, 1984), 23. Lamentations would of course at some point be adopted by Jewish communities for liturgical reading on the Ninth of Av to commemorate the destruction of both the First and Second Temples.

51. Peter R. Ackroyd, *Exile and Restoration: A Study of Hebrew Thought of the Sixth Century B.C.*, OTL (Philadelphia: Westminster John Knox Press, 1968), 232–256. Cf. also Knibb, "The Exile," and a more recent collection of essays, *Exile: Old Testament, Jewish, and Christian Conceptions*, ed. James M. Scott, JSJSup 56 (Leiden: Brill, 1997).

52. Bradley C. Gregory, "The Postexilic Exile in Third Isaiah," *Journal of Biblical Literature* 126, no. 3 (2007): 475–496, at 489.

Zechariah provides evidence that during the Second Temple period, there
was institutionalized fasting and mourning for the destruction of the First
Temple and the destruction of Jerusalem under the Babylonians (Zech 7:5,
8:19).[53] The practice of confessional prayer, first witnessed in Persian-period
texts and discussed at length in the previous chapter, continues into the
later Greco-Roman period (cf. Baruch 1:15–3:8; PrAzariah, PrManasseh).
This was connected in its inception to the Deuteronomic understanding
of the need to repent for sins resulting in exile.[54] Indeed, the ending of
the oft-ignored book of Baruch also reflects a participation in this exilic
trauma-restoration trend by weaving together the figure of Zion in need of
consolation with the discourse of Second Isaiah. Such prayers continued to
be composed and even institutionalized liturgically during the later Second
Temple period. Nonsectarian confessional prayers 4Q504–506 (Words of
the Luminaries), which were composed for daily use and recounted the history of Israel through the exile into the contemporary period, and 4Q393
(Communal Confession) provide further evidence of a broader practice in
which the memory of exile and the need to overcome it through liturgical
means was enshrined.

Memory and Purposeful Forgetting

I have gone to some lengths to demonstrate that the event of the exile and
the language of affliction and consolation cast a large shadow over much of
early Jewish thought and practice. The language would have been so common as part of the cultural script of early Judaism that to those familiar
with Jewish practices the words "consolation" and "affliction" would have
summoned up this powerful cultural memory. Yet given this deep well of
memory about exile, the question arises why the exile, *qua se*, is never explicitly mentioned, as it is in other Second Temple Jewish discourse. Both
the connection to Second Isaiah and the thematic omission of exile have
not been missed by many New Testament scholars, who illustrate in their
scholarship a lack of familiarity with Jewish traditions and a much closer
acquaintance with Greco-Roman or classical sources and practices.

53. Adele Berlin, *Lamentations*, OTL (Louisville, KY: Westminster John Knox Press, 2002), 35.

54. Westermann, "Struktur und Geschichte." On the scholarly genealogy of research into this topic, see the discussion of Samuel Balentine, "'I Was Ready to Be Sought Out by Those Who Did Not Ask,'" in *Seeking the Favor of God*, vol. 1, *The Origins of Penitential Prayer in Second Temple Judaism*, ed. Mark Boda, Daniel K. Falk, and Rodney A. Werline, SBLEJL 21 (Atlanta: SBL, 2006), 2–10.

I would argue, however, that the lack of explicit mention of exile in the introductory blessing of 2 Corinthians is a purposeful omission. Though it is thick with the lexicon of divine and human consolation, Assmann's first "fixed point" of exile is forgotten by Paul. Paul is intent on forging a new community through what Paul Connerton has called one of the seven types of cultural forgetting, that is, "a forgetting that is constitutive in the formation of a new identity."[55] This forgetting is not so much a loss as, in Connerton's words, "a gain that accrues to those who know how to discard memories that serve no practicable purpose in the management of one's current identity and ongoing purposes."[56] An example of such forgetting on a personal level lies in relinquishing the details of a former partner from a previous marriage in order to cultivate a new relationship. Not to forget might be to provoke too much cognitive dissonance in forming new marriage bonds and habits. On a broader social scale, Connerton refers to ethnographic accounts of Southeast Asian societies in which such forgetting serves a contemporary social purpose. A number of societies in Borneo, Bali, the Philippines, and rural Java lack knowledge of ancestors, which is a kind of a purposeful forgetting. Their focus lies on horizontal sibling kinship relations rather than vertical ancestral connections. This reflects the high degree of mobility among the island populations of that region. Remembering the ancestors, characteristic of less mobile cultures, does not serve a useful purpose in a new island setting.

Second Isaiah itself offers a prime example of Connerton's kind of forgetting in order to forge a new identity. While we have noted that the presence of the past is in full evidence through Isaiah's many allusions to and reversals of Jeremiah and Lamentations, forgetting is also enjoined. The instruction is repeated: "Remember not the former things [*devarim*]; nor consider things of old. Look, I am doing a new thing [*davar*]" (Isa 43:18; cf. Isa 42:9, 46:9, 65:17). Along with the language of consolation, the juxtaposition of former events and new events is a leitmotif that serves as a summons to memory while at the same time reshaping the old in the context of the new situation. The rhetoric of Second Isaiah imaginatively combines both the language of earlier prophets with the language of creation, so there is a forging of a new identity for the new project of return from exile. The messianic promise to David is attached to a non-Israelite Persian king, Cyrus, in an astonishing feat of memory suppression for a post-monarchic age.

55. Paul Connerton, *The Spirit of Mourning: History, Memory and the Body* (New York: Cambridge University Press, 2011), 36.
56. Connerton, *Spirit of Mourning*, 37.

What does Paul remember and what does he forget about the "fixed point" of the exilic experience in framing a blessing for his letter? How does his new "fixed point," centered around his own understanding of the death and resurrection of Jesus, inform the shaping of a new communal identity? Like the creative author of Second Isaiah, the Pauline author of the blessing in 2 Cor 1:3–11 both remembers and forgets. He draws on the language of scripture while at the same time conceiving of something new for a new historical moment. He forgets the recollection of exile and hope for ingathering of the people, because of his broadening understanding of community. He is intent on extending the bonds of community beyond an exclusive kinship relationship with his fellow Israelites.

In sum, the introductory blessing serves as a means of communicating a corporate memory that rekeys the meaning of the trauma of exile and restoration from it. Overcoming this trauma involves corporate and shared suffering. The strong memory of the suffering righteous individual whose identity is enmeshed with the corporate identity, such as we see in the bereft mother or the suffering servant in Deutero-Isaiah, is retained. The suffering one now inheres in the emergent identity of a particular leader, Paul, who is "forgetting" the explicit connection to the exile in order to forge a new community, not only with Judeans but with a range of peoples in Asia Minor.

Paul Who Embodies Christ's Death in Suffering

Now that we have traveled this route of cultural memory and its reshaping by Paul, it is instructive to return to the blessing once again with an eye to the way in which the community is drawn into Paul's own role as an exemplary sufferer.

> Our hope for you is unshaken; for we know that as you share in our sufferings, so also you share in our consolation.
>
> We do not want you to be unaware, brothers and sisters, of the affliction we experienced in Asia; for we were so utterly, unbearably crushed that we despaired of life itself. Indeed, we felt that we had received the sentence of death so that we would rely not on ourselves but on *God who raises the dead*. He who rescued us from so deadly a peril will continue to rescue us; on him we have set our hope that he will rescue us again, as you also join in helping us by your prayers, so that many will give thanks on our behalf for the blessing granted us through the entreaties of many. (2 Cor 1:7-11)

Not only does Paul exhort his community to pray for him, but he embodies the substance of his prayer in his continual suffering. The afflicted body of Paul is evident not only in the blessing but throughout the letter. In a potent mixed metaphor, Paul depicts himself as a slave and fragrant offering in a triumphal victory procession (2 Cor 2:14–17), deftly combining the spectacle of Roman war triumph with imagery from Judean temple ritual. His own body serves as an incense-like aroma: "To the one a fragrance from death to death, to the other a fragrance from life to life" (2 Cor 2:16).

Paul's suffering and his authoritative status in relation to competing Judean "super-apostles" are a central issue in 2 Cor 10–13. Jennifer Glancy has called attention to a common misreading of Paul's hardship catalogues in contemporary scholarship that regards these as accounts of heroic feats of endurance, and the scars as marks of virtue.[57] Rather, she observes, the cultural meaning of a breast pierced by a sword as a sign of martial valor is quite distinct from a back welted by a whip: "In boasting of beatings, Paul boasts not of his manly courage but of his humiliating corporal vulnerability."[58] What we might best describe as an intercultural encounter in bodily debasement is depicted as well in 2 Cor 11:22–29, where Paul mentions that on five occasions he received a penalty of thirty-nine lashes from his fellow Judeans. The fact of his willingness to submit to this penalty suggests his continuing involvement in synagogue worship and practice.[59] He also recounts three beatings by the Roman rod. In light of my argument above that the consolation language in 2 Corinthians draws on more than one cultural context, both pagan and Judean, so too we might say that Paul's body "knows" about suffering from these two cultures and their imprints on his body. His intercultural bodily habitus helps parse the letter's rhetorical aims for a putative mixed audience of Corinthians and Achaians, whether Judeans or Gentiles. The debased body of Paul unites him in experience to Jesus. Glancy offers further insights about the significance of Paul's debased body. She argues that in

> the repeated violation of his body Paul claims a corporal knowledge that unites him with Jesus. Paul does not try to represent this corporal knowledge as glorious. The whip teaches abasement and humiliation. Nonetheless, because his

---

57. Jennifer Glancy, *Corporal Knowledge: Early Christian Bodies* (New York: Oxford University Press, 2010), 26. Glancy cites in particular the work of John T. Fitzgerald in this regard, *Cracks in an Earthen Vessel: An Examination of the Catalogues of Hardships in the Corinthian Correspondence*, SBLDS (Atlanta: Scholars Press, 1988), 43.

58. Jennifer Glancy, *Corporal Knowledge*, 26.

59. J. Paul Sampley, *2 Corinthians*, NIB 11 (Nashville, TN: Abingdon Press, 2000), 22. The thirty-nine lashes as punishment is mandated in Deut 25:3.

experiences of physical abuse unite him with Jesus, Paul presents his abject body as evidence of his authority.[60]

The source of Paul's authority lies in this embodied condition in relation to Christ and this transformed cultural memory. In attending to a new community, in his introductory blessing Paul remembers most clearly the role of the afflicted sufferer and affixes it to himself as a sufferer in Christ. Like Isaiah before him, he remembers God as the source of all comfort (Isa 51:12) in affliction, even from death. He knows his sole dependence on the God "who raises the dead." This includes the God who restored Israel from the death of exile, and who promises to do it again. It includes as well a God who in Paul's understanding is doing a new thing, by forging a community through a renewed understanding of mutual suffering and consolation, mediated by Paul, the prophetic and afflicted sufferer who offers himself to console others.

The performative punch line of the blessing occurs in its last verse: "as you also join in helping us by your prayers, so that many will give thanks on our behalf for the blessing granted us through the entreaties of many." It is not just God who comforts, but the humanly mediated and reciprocal act of consolation in the face of affliction and suffering that effects restoration. The endgame in this case, just as in the case of the community benefaction, is to increase the tide of thanksgiving on the part of those joined in the community.

3.3 RITUALIZING THE LETTER THROUGH PERFORMANCE

I have argued that two practices imbedded in 2 Corinthians are intended for the formation of community, the collection for Jerusalem in 2 Cor 8–9 and the prayer for Paul in 2 Cor 1:3–11. Both implicate the mediation of Paul and occur through reciprocal liturgical action and the rendering of thanksgiving. I have described the communal shaping that would result from them when in fact, because we have only examined the textual description of these activities, they only bear the *potential* of being enacted in congregations. The astute reader may have already noted this and wondered about this disjuncture between the portrayal of the practices in 2 Corinthians and the social context in which they might come to life. I thus want now to turn

60. Glancy, *Corporal Knowledge*, 27.

to another practice that is less overt in its liturgical aspects, but ultimately the most important in understanding the transformation of this letter into scripture. The third practice is the performance of the letter, perhaps better imagined as a series of continuing performances of the letter or letters that constitute this composition.

Constituting a Communal Reality Through Text

I would argue that, rather than reflecting events, the redacted letter of 2 Corinthians seeks to shape them in relation to assembly practices and perception of Paul. To return, then, to our initial question: how does the letter of Paul become scripture? The answer is through the process of its ongoing performance. Catherine Bell has called attention to the social and performative aspects of the texts in constituting a social reality:

> What is the significance or functional effect of writing ritual down, both vis-à-vis ritual and as a written text? How does writing a text or depicting ritual in a text act upon the social relations involved in textual and ritual activities? Ultimately, how are the media of communication *creating* a situation rather than reflecting it; how are they restricting social interactions rather than merely expressing them?[61]

She refers to this process as the "textualization of ritual" and the simultaneous "ritualization of text."[62] Bell understands "ritualization" as a strategic way of acting that serves to differentiate certain actions from others and to constitute social relations. Bell uses a processual term to argue that ritual is constituted by practices that define and shape social interaction.[63]

In the case of 2 Corinthians, ritualization occurs through establishing specific claims about Paul as thanksgiver and bearer of Christ in his body, which shapes his self-image in relation to the congregations. The process of ritualization occurs through the repeated performances of the letters, and through their editing. 2 Corinthians does not simply reflect in a straightforward way the situation at Corinth but in fact takes part in shaping not only the Corinthian community but other congregational practices,

---

61. Catherine Bell, "The Ritualization of Text and the Textualization of Ritual in the Codification of Taoist Liturgy," *History of Religions* 27, no. 4 (1988): 366–392, at 368–369.

62. Bell, "Ritualization of Text." She also discussed the concept in her signal *Ritual Theory, Ritual Practice* (New York: Oxford University Press, 2009).

63. Bell, *Ritual Theory*, 74.

and not just in the region of Achaia but implicitly in other (and future) *ekklesiae*. 2 Corinthians promotes Paul as the author and inaugurator of a textual tradition and secures his place as the absent voice of the apostle. He directs congregations from a distance, both spatially and in temporal terms, as his own written legacy becomes part of the fabric of community worship over time. 2 Corinthians is thus as much a commemoration of the role of the founding apostle as it is strictly a communication of Pauline or early church teaching.

Performing Paul

In this sense, it is crucial to imagine the performative character of these texts as compositions that would have been recited, heard, and transmitted by a community as part of a collection of texts, in the case of 2 Corinthians as a collection of letters deriving from a community, as opposed to a singular author.[64] There remains a consensus, even though recently questioned, that 2 Corinthians is the product of redaction, whether by Paul himself in shaping his letter collection or by his followers at a later date.[65] Because the earliest manuscript evidence for the Pauline letters, P46, dates from the second century CE and already contains a collection of Pauline correspondence, however, it is not possible to trace all steps in the editorial

64. On this point, see especially the insightful argument of Cynthia Briggs Kittredge, "Rethinking Authorship in the Letters of Paul," in *Walk in the Ways of Wisdom*, ed. Shelly Matthews et al. (Harrisburg, PA: Trinity Press International, 2003), 318–333. Kittredge problematizes the notion of "the mind of Paul" as singular author: "Allowing liturgical formulas, hymns, and doxologies to keep some role of the community in the production of Scripture and the creation of the canon. In their focus on individual authors, particularly Paul, scholars overlook the role of community and tradition in shaping Scripture. The move of various commentators to insist that the only legitimate object of study is Paul's use of early Christian traditions causes the loss of the communal dimension of these traditions" (331).

65. I understand 2 Corinthians to comprise at least two redacted parts, chapters 1–9 and 10–12. A brief overview and convenient outline of the four major hypotheses about the composition (with variations) and prominent proponents of each (a single letter, or two, three, or five letters) can be found in Calvin J. Roetzel, "2 Corinthians," in *The Blackwell Companion to the New Testament*, ed. David E. Aune (Oxford: Wiley-Blackwell, 2010): 437–443. On the various theories regarding the Pauline letter collection, see Stanley Porter, *Paul's Letter Collection: Tracing the Origins* (Minneapolis: Fortress, 1994); Harry Y. Gamble, *Books and Readers in the Ancient Church: A History of Early Christian Texts* (New Haven, CT: Yale University Press, 1995); David Trobisch, *The First Edition of the New Testament* (New York: Oxford University Press, 2000); and William Arnal, "The Collection and Synthesis of 'Tradition' and the Second-Century Invention of Christianity," in *Method and Theory in the Study of Religion* 23 (2011): 193–215.

process, let alone know the details of 2 Corinthians' circulation before being collected with other letters.

In understanding the circulation of letters, there is the historical evidence related to the sending of letters in antiquity. Letters were communicated in an author's absence by those he sent as trusted emissaries to convey the contents. We know from the transmission of Roman letters that in many cases letter carriers were expected to supplement and interpret the written content of the letter they delivered orally.[66] The author's presence is recreated by someone else who reads them, interprets them for the audience, and answers questions about the communication. Given the length of Paul's letters and the quasi-public nature of the correspondence, we can expect that Paul too would have expected his trusted carriers to be so equipped. We have discussed Betz's idea that the liturgical elements in the text provide an invitation of sorts for community participation. The process of transmission was thus a communal one.

Yet on the other hand, we should weigh the historical evidence against the rhetorical claims about performance of letters in 2 Corinthians itself. At two points in 2 Corinthians it becomes clear that the performance of the letter was understood as superior to Paul's personal presence in the congregation. One is the passage in 2 Cor 7, already discussed, in which Paul recounts his lack of regret in sending the letter that caused such deep emotion among the congregation, news of which was brought by Titus (2 Cor 7:6–8). Another is 2 Cor 10:10, in which an emissary's reading of Paul's letters provides a heightened impact in the community, even more so than his own voice.[67] The fact that such an assertion is put in the mouths of his rivals in Corinth, the so-called Judean super-apostles, invests the statement with even more rhetorical force. "For they say, 'His letters are weighty and strong, but his bodily presence is weak, and his speech contemptible.'" It thus vests the letter with even more authority, but only as it is transmitted and circulated by someone other than its nominal author. To see this through Bell's eyes is to see these performative clues as a means of shaping the authority of the Pauline letter, rather than as reflecting straightforwardly the potency of the Pauline missive in its circulation.

---

66. For knowledge of Roman letter carriers and the oral aspect of letter composition and delivery, see Lincoln H. Blumell, "The Medium and the Message: Some Observations on Epistolary Communication in Antiquity from the Papyri," *Journal of Greco-Roman Christianity and Judaism* 10 (2014): 24–67.

67. Although he is more invested in a historical "Paul" and the idea of 2 Cor 10–12 as its own separate letter, cf. the cogent argument of Richard F. Ward about the performance of Paul's letters, "Pauline Voice and Presence as Strategic Communication," *Semeia* 65 (1995): 95–107.

The redacted letter of 2 Corinthians thus serves three purposes that transform it into scripture.[68] First, it bolsters the apostolic authority of Paul as a Christ-like sufferer. He bears a revelatory status in his very being. Second, and not entirely separable from the first, it institutes ritual practices of reciprocal prayer and financial offerings meant to forge not only a tight community but an intra-Christian community. Third, as a letter with "missing pieces," it requires active interpretive input from its audience in order to make sense of it. Its rhetorical aims are secured through recalibrating the concept of pain and transforming it into social emotions that foster cohesive community, whether that be in the Corinthian *ekklesia* or other congregations where the correspondence circulated. Thus it is a work intended to shape a social reality over time, beyond the immediate situations to which the correspondence was addressed.[69] The letters cross spatial and temporal dimensions through embodied performances. 2 Corinthians is in no small part about the means by which interpretation happens through bodily agency.

CONCLUSION

I have argued in this chapter that practices of community formation embedded in this letter to the Corinthians served the purpose of forging indelible links to Paul and his revelatory body. In making this argument, we have shifted attention from the customary locus, the body of the letter and its theology, to liturgical practices within it. We have also shifted attention to its performative role in the social life of congregations.

We have seen that the collection for the population in Jerusalem serves the purpose of forging strong inter-ecclesial bonds. The second practice of reciprocal prayer lodged in Paul's initial blessing retrieves and rekeys the cultural memory and legitimizes Paul in his role as leader. Paul's initial blessing plays a crucial role in cementing community self-understanding as a suffering and restored corporate body of various socioeconomic strata. Paul's exhortation to the Corinthians to pray on his behalf and share in his suffering serves a dual purpose: to bolster his own embodied authority as

---

68. I agree with the majority of scholars who hold that the "letter" is actually a redacted compilation of shorter letters or letter excerpts.

69. For a discussion of the development of a specifically Christian book culture in the second century CE and beyond including the depiction of a highly literate Paul in 2 Timothy and Acts, see John S. Kloppenborg, "Literate Media in Early Christ Groups: The Creation of a Christian Book Culture," *Journal of Early Christian Studies* 22 (2014): 21–59.

a Christ-like sufferer and to institute communal practices that enhance social cohesion. Indeed, the two purposes and functions cannot be separated.
But it is the third practice, that of the performance of the letter as read by
Paul's co-workers or others in the early years of the movement, that would
ultimately ritualize the text as part of a growing corpus of texts attributed
to Paul.[70] Performing the letter constitutes an act of author construction
and community formation. The reading of the letter enacts the letter as
scripture.

If we take seriously Paul's or his heirs' role in shaping the textual legacy,
then we will see that it assumes the rhetorical shaping implicit in the editorial activity result in 2 Corinthians. Thus Paul or "Paul" in part creates his
own social reality. The text serves to shape the social setting and community rather than simply and straightforwardly reflect it. This amounts to
more than simply reflecting "Paul's" own rhetorical perspective, his side of
an argument. I have argued in particular that the performative cues imbedded in the letter are in fact clues to the way in which the letter served to
become "ritualized," that is, a regularized part of the liturgical gathering
of early Christian communities, beyond its putative original setting in
Corinth and beyond the eucharistic body of Paul himself.

70. Indeed, while it lies beyond the parameters of this project, the way in which such
deutero-Pauline letters as Ephesians and Colossians contributed to the creation of an
even heightened liturgical body of Paul, who completes the suffering of Christ in his
own body, is worth further study.

CHAPTER 4

⌒∿⌒

The Hodayot and the Formative Process
of Performing Scripture

One of the most frequently read parts of the Bible has been the book of Psalms. Tradition attributes these prayers to King David and the psalms were quoted and interpreted in antiquity, from the Qumran pesharim to the book of Acts, as if they were prophetic oracles. The Psalms thus present a puzzle: how did a collection of prayers addressed to God come to be included and understood as part of sacred scripture, as revelatory words for believing communities? The answer has to do with how the psalms were thought to originate from David, who was not just a king but by the Second Temple period was considered a sage with prophetic gifts. In this final chapter, I want to draw attention to another collection of psalms that represents a similar hermeneutical shift. The Qumran Hodayot (Thanksgiving Hymns) are a collection of psalms that are connected to a central leadership figure in the movement, the Maskil. Unlike the texts examined up to this point, the Hodayot never entered any community's Bible, yet like the Psalms of David or the oracles of Isaiah, the collection was of central importance to the Yaḥad. The Hodayot, and especially the youngest scroll, 1QHᵃ, shed light on the dynamics involved in the formation of scripture and its entwinement with teaching, interpretation, and worship practices in the service of shaping self and community.

The communities connected to the finds from the Dead Sea Scrolls left abundant contemporaneous information about their social organization, the rules that governed community life, and associated practices. By contrast, the letters of Paul provide little information about the organization of the congregations to which they were sent and even less about the way in which the one-sided correspondence was initially performed and preserved. In the Hodayot, we can see the formation of both sectarian self and community through the performative words and deeds of the Maskil. His words of thanksgiving are depicted as inspired, revelatory words that serve both as teaching and as worship through their performance.

I begin this chapter by situating the Hodayot in their larger social context. They make up part of the literary corpus of a textual community in which the Maskil played a chief role. I then evaluate the psalms of the Maskil from two perspectives. The first assesses the Maskil as the performer of confession that interprets and extends scripture. The second considers the unique role enacted by the Maskil in his acts of prostration. Finally, I turn to the issue of the ritualization of the collection in the 1QH[a] scroll. I will argue that the Maskil's role as keeper of esoteric knowledge and performer of psalms as depicted in 1QH[a] provides a context for understanding the ongoing interpretive shaping of scripture. This is true not only for the Qumran Yaḥad but for other textual communities as well, even those devoted to less extreme practices.

4.1 READING, STUDYING, AND BLESSING IN A TEXTUAL COMMUNITY

The first generation of Qumran scholars confidently reconstructed historical details about a singular dissident movement of priests led by a Teacher of Righteousness who fled to the desert settlement by the Dead Sea in the second century BCE at the time of the rise of the Hasmoneans. Recent scholarship has largely dismantled this description and been much more tentative about the ability to reconstruct a full-blown historical account based on the literary finds.[1] An emerging consensus is that there was no single

1. On the changing scholarly perspective on the Teacher of Righteousness, see Angela Kim Harkins, "How Should We Feel About the Teacher of Righteousness?" and Reinhard Kratz, "The Teacher of Righteousness and His Enemies," in *Is There a Text in This Cave? Studies in the Textuality of the Dead Sea Scrolls in Honour of George J. Brooke*, ed. Ariel Feldman, Maria Cioată, and Charlotte Hempel, STDJ 119 (Leiden: Brill, 2017), 493–514, 515–532. Three factors lie behind this scholarly shift. The first was the complete publication of the Dead Sea Scrolls in the 1990s, including manuscripts from Cave 4. The second is an archaeological assessment redating the earliest possible settlement of Khirbet Qumran to the first century BCE, for which see Jodi Magness, *The Archaeology of Qumran and the Dead Sea Scrolls* (Grand Rapids, MI: Eerdmans, 2012), 63–66. A third, and perhaps the most significant, is the deployment of different methodological tools and frameworks in approaching the texts, including cultural memory theory, rhetorical analysis, and tools from the social sciences.

"Qumran community" located at Khirbet Qumran alone, but in fact there was a larger, more geographically dispersed movement that surely evolved in terms of organization and practices over time.[2] Of the two principal works that describe the life of the movement, the Damascus Document and the Rule of the Community (the Serekh), the latter is especially illustrative of the entwinement of liturgical practices and scripture because of the distinctive role played by the Maskil.[3]

The Textual Community of the Hierarchical Yaḥad

The Serekh reveals the centrality of scriptural study to the life of the movement.[4] Borrowing from Brian Stock's conception of a "textual community," Charlotte Hempel has drawn a portrait of life in the Yaḥad as one in which the cultural value of texts and their study had great currency.[5] Unlike a modern-day book club, however, private copies of manuscripts were not owned by all members. Indeed, the formation of a textual community in antiquity did not require literacy on the part of all who participated. Teaching and learning could nonetheless occur in a largely oral environment, with text specialists positioned in a privileged station. In Hempel's words: "It seems inevitable that the top-tier scribal and intellectual elite did not start out in the back row."[6] Years of training would be required to attain a thorough knowledge of both the cultural repertoire and the scribal

2. For an overview of the pertinent issues, see the eight essays in *Dead Sea Discoveries* 16, no. 3 (2009) devoted to this topic, including an overview by Michael A. Knibb, "The Community of the Dead Sea Scrolls: Introduction," 297–308. The 1QS manuscript was copied between 100 and 75 BCE. The relationship among the serekh manuscripts (S) and the Damascus Document manuscripts (D) is quite complex. Both traditions show significant signs of redaction and points of interrelationship. See Charlotte Hempel, *The Qumran Rule Texts in Context: Collected Studies*, TSAJ 154 (Tübingen: Mohr Siebeck, 2013).

3. Both documents nonetheless reflect different instantiations of the same sectarian movement. See Cecilia Wassén and Jutta Jokiranta, "Groups in Tension: Sectarianism in the Damascus Document and the Community Rule," in *Sectarianism in Early Judaism: Sociological Advances*, ed. David J. Chalcraft (London: Equinox, 2007), 205–245.

4. The insights of an early study by Steven D. Fraade have only been reinforced in this regard; "Interpretive Authority in the Study Community at Qumran," *Journal of Jewish Studies* 44 (1993): 46–69.

5. Charlotte Hempel, "Reflections on Literacy, Textuality, and Community in the Qumran Dead Sea Scrolls," in *Is There A Text in This Cave?*, ed. Feldman, Cioată, and Hempel, 69–82; Brian Stock, *The Implications of Literacy: Written Language and Models of Interpretation in the Eleventh and Twelfth Centuries* (Princeton, NJ: Princeton University Press, 1983).

6. Hempel, "Reflections on Literacy," 81.

skills of reading and writing. It is likely that only a small percentage of members were fully literate. She highlights the hierarchical character of the movement as a textual community, in which authority was invested in an elite leadership and daily life was governed by control of both speech and actions.

The Yaḥad was centered around texts in a way that shaped the self in relation to the tight cohesion of the movement. Unlike the father-son, teacher-student model of study of Ben Sira, the Yaḥad's formation was both communal and internally ranked. The ideal of the perfected community involved separation from others with a two-year process of gradual inculcation into the life of the community before attaining full membership:

> When such men as these come to be, as a community [*bayyaḥad*], in Israel, according to these rules, they shall separate from the dwelling of wicked men to go to the wilderness, to prepare there his way, as it is written, "In the wilderness prepare the way of the LORD, make straight in the desert a path for our God" (Isaiah 40:3). This means the interpretation of the Torah, which he commanded by the hand of Moses according to all that is revealed from time to time, and according to what the prophets have revealed by his holy spirit. (1QS 8:12b–16a)

The passage highlights the centrality of the study of scripture, revealing both the importance of written text through its explicit quotation of Isa 40:3 and the distinctive understanding of interpretation from the Yaḥad's perspective.[7] The interpretation of Isa 40:3 understands the preparation for the divine theophany in the wilderness to require the study of the Torah of Moses. There are, moreover two distinctive aspects of this interpretation. The first relates to the distinctive temporal perspective of the Yaḥad, which conceived itself as living in "the latter days." "According to all that is revealed from time to time" refers specifically to the proper understanding and observance of the Torah as interpreted by the leaders of the sectarian community.[8] Revelation related to the interpretation of the Torah is understood as intermittently revealed, "from time to time."[9] Alex Jassen

---

7. We can only here note the complex textual history of 1QS 8:15b–9:11 which is absent from 4Q259 (4QSᵉ) entirely and contains multiple scribal corrections suggesting its importance to the community over time. 4Q259 also lacks the final hymn of the Maskil that we will discuss below.

8. Jassen, *Mediating the Divine: Prophecy and Revelation in the Dead Sea Scrolls and Second Temple Judaism*, STDJ 68 (Leiden: Brill, 2008), 337–339.

9. Devorah Dimant, "Time, Torah, and Prophecy at Qumran," in *History, Ideology, and Bible Interpretation in the Dead Sea Scrolls: Collected Studies*, FAT 90 (Tübingen: Mohr Siebeck, 2014), 301–314.

identifies the interpretation strictly with the formulation of new law for the community, but such a restrictive understanding related only to halakhah may be too narrow. Interpreting and recasting the Torah of Moses also occurred in narrative forms, such as the so-called para-biblical texts or rewritten scripture texts that were found in the 4Q Reworked Pentateuch. It also occurred, as we shall see, in the form of liturgical poetry such as we find in the Hodayot.

A second distinctive aspect of interpretation in the Yaḥad relates to prophecy. The interpretation of the Torah of Moses should also be according to what the prophets have revealed "by his holy spirit." The perspective on prophecy is self-referential to the passage itself, because it includes an interpretation from the prophet Isaiah. The realization of the prophecy of Isaiah was to be a continuation of interpretation by inspired figures in the movement. Its fulfillment of the oracle thus was not understood as complete in a single moment, but rather points to the diachronic. The understanding of prophecy at Qumran was that revelation and inspiration constituted an evolving and unfolding process.[10]

Another passage illuminates the daily activity in the movement:

> In any place where the ten gather there shall not be lacking one to interpret the Torah, day and night, continually, each one taking his turn. The Many [*rabbim*] will be on watch together [*bayyaḥad*] for the first third of every night of the year, to read in the scroll, to explain the regulation, and to bless together [or *bayyaḥad*]. (1QS 6:6–8)

The importance of daily study of the Torah and communal prayer is clearly evident from this passage. Three activities represented in the last clause are of most importance for our discussion: "to read in the scroll, to explain the regulation, and to bless together" (*liqro' bassefer, lidrosh bammishpat, uvarekh bayyaḥad*).[11] While much attention has been paid to the first two activities mentioned, reading from the scroll and interpreting law, little attention has been paid to the third activity, blessing together. Based on their use not just in this passage but elsewhere in the sectarian scrolls, George Brooke has offered a cogent argument that these three activities

---

10. Jassen, *Mediating the Divine*, 379.

11. In translating the verb *darash* as "explain," I am siding with George J. Brooke and others who allow for a semantic shift of the verb during the Second Temple period, against the view of Johann Maier, who understands the verb narrowly as a technical term; see Brooke's discussion, "Reading, Searching, Blessing," in *The Temple in Text and Tradition: A Festschrift in Honour of Robert Hayward*, ed. R. Timothy McLay (London: Bloomsbury, 2015), 140–156, at 147–150.

reflect a sequential and interrelated process.[12] Reading from the scroll involved the active participation of the reader. Searching or interpreting the
law represents the engaged interpretation not simply from the Torah but
also from psalms, prophets, and other works authoritative to the Yaḥad,
such as the book of Jubilees or the Temple Scroll.

The third activity, blessing, proves especially relevant to our discussion
of the Hodayot. Brooke wonders what the content of such blessings might
be and considers the initial blessing pronounced by the priests during the
entry ceremony into the Yaḥad in 1QS 2:2–4 as one possible example. The
blessing is an expansion of the priestly blessing in Num 6:24–26. Each
clause of the Aaronic blessing is expanded with a phrase from scripture.
The resulting blessing is thus a scripturalized prayer that endorses a particular community perspective through its own interpretation of the Torah.
He identifies two purposes in the activity of blessing:

> The first function of those prayers of blessing was to interpret and reinterpret
> earlier scriptural materials to extend the repertoire of prayer. . . . [T]he second
> intertwined function of blessing was to endorse the kinds of right interpreta-
> tion that had been the subject of the earlier searching study of both the Law and
> the Prophets and some other authoritative texts.[13]

Brooke suggests that such daily sessions involving performative reading,
intensive searching of texts, and blessings likely would have been a time for
offering one or more of the Hodayot. Because of the hierarchical character
of the community described in the Cave 1 version of the Serekh, with ordered seating at community gatherings and tight control over speech and
participation (1QS 6:8–16), it is likely that only certain members would
have played a prominent role in such communal study sessions, according
to their status, knowledge, and longevity in the community. Chief among
such leaders would have been the Maskil.

The Maskil as Chief Teacher and Exemplar in the Yaḥad

The Maskil is a sage with a different profile from others we have discussed
so far. While the Teacher of Righteousness, the presumed founding figure,
is arguably the most well-known teacher from the sectarian scrolls, the

---

12. Brooke, "Reading, Searching, Blessing."
13. Brooke, "Reading, Searching, Blessing," 153.

Maskil eclipses him as a prominent teacher, both because of the amount of literature describing his role and because of the number of texts connected to him. Scant attention has been paid to the role of this sage in relation to the collection of the Hodayot, however, but there we see him teaching others in both word and deed.[14] Like the scribal figures Ben Sira and Baruch, the Maskil was centrally concerned with both discerning and teaching wisdom. Yet the kind of knowledge attained and mediated by the Maskil was markedly different. His claim to esoteric knowledge available only to an elect group is much more akin to Daniel's visionary wisdom. Indeed, the term "Maskil" likely derives from the Daniel tradition, in which the *maskilim* living in the latter days "would shine like the stars and lead many to righteousness" (Dan 12:3; cf. Dan 11:33, 35; 12:10).[15]

Within the context of ongoing intensive study in the long life of the communities associated with the Yaḥad, the Maskil played a unique role. Carol Newsom aptly describes him "not only as an apotheosis of sectarian selfhood but of the sect itself . . . He is the master of all revealed torah, the knowledge of the ages, and the rule of each time."[16] To him is attributed the so-called treatise of two spirits, in which he is charged with instructing the "sons of light" concerning the nature of the two spirits of light and darkness that govern humanity (1QS 3:13–4:26). The most explicit

14. While there has been attention to the figure of the Maskil in parts of articles and books, a full-scale treatment in a monograph remains a desideratum. Charlotte Hempel, "The Qumran Sapiential Texts and the Rule Books," in *The Wisdom Texts from Qumran and the Development of Sapiential Thought*, ed. Charlotte Hempel, Armin Lange, and Hermann Lichtenberger, BETL 159 (Leuven: Peeters, 2002), 277–295, esp. 286–294. For a comprehensive survey of all occurrences of the term, see Robert Hawley, "On *Maskil* in the Judean Desert Texts," *Henoch* 28 (2006): 43–77; Hans Kosmala, "Maśkîl," *Journal of the Ancient Near Eastern Society of Columbia University* 5 (1973): 235–41; Carol A. Newsom, "The Sage in the Literature of Qumran: The Functions of the Maśkîl," in *The Sage in Israel and the Ancient Near East*, ed. John G. Gammie and Leo G. Perdue (Winona Lake, IN: Eisenbrauns, 1990), 373–382; Armin Lange, *Weisheit und Prädestination: Weisheitliche Urordnung und Prädestination in den Textfunden von Qumran*, STDJ 18 (Leiden: Brill, 1995), 144–164; Charlotte Hempel, "Community Structures in the Dead Sea Scrolls: Admission, Organization, Disciplinary Procedures," in *The Dead Sea Scrolls After Fifty Years: A Comprehensive Assessment*, vol. 2, ed. Peter W. Flint and James C. VanderKam (Leiden: Brill, 1999), 67–92; Joseph L. Angel, "Maskil, Community, and Religious Experience in the *Songs of the Sage* (4Q510–511)," *Dead Sea Discoveries* 19 (2012): 1–27. Aryeh Amihay has recently argued for the eschatological character of the Maskil's leadership in 1QS, but does not attend to his role in the Hodayot, *Theory and Practice in Essene Law* (New York: Oxford University Press, 2017), 146–152.

15. For a nuanced discussion of this relationship, see Charlotte Hempel, "The Community Rule and the Book of Daniel," in *Qumran Rule Texts*, 231–252.

16. Carol A. Newsom, *The Self as Symbolic Space: Constructing Identity and Community at Qumran*, STDJ 52 (Leiden: Brill, 2004), 190.

representation of the Maskil's responsibilities appears at the culmination of the Community Rule (1QS 9:12–11:22).[17]

If the apostle Paul is concerned with breaking down barriers between Judeans and non-Judeans, the Maskil's job entails the opposite. One of his chief roles was to serve as the boundary marker of the community and to evaluate the status of those within it. He was to exercise a negative role by concealing esoteric knowledge from outsiders. He was to exercise a positive role by learning that which has been revealed from time to time (cf. 1QS 8:15) and teaching community members. His claim to a revelatory vision of God and internal transformation resulted in esoteric knowledge: "For from the spring of his knowledge, he has released my light and my eyes have observed his wonders in the light of my heart, the mystery that shall be and which is eternal" (1QS 11:3b-4a).

The Maskil's responsibilities also centrally involve discerning and observing the divinely ordained times for prayer for all days and seasons and feasts.[18] It is well known that differences over the calendar were at the heart of the division between the Yaḥad and other segments of the Judean population. This liturgical responsibility was crucial to the maintenance of the Yaḥad's well-being which understood itself in a priestly vein as a sanctuary of men (1QS 8:5–9; 4Q174) because their worship was understood to fulfill the place of Temple sacrifice.[19]

In this regard we should note a special phrase that occurs uniquely in connection with the Maskil: "engraved statute." "As long as I live an engraved statute is on my tongue as a fruit of praise, the portion of my lips" (1QS 10:8; cf. 1QS 10:6). Another reference to the engraved statute refers to the Maskil's sins (1QS 10:11), which will always be visible before his eyes as a testament to God's righteousness and justice. The Hebrew verbal root for "engrave" (*ḥarat*) occurs just once in the Hebrew Bible, in Exod 32:16 to refer to God's own engraving of the tablets of law at Sinai.[20] It thus conveys

---

17. The complex redaction history of the Cave 1 and Cave 4 serekh manuscripts will not be taken up here, though it is relevant for a complete diachronic understanding of the development of community functionaries.

18. Sarianna Metso, *The Serekh Texts*, LSTS 62 (New York: T. &T. Clark, 2007), 14.

19. See, for example, Georg Klinzing, *Die Umdeutung des Kultus in der Qumrangemeinde und im Neuen Testament*, SUNT 7 (Göttingen: Vandenhoeck & Ruprecht, 1971), 50–106; George Brooke, "Miqdash Adam, Eden, and the Qumran Community," in *Gemeinde ohne Temple = Community Without Temple: zur Substituierung und Transformation des Jerusalemer Tempels und seines Kults im Alten Testament, antiken Judentum und frühen Christentum*, ed. Beate Ego, Armin Lange, and Peter Pilhofer (Tübingen: Mohr Siebeck, 1999), 285–301.

20. While there is a similar verb (*ḥarash*, חרש) that also means "to engrave," the verb *ḥarat* is confined to engraving in wood, stone, or metal and is nowhere connected with the inscription of laws as it is in Exod 32:16.

the sanctity and uniqueness of the medium on which the divine teaching appears. In this section of the Rule of the Community, the engraved statue is connected uniquely to the prayer and song offerings pledged by the Maskil.[21] A legal statute associated with Sinai is thus metaphorically inscribed on the teacher's mouth, the divine gift of speech issuing in prayer and praise, as well as acknowledgment of sin. Implicitly, then, we can see that the interpretation of the Torah of Moses at Sinai is deeply, if subtly, entwined with the speech of the Maskil, though this esoteric knowledge is not available to all.

A third role of the Maskil was to serve as pious exemplar. This is implicit in the final section of 1QS, a long first-person psalm (1QS 10:6–11:22). Because of the psalm's placement at the end of the description of the Maskil's duties, it plays the role of a kind of exemplary teaching. That this should appear in the heightened rhetorical form of poetry may itself be meaningful though the significance of the poetic medium deserves more attention than can be devoted to it here.[22] The psalm rehearses many of the Maskil's duties described at the beginning of the passage in the third person, including regulating the times for prayers and concealing knowledge from unworthy recipients, and makes claims for the Maskil's own esoteric knowledge even in the face of his lowly condition as a member of the "assembly of deceitful flesh." The composition provides a linkage to the larger collection of Hodayot.

The Indigenous Psychology of the Yaḥad

Situating the Hodayot in relation to the formation of self and community requires some consideration of the "indigenous psychology" of the Yaḥad, as was discussed in the first chapter in relation to Ben Sira. The default self of the human being in Ben Sira was rooted in the understanding of a "divided heart." Ben Sira offers a positive view of human nature, of humans

---

21. This unique use carries over into the use of the verb in the sectarian scrolls, where it appears only in sectarian texts, the War Scroll, the Community Rule, the Shirot, 4Q Instruction, and the Berakhot (4Q511), thus almost exclusively in texts connected with the Maskil, and it always refers to a heavenly or divinely engraved medium. In addition to the Community Rule, it appears in the three other S manuscripts four times, twice in the D manuscripts, once in the War Scroll, once in a purification liturgy (4Q284 3, 4), four times in the Shirot, once in the Berakhot (4Q511 63–64ii3), and 4Q180, a pesher concerning the latter days, which makes reference to the engraved tablets of the sons of men.

22. It is worth noting, however briefly, that all the works but one (1QS) associated with the Maskil are written in poetry.

made in the divine image and filled with understanding from their creation. Humans were created for the purpose of praise. Ben Sira's view of
moral agency, like that of the Hebrew Bible, is that humans are free to
choose whether or not to sin.

By contrast, the kind of self envisioned in the Yaḥad is distinctive in
both its expanded conception of interiority and its negative view of human
creaturehood and moral agency. The default notion of the self is best understood in relation to descriptions of the self found in the *Niedrigkeitsdoxologie*
(the term was first coined by Hans Kuhn), which relate to the negative
view of the lowliness of humans set against the stark recognition of divine
righteousness.[23] The passages are found only in the Hodayot, in the psalm
at the end of 1QS (1QS 10:6–11:22), and in the Songs of the Maskil (4Q
510–511). Passages repeat similar phrases such as "a creature of clay and a
thing kneaded with water, a foundation of shame and a spring of impurity,
a furnace of iniquity and a structure of sin" (1QH 9:23–24). Carol Newsom
has coined a term, the "masochistic sublime," to describe this perspective
of wallowing in human unworthiness.[24] The created state of humans is understood to be sinful, according to the Hodayot, and not resulting from any
particular transgressions.[25]

A second aspect of the anthropological view relates to the development of
the concept of spirit in the Hellenistic-Roman era. The language of spiritual
warfare, with spirits doing battle even within each person, is another characteristic part of this indigenous psychology that is on particular display
in the Hodayot and other liturgical texts such as 4Q444, 4QIncantation,
which seeks protection from wicked spirits. Such a perspective reflects the
influence not only of the scriptures now constituting the Tanakh but also
of other works such as Jubilees and Enoch. Spirit language is rife in the
Hodayot. A number of the psalms reflect a battle between wicked spirits
that were unleashed after the fall of the Watchers.[26]

---

23. Heinz-Wolfgang Kuhn, *Enderwartung und gegenwärtiges Heil: Untersuchungen
zu den Gemeindeliedern von Qumran*, SUNT 4 (Göttingen: Vandenhoeck & Ruprecht,
1966), 16–33.

24. Newsom, *The Self as Symbolic Space*, 220.

25. Miryam T. Brand, *Evil Within and Without: The Source of Sin and Its Nature as
Portrayed in Second Temple Literature*, JAJSup 9 (Göttingen: Vandenhoeck & Ruprecht,
2013), 60.

26. Loren Stuckenbruck makes the point that the texts associated with Enoch bear
no marks of being sectarian as such, in the sense of being connected to the Yaḥad
movement. See his nuanced discussion of the various wicked spirits that appear in
the Hodayot, 4Q444, and Songs of the Maskil (4Q510–511); *The Myth of Rebellious
Angels: Studies in Second Temple Judaism and New Testament Texts* (Tübingen: Mohr
Siebeck, 2014; Grand Rapids, MI: Eerdmans, 2017), 87–90.

If the default state of humanity is one in which "sinful guilt is his foundation, obscene shame, and a source of impurity" (1QH^a 5:31–32), how is the ideal self achieved? In our discussion of Ben Sira, we described the way in which prayer might serve the purpose of decentering the self. Ritual practices that engage religious narratives and ideals can provide a way to achieve a unified self with strong conscious agency. As we will see, according to the ideals of the Yaḥad, the self does not stand alone and independent of its close connection to the community.

As is widely recognized, repentance played a large role in the self-conception of the Qumran movement. The importance of repentance to the maintenance of the community is reflected in the frequent self-designation of its members as the *shavei pesha*, "those who turn from sin," a phrase drawn from Isa 59:20.[27] But *shuv* in Qumran parlance takes on a different meaning in that it signals a turn toward the adoption of sectarian practice.[28] This can be seen in the admission ceremony described in the collective annual covenant renewal, with its entry rites and ritualized confession (1QS 1:16–2:12). It is also evident in the Hodayot. The antidote for human sinfulness comes not from human initiative but rather through divine determination. Moreover, the understanding of sin and its therapy is different from that seen in Sirach or Baruch. The relief from sin is related both to the priestly outlook of the movement and to its distinctive perspective that collapses ritual and moral purity.[29] Whereas ritual purity is kept distinct from moral issues in the Hebrew Bible, in the Yaḥad sin is considered something that *ritually* defiles as well. This is related to the underlying conceptual understanding of the community and its members as a temple, whose sanctity requires maintenance of both ritual and moral spheres.[30] Relief from sin is thus described as a kind of cleansing, with the end result of purification. The

---

27. Cf. 1QS 10:20; CD 2:5; 20:17; or the *shavei Israel* (CD 8:16; 19:29). The phrase *shavei pesha* occurs three times in the Hodayot (1QH^a 6:35; 10:11; 14:9; cf. 8:35, "those who return to you"), signaling an affiliation with this community self-understanding. Bilhah Nitzan, "Repentance in the Dead Sea Scrolls," in *The Dead Sea Scrolls After Fifty Years*, ed. Peter W. Flint and James C. VanderKam (Leiden: Brill, 1999), 2:145–170. Cf. David A. Lambert, *How Repentance Became Biblical: Judaism, Christianity, and the Interpretation of Scripture* (New York: Oxford University Press, 2016), 133–142.

28. David A. Lambert, "Was the Dead Sea Sect a Penitential Movement?," in *The Oxford Handbook of the Dead Sea Scrolls*, ed. Timothy Lim and John J. Collins (New York: Oxford University Press, 2010), 501–513, at 507.

29. See Jonathan Klawans, *Impurity and Sin in Ancient Judaism* (New York: Oxford University Press, 2000), 80–85.

30. Newsom, *The Self As Symbolic Space*, 125.

result of divine forgiveness is understood not as a simple debt relief but as a real transformation. As David Lambert has observed: "God does not simply forgive past sin; his purification literally changes human nature, enabling members of the sect to attain a new kind of glory, 'the glory of Adam,' which may even have a visible dimension."[31] This amounts to a divine recreation.

A final aspect of the Yaḥad's indigenous psychology relates to this human transformation from the debased portrayal of the *Niedrigkeitsdoxologie*.[32] A hallmark of the sectarian perspective is the understanding that the purified, perfected community members were worshipping in the company of the angels.[33] While the degree to which such angelic communion affected the ontological status of the worshippers has been debated, what is clear is that angels and heavenly worship were thought to be accessible within the Yaḥad.[34] This marks a clear difference from the worldview of Sirach or Baruch, where no such mediating angels are mentioned. The Songs of the Sabbath Sacrifice reflect such angelic intimacy, as does a composition reconstructed in the Hodayot that is connected to the Maskil (1QH^a 25:34–27:3?), also known as the Self-Glorification Hymn.[35]

A closer examination of the Hodayot can illustrate the way in which their liturgical performance does not simply reflect a static anthropological concept but enacts this transformation of self and community. As chief teacher of the Yaḥad, the Maskil played a unique role of enacting this transformation of self-in-community in both word and deed.

31. Lambert, "Was the Dead Sea Sect a Penitential Movement," 509. The visible dimension relates in part to the "shining face" of the teacher figure described in some of the Hodayot (e.g., 1QH 12:6–7, 24–30; 15:26–28), which is thought to draw from the depiction of Moses after descending from Sinai. See my essay "Covenant Renewal and Transformational Scripts in the Performance of the Hodayot and 2 Corinthians," in *Jesus, Paulus, und die Texte von Qumran*, ed. Jörg Frey, Enno Edzard Popkes, and Sophie Tätweiler (Tübingen: Mohr Siebeck, 2015), 291–330, at 305–307.

32. John J. Collins, "The Angelic Life," in *Metamorphoses: Resurrection, Body and Transformative Practices in Early Christianity*, ed. Turid Karlsen Seim and Jorunn Økland, Ekstasis 1 (Berlin: De Gruyter, 2009), 291–310, at 302.

33. Bjørn Frennesson, *"In a Common Rejoicing": Liturgical Communion with Angels in Qumran* (Uppsala: Uppsala University Library, 1999).

34. Though followed by few, Crispin H. T. Fletcher-Louis has argued for an ontological transformation of humans into angels; *All the Glory of Adam: Liturgical Anthropology in the Dead Sea Scrolls*, STDJ 42 (Leiden: Brill, 2002).

35. Eric Miller, "The Self-Glorification Hymn Reexamined," *Henoch* 31 (2009): 307–324; Angela Kim Harkins, *Reading with an "I" to the Heavens: Looking at the Qumran Hodayot Through the Lens of Visionary Traditions*, Ekstasis 3 (Berlin: De Gruyter, 2012), 17, 247–250.

4.2 THE HODAYOT AND THE FORMATION
OF COMMUNAL IDENTITY

The Hodayot offer first-person thanksgivings or blessings to God for deliverance, salvation, knowledge, and divine mercy. The roughly thirty psalms extant from the twenty-eight reconstructed columns of 1QH^a represent the longest and most complete collection.[36] Each hodayah begins with one of two standard formulations, either "I thank you, God" or "Blessed are you, O God." Scholars have traditionally divided the hymns into two groups, Teacher Hymns (TH) and Community Hymns (CH). In 1QH^a the so-called Community Hymns are sandwiched around the Teacher Hymns (CH in cols. 1–9; 19–28; TH in cols. 10–18). Newsom, for example, makes a clear distinction between the hymns of the community and the teacher hymns in 1QH^a. Eschewing a prevalent notion that teacher hymns represent the personal poetry of the historical Teacher of Righteousness, she understands them as psalms that could be adopted by any leader in the community. They serve to model a leadership role and to draw sharp lines between the sect and its rivals.[37] The community hymns, by contrast, model "the character implied by the teachings of the sect." They serve in the shaping of an alternative subjectivity, creating new selves of those who have joined the group.

This strict bifurcation has been called into question by a number of scholars.[38] The Teacher Hymns are recognized as a more cohesive group of psalms that depict a divinely inspired teacher giving thanks to God for having survived persecution by vicious foes. The Community Hymn designation is more diffuse and nebulous.[39] Some are more closely connected to language in the Community Rule and other texts that were found in

---

36. For a discussion of these issues and a new critical edition of the Hodayot, see Eileen Schuller and Hartmut Stegemann, eds., *Qumran Cave 1.III: 1QHodayota^a and 4QHodayot^{a-f}*, DJD 40 (New York: Oxford University Press, 2009). Schuller has rightly suggested that the compositions be called psalms rather than hymns based on their form-critical similarities to biblical psalms. Eight copies of hodayot manuscripts reflect variant orderings of the psalms and collections of different character.

37. Newsom, *The Self as Symbolic Space*, 345–46.

38. Trine Bjørnung Hasselbalch provides an overview of those who have found the TH/CH bifurcation problematic in *Meaning and Context in the Thanksgiving Hymns: Linguistic and Rhetorical Perspectives on a Collection of Prayers from Qumran*, EJL 42 (Atlanta: SBL Press, 2015), 2–12. Her point is well made: it is problematic that even scholars who reject the idea that the "Teacher Hymns" were written by the Teacher of Righteousness continue to use the categorization.

39. Sarah Tanzer sought to differentiate among the Community Hymns by designating two subgroups, "Deuteronomic" and "*Niedrigkeitsdoxologie*" hodayot; "The Sages at Qumran: Wisdom in the *Hodayot*," PhD dissertation, Harvard University, 1987, 141–149. See also Angela Kim Harkins, "The Community Hymns Classification: A Proposal for Further Differentiation," *Dead Sea Discoveries* 15 (2008): 121–154.

the caves, such as 4QInstruction and the Book of the Watchers from Enoch. Other hodayot, such as a long creation psalm in 1QH 9, have been recognized as hybrid with characteristics that reflect both a teacher and community. Thus while Newsom's insightful work has been highly influential, her argument that the community hymns could be adopted by any member of the sect is less convincing and needs refinement. While she recognizes that certain psalms are connected to the Maskil, she sees them all containing "a stereotypical set of topoi, motifs, concepts, and patterns of emotion."[40] This is to overlook the distinctiveness of the psalms attributed to the Maskil.

The hodayot related to the Maskil form one group of psalms that has not been sufficiently analyzed for the role they play in molding the community. Four hodayot are explicit in their connection to the Maskil through the use of a superscription (1QH[a] 5:12–6:33; 7:21–8:41; 20:7–22:42; 25:34–27:4?).[41] In addition, two other hodayot bear marks of similarity to the Maskil psalms (1QH[a] 4:21–40, 19:6–20:6) and were likely assigned to the Maskil as well.[42] Several features of these psalms distinguish them from others in the collection and point to his unique role in modeling the perfected member of the Yaḥad. Three features in particular may be singled out: one is the first-person affirmation of knowledge as a kind of confession, the second is the use of petitions directed to God, and the third is the posture of the Maskil as a penitent who prostrates himself during supplication. These "Maskil hymns" are consistent with his portrayal in the Serekh as a teacher and a penitent leader of the Yaḥad, but one who also reflects the ideal transformed with an elevated angel-like status of the Self-Glorification Hymn.

A closer examination of extended excerpts of a psalm associated with the Maskil in 1QH[a] 7:21–8:41 can illustrate these points.

40. Newsom, *The Self as Symbolic Space*, 204.

41. Psalm divisions follow those of Harmut Stegemann as found in Eileen Schuller and Carol A. Newsom, *The Hodayot (Thanksgiving Psalms): A Study Edition of 1QH*[a], EJL 36 (Atlanta: SBL Press, 2012), 9–11. English translation of the psalms follows Newsom with occasional adjustments.

42. Émil Puech has suggested that the Maskil hymns mark five different sections in the Hodayot of 1QH[a] akin to the book of Psalms; "Quelques aspects de la restauration du Rouleau des Hymnes (IQH)," *Journal of Jewish Studies* 39 (1988): 38–55, at 52–53. Subsequent research on the Hodayot since the publication of the manuscripts from Cave 4 indicate there were not likely fixed Maskil groups of psalms; nonetheless, there are certain hymns that are associated with the Maskil throughout the collection. Justin L. Pannkuk, "Are There למשכיל Sections in the Hodayot? Evidence from Cave 4 (1)," *Revue de Qumran* 28 (2016): 3–13.

The Maskil's Confession of Knowledge

I.

And as for me, **I know,** by the understanding that comes from you, that it is not through the power of flesh [that] an individual [may perfect]

(26) his way, nor is a person able to direct his steps.

And I know that in your hand is the inclination of every spirit, [and all] its [activity] (27) you determined before you created it. How could anyone change your words?

You alone [crea]ted (28) the righteous, and from the womb you prepared him for the time of favour, to be attentive to your covenant and to walk in all (your way), . . .

But the wicked you created for the [purpose of your wrath, and from the womb you dedicated them for the day of slaughter . . .

(34) But what is flesh that it should have insight into [these things? And] how is [a creat] ure of dust able to direct its steps? *Vacat* (35) You yourself have formed the spirit and determined its activity [from of old]. And from you (comes) the way of every living being.

And as for me, I know that (36) no wealth can compare with your truth and there are none in the world like] your holy [angels].

I know that you have chosen them above all (others), (37) and they will serve you forever. You do not accept a bribe [for evil acts,] nor do you take a ransom for guilty deeds. For (38) you are a God of truth, and all iniquity you will destroy forever] and no wickedness will exist in your presence.

II.

(22) **And I know** that by [your] goodwill toward a person you have multiplied his inheritance in [your] righteous deeds [ ] *r* your truth in all [ ](23) and a righteous guard over your word that you have entrusted to him lest he stray [from your commandments and so as not to stumble in any of [his] dee[ds. For] (24) through my knowledge of all these things I will find the proper reply, *falling prostrate and begging for mercy [continuously] on account of my transgression*, and seeking a spirit of understanding], (25) and strengthening myself through your holy spirit, and clinging to the truth of your covenant, and serving you in truth and (with) a perfect heart, and loving the word of [your] mouth.

(26) Blessed are you, O Lord, great in counsel and mighty in deed, because all things are your works. Now you have determined to do me gr[eat] (27) kindness, and you have been gracious to me in your compassionate spirit and for the sake of your glory. *Righteousness belongs to you alone, for you have done all these things.* (28) Because

I know that you have recorded the spirit of the righteous, I myself have chosen to cleanse my hands according to your wil[l]. The soul of your servant abhors every (29) malicious deed.

III.

I know that no one can be righteous apart from you, and so I entreat you with the spirit that you have given to me that you make (30) your kindness to your servant complete [for]ever, *cleansing me by your holy spirit* and drawing me nearer by your good favor, according to your great kindness which you have shown (31) to me, and causing my feet to stand in the whole station of your good favor, which you have chosen for those who love you and for those who keep your commandments that they may take their stand (32) before you forever, and [atone for iniquity], and savo[r] what is pleasing, and mingle myself with the spirit of your work, and understand your deed[s] *l*[. . .] (33) . . . . not [. . .] and let there not c[o]me before him any affliction (that causes) stumbling from the precepts of your covenant, for [. . .] (34) your face.

And I kno[w that you are a God] gracious and compassionate, patient and abounding in kindness and faithfulness, one who forgives transgression and unfaithful[ness . . .], (35) moved to pity concerning all the iniquity of those who love] you and keep [your] commandments, [those] who have returned to you in steadfastness and (with) a **perfect heart** *[. . .] (36) to serve you [in . . . to do what is] good in your sight. Do not turn away the face of your servant [and do no]t reject the son of your handmaid. [. . .]*[43]

The Scripturalized Confession of the Maskil

The hodayah is a confession in two senses of the word, as a statement of what the psalmist knows and as an acknowledgment of sinfulness. In relation to the first sense of confession, the Maskil proclaims his knowledge of different aspects of divine reality. Indeed, the statement "I, I know" (*'ani yadati*) occurs seven times in this psalm. This stands in contrast to the very rare use of this emphatic first-person confession of knowledge elsewhere in the Hodayot.[44] Aside from its conspicuous use in this and other Maskil psalms, "I, I know" occurs also in the Teacher Hymns, which begin with the affirmation "I, I know there is hope" (1QH[a] 11:21, 14:9, 17:14), in relation to divine redemption of the psalmist. The use of the first-person pronoun in addition to the conjugated verb is a rhetorical way of heightening the voice and standing of the speaker. It suggests as well not a simple prayer directed to God but a series of affirmations to witnesses who hear it. It could be said to function like a creedal statement read in communal worship. For example, the Nicene Creed was written and is recited in churches in order to affirm a particular view of Christology as well as to differentiate the group that recited it from others through the ages who did not adhere to the Nicene perspective. On one hand, "I believe" is part of what "we" the community of worshippers believe. In addition, from the perspective of

43. Translations of the Hodayot are adapted from those of Carol Newsom in Schuller and Stegemann, eds., *Qumran Cave 1.III.* For a division of the contents of the scroll into discrete hymns proposed by Hartmut Stegemann, see Schuller and Newsom, *The Hodayot,* 9–10.

44. Other occurrences of the emphatic first-person "I know" in Maskil psalms: three times in 1QH[a] 5:12–6:33; four times in 1QH[a] 20:7–22:42. Cf. the single instances in 1QH[a] 9:23, 12:31, and 19:10.

liturgical performance, ritual theorists such as Joseph Schaller agree that the "use of language does more than communicate *about* a given state of affairs: a state of affairs is established *in* communicating."[45] The rhetoric of first-person knowledge serves to create a new reality for those who speak it or those who witness it. It constructs the community and its boundaries.

In the context of the Hodayot, the repeated affirmations of knowledge raise the question of what it is the Maskil *knows* so emphatically and how his ritual performance of these words shapes the self and community. I have divided the excerpted composition into three parts in order to expound on some of this special knowledge.

In Part I of this psalm, the Maskil shares knowledge of the dualistic and predetermined moral order created by God. The understanding comes from God and reflects the perspective of the Yaḥad, in which humanity is divided into spheres of righteous and wicked. This knowledge notably, if implicitly, includes the meaning of scripture framed through the indigenous psychology of the Yaḥad. The speaker knows about the abased character of humans in their unredeemed state as a "creature of dust." This knowledge of the lowliness of flesh seems to have been gained because of the redeemed and elevated status of the one who professes knowledge about the angels and can stand with them forever. But the roots of this anthropology also derive from the interpretation of a number of scriptural texts.[46] One of them is the second creation account in Gen 2:7, where the human is formed as a shape of clay. Jer 18:3–6, Isa 29:16, Isa 45:9, and Job also inform this perspective.[47]

Of the texts from the scrolls, the Hodayot likely have the densest concentration of scriptural allusions.[48] This psalm is no exception. Julie Hughes has recently undertaken a focused study of the use of scripture in the Hodayot.[49] Her work has confirmed the frequent use of the prophets

45. Joseph J. Schaller, "Performative Language Theory: An Exercise in the Analysis of Ritual," *Worship* 62 (1988): 415–432, at 416.

46. See Nicholas A. Meyer, *Adam's Dust and Adam's Glory in the Hodayot and the Letters of Paul*, NTSup 168 (Leiden: Brill, 2016), 6–11.

47. Wally Cirafesi, "'Taken from Dust, Formed from Clay': Compound Allusions and Scriptural Exegesis in 1QHodayot[a] 11:20–37; 20:27–39 and Ben Sira 33:7–15," *Dead Sea Discoveries* 24 (2017): 1–31; Carol A. Newsom, "Deriving Negative Anthropology Through Exegetical Activity," in *Is There a Text in This Cave?*, ed. Feldman, Cioată, and Hempel, 258–274.

48. This was noticed in the earliest scholarship on the Hodayot. See Jean Carmignac, "Les citations de l'Ancien Testament et spécialement des Poèmes du Serviteur, dans les Hymnes de Qumran," *Revue de Qumran* 2 (1959–1960): 357–394, and Svend Holm-Nielsen, *Hodayot: Psalms from Qumran*, ATD 2 (Aarhus: Universitetsforlaget, 1960).

49. For an overview, see Sarah Tanzer, "Biblical Interpretation in the Hodayot," in *A Companion to Biblical Interpretation in Early Judaism*, ed. Matthias Henze (Grand Rapids, MI: Eerdmans, 2012), 255–275. Julie A. Hughes offers a thorough treatment

and psalms, particularly Isaiah and Jeremiah. Hughes describes 1QH[a] 7:21–41 as a "meditation on Jeremiah 10–12."[50] She notes, for example, a framing device in 1QH[a] 7:26 and 7:34 that alludes to Jer 10:23: "I know, O LORD, that the way of a human is not in his control, nor can a person direct his steps." Allusions to this verse appear in other Qumran texts, in a context in which divine predestination is also a theme.

The poetic weaving of scriptural phrases and expressions is not the explicit interpretation known from the distinctive pesher commentaries from Qumran, which cite a verse from a prophet and then expound its relevance for their contemporary time, conceived as the latter days. Rather, this interpretive activity is much more subtle and erudite. The allusions derive not only from the books of what would become the Pentateuch but also, and especially, from prophetic discourse. Here we should recall the discussion of George Brooke about the scripturalization of prayers such as the amplified Aaronic blessing used in the sectarian entrance ritual. Such scripturalization might well be seen as the interpretive harvest from the daily study sessions of the Yaḥad described in 1QS 6:6–8.

Part II builds on this statement of knowledge. Because of his knowledge, the Maskil is able to find "the *proper reply*, falling prostrate and begging for mercy [continuously] on account of my transgression." We will discuss the Maskil's prostration below. What is significant in this section of the psalm is not only the psalmist's affirmation of divine righteousness, which is always an element of prayers that confess sin, but that the Maskil is able to offer the "proper reply" or literally an "answer of the tongue" (*ma'aneh lashon*). The distinctive phrase is found only in the Hodayot and in one pesher, 4Q 171. It seems to derive from the unique appearance of the phrase in Prov 16:1: "The plans of the heart derive from mortals, but the answer of the tongue is from the Lord." Its use in Proverbs thus underscores that this particular reply is understood to derive from a special divine gift.[51] Moreover, the phrase is connected to the internalized spirit of the Maskil (1QH[a] 4:29, 8:24) and the teacher's ability to deliver the proper

of five poems along with a methodological discussion for identifying allusions and intertexts in *Scriptural Allusions and Exegesis in the Hodayot*, STDJ 59 (Leiden: Brill, 2006). See also the brief treatment in Armin Lange, "The Textual History of the Book of Jeremiah in Light of Its Allusions and Implicit Quotations in the Qumran *Hodayot*," in *Prayer and Poetry in the Dead Sea Scrolls and in Related Literature: Essays in Honor of Eileen Schuller on the Occasion of Her 65th Birthday*, ed. Jeremy Penner, Ken M. Penner, and Cecilia Wassen, STDJ 98 (Leiden: Brill, 2012), 251–284.

50. Hughes, *Scriptural Allusions and Exegesis*, 81–92.

51. Daniel Falk, "Petition and Ideology in the Dead Sea Scrolls," in *Prayer and Poetry*, ed. Penner, Penner, and Wassen, 135–159, at 141.

words (1QHª 10:9; 15:14, 16; 19:31, 37). This particular kind of speech thus highlights the status of the Maskil as one who is privy to esoteric and divine knowledge.

Tradition and Innovation in Confession

In the final part of the psalm appears the second sense of confession, in the sense of acknowledging sinfulness. The confession intensifies, with the culmination occurring as the Maskil petitions God: "I know that no one can be righteous apart from you, and so I entreat you with the spirit that you have given to me that you make your kindness to your servant complete forever, cleansing me by your holy spirit and drawing me nearer by your good favor." Esther Chazon has analyzed this psalm against the backdrop of confessional prayer in Second Temple literature more broadly. She draws attention to five features typical of confessional prayer that are evident in this composition: a confession of sin; supplication for forgiveness (1QHª 8:24); repentance-like statements, most petitionary (1QHª 8:25, 29–31, 35); a proclamation of divine justice (1QHª 8:27–28); and a recitation of the thirteen divine attributes deriving from Exod 34:6–7 (1QHª 8:34–35).[52] Chazon observes three aspects of the confession that are distinctively sectarian: there is no recitation of specific acts for which divine punishment was meted out, but rather an emphasis on God's merciful deeds; the speaker is counted among the preordained elect; and the very knowledge and ability to address God and petition are attributed to God.[53]

There is more to say about the distinguishing features of this confession as it contrasts with many others in the larger tradition. First concerns the character of the Maskil's petition. The act of petition is exceedingly rare in the sectarian liturgical material.[54] Thus it is striking that almost

52. Esther Chazon focuses in particular on the Hodayot's use of the proclamation of divine justice. The *Tsiduk Ha-Din* would become an integral part of confessional and penitential liturgies in the earliest Jewish prayer books of the ninth and tenth centuries. Chazon, "Tradition and Innovation in Sectarian Religious Poetry," in *Prayer and Poetry*, ed. Penner, Penner, and Wassen, 55–68, at 62–63.

53. Chazon, "Tradition and Innovation," 65.

54. Eileen Schuller shows the predominantly doxological character of Qumran liturgical material; "Petitionary Prayer and the Religion of Qumran," in *Religion in the Dead Sea Scrolls*, ed. John J. Collins and Robert Kugler, SDSSRL (Grand Rapids, MI: Eerdmans, 2000), 29–45. The only petitions in the Hodayot are in 1QHª 4:35, 8:29–36, 22:37, and 23:10. References to petition, but not actual petitions, appear in 1QHª 17:10–11, 19:36–37, and 20:7. A petition appears in the Maskil's psalm in 1QS 11:15–17.

all petitions are limited to the Maskil. Only this figure is permitted such kind of direct entreaty to the creator. He requests the act of cleansing and forgiveness so that he is able to stand in the company of the angels and with all the elect who keep the commandments.[55] The petitions are in fact for something that the psalmist has already acknowledged God has given to him.[56] The language of cleansing is part of a priestly lex-icon, as noted above, in which moral turpitude is understood in ritual terms, sin requiring a purification that can only be divinely provided. The wording of the confession and the divine attribute formula is tweaked with priestly language of atonement and associated with the cleansing gift of the holy spirit. It reflects the heightened sense of interiority in which good and bad spirits are at work both internally and in the cosmos during the latter days. The language is likely drawn in part from Psalm 51: "Create in me a clean heart, O God, and set a new and right spirit within me" (Ps 51:12).[57] A similar use of Psalm 51 in the prayer of Moses appears in the book of Jubilees and seems to have influenced the confes-sional prayer in 4Q393.[58] Cleansing that results in a "perfect heart" can only and uniquely be effected by God. Yet in the Hodayot, the language is reinflected, signaling that transformation comes through the Maskil's

55. Carol Newsom has recently argued that the language of spirit within the heart likely points to a new anthropological understanding of interiority. She understands this to be a development of the promise of a new heart of Ezek 11:19 and 36:26–27; "Flesh, Spirit, and the Indigenous Psychology of the Hodayot," in *Prayer and Poetry*, ed. Penner, Penner, and Wassen, 339–354. I will not take up her intriguing argument here, except to note that she does not consider the possibility of discourse distinctively linked to the Maskil, which might qualify her claims. The language of cleansing as well as the purification of the heart also reflects an intricate reworking of language from Psalm 51. See Anja Klein, "From the 'Right Spirit' to the 'Spirit of Truth': Observations on Psalms 51 and 1QS," in *The Dynamics of Language and Exegesis at Qumran*, ed. Devorah Dimant and Reinhard G. Kratz, FAT 2.35 (Tübingen: Mohr Siebeck, 2009), 171–191. As discussed, this traditioned interpretation is also reflected in Jub 1:19–21.

56. Israel Knohl, "Between Voice and Silence: The Relationship Between Prayer and Temple Cult," *Journal of Biblical Literature* 115 (1999): 17–30, at 29–30.

57. Anja Klein has cogently argued that Psalm 51 represents a later tradition that postdates Ezekiel and in which the psalmist is petitioning for the fulfillment of that divine promise in Ezekiel. This in turn influenced the author of the two spirits treatise of 1QS; "From the 'Right Spirit' to the 'Spirit of Truth.'"

58. At the end of his prayer of petition for divine mercy, Moses uses wording from Psalm 51: "Create a pure heart and a holy spirit for them. And do not let them be ensnared by their sin henceforth and forever." God responds by promising both to cre-ate a holy spirit and purify them, as well as circumcising the foreskins of their hearts with the result that "they will be called the sons of the living God.'" Jub. 1:21, 23, 25 (trans. Orval S. Wintermute, *OTP*). On 4Q393, see Daniel K. Falk, "Biblical Adaptation for 4Q392 *Works of God* and 4Q393 *Communal Confession*," in *The Provo International Conference on the Dead Sea Scrolls: Technical Innovations, New Texts, and Reformulated Issues*, ed. Donald W. Parry and Eugene Ulrich, STDJ 30 (Leiden: Brill, 1999), 126–146.

privileged knowledge of God as leader of the elect. The reworking of scripture is not direct "exegesis" from scripture. Rather, this cluster of what might be called "priestly" confessional prayers, Jub 1:19–21, 4Q393, and 1QH^a 7:21–8:41, concerned with ritual cleansing for moral failings suggests an ongoing interpretative tradition that is entwined with the continuing practice of prayer.

Another remarkable difference from the larger confessional prayer tradition is that this confession has nothing to do with the people of Israel as a whole, nor their history, nor the end of exile, nor the return of the diaspora people to the land, as is the case in other confessional prayers. The psalm is focused on a single individual. The Maskil is adapting the practice of confession by reshaping the liturgical tradition in a vein that accords with the indigenous psychology of the Yaḥad. The psalm exhibits a creative intimacy with scripture in its allusions but also knowledge of contemporary liturgical texts that were part of the broader swath of early Jewish confessional prayer practices. The prayer, then, exhibits a virtuoso's ability to adapt traditional formulas. The psalm can thus be understood as heavily scripturalized, and indeed, given its ongoing use by the community, it can be characterized as scripturalizing. It draws on traditions of scriptural language and interpretation in their composition, but also in its use in ongoing performances it becomes an authoritative script as well as a creed. The Maskil serves as an exemplary performer of this confessional rite.

4.3 THE MASKIL'S EMBODIED PERFORMANCE OF CONFESSION

The Maskil not only confesses his knowledge with his mouth but embodies his relationship to the divine through prostration. Two of the Maskil psalms provide an effective rubric in the superscription that the Maskil must prostrate himself in prayer (1QH^a 5:12; 20:7). A third psalm, already discussed, describes the act of prostrating and supplicating for forgiveness within the prayer itself, in which he prostrates and begs for mercy (*lehitpallel welehithannen*) continuously on account of his sin (1QH^a 8:24).[59]

---

59. Eileen Schuller thinks col. 4 comprises a long psalm that begins at some point in the missing first twelve lines and ends at 1QH^a 4:40. Daniel Falk has noted that it is likely that the hymn in col. 4 was also a Maskil hymn, given its overlap with 1QS 10–11; "Petition and Ideology," 142 n. 27. This is cogent especially because of its mention of the "answer of the tongue" and the location of spirits within the psalmist (1QH^a 4:29), as noted above.

The mention of prostration is one of the few clues provided in Qumran liturgical material about posture during prayer, and this action is uniquely connected to the Maskil.

In evaluating the Maskil's body engaged in the technique of prostration, it is helpful to recall the three levels of mindful body distinguished by Scheper-Hughes and Lock, discussed in the introduction. The mindful body of the Maskil encountered in the Hodayot can be evaluated in its phenomenological/biological and sociopolitical aspects, and they are not entirely separable. We should consider not only the biologically functioning and socially constructed body but also the inculcation of a practice performed in a ritual setting governed by its own formal rules. In his work on ritual, Roy Rappaport understands the special significance of embodied actions: "Acts . . have virtues of their own, virtues possessed by neither the words of ritual nor the objects and substances that rituals may employ."[60] Rappaport distinguishes between two classes of messages that are transmitted in any performance, the self-referential and the canonical.[61] The self-referential pertain to the immediate experience relating to the enactor's current physical, psychic, or social state, which corresponds to a certain extent to the biological-phenomenological body of Scheper-Hughes and Lock. For example, the prostration of the Maskil may be especially painful some days because of his arthritic knees and the fact that he really just does not want to do it. Perhaps the prostration is incomplete, or might have been interrupted by his wheezy cough. Thus the gesture both has physiological effects on the performer himself and can be "read" in a literal sense by other participants who may notice this. The self-referential message does not extend beyond the particulars of that performance. The second messages are ones that are not encoded by the performer himself but are in his terms "canonical" ones, which transcend the particular state of being of any individual, or any one instantiation of the ritual. Here we may begin to consider the social and cultural aspects of the posture. The "canonical" (or, perhaps better, abiding) message of the gesture is not to communicate the interior state of the prayer but rather to communicate a timeless message or messages about the relationship of the created to the Creator as well as the prostrate Maskil to his fellow worshippers.

60. Roy A. Rappaport, *Ritual and Religion in the Making of Humanity* (New York: Cambridge University Press, 1999), 145.
61. Rappaport, *Ritual and Religion*, 52–54.

Seeing and Feeling Prostration

Rappaport does not attend in great depth to the biological responses of ritual performers, but we can delve further into the physiological effects of prostration not only on the Maskil but on those who witness it. The visual aspect of ritual posture can be a very powerful form of communication. From a neurophysiological perspective, facial expression and posture work at the pre-objective level of consciousness, especially when this involves a base emotion such as fear, which activates the amygdala.[62] Visual images have potency and do their work subconsciously even before they are brought to mind consciously. This involves the neurophysiological aspect of mirror neurons, which are dedicated cells in the central nervous system. They are "excitable," sending signals to the organism's body and to the outside world, and receiving from both signals that provide images to the mind.[63] In the words of Antonio Damasio, "As we witness an action in another, our body-sensing brain adopts the body state we would assume were we ourselves moving."[64] If we see someone performing an action, the sight activates our own brains within the same "somato-sensing regions." What is particularly striking about the recent discovery of mirror neurons is that they suggest that the boundaries of self and other are porous because neuronal signals are able to activate between and among selves. The activation of mirror neurons is understood as the likely cause of what enables empathy.[65]

The submissive posture of the Maskil before God and the congregation can be understood to work in this way, though codified in ritual form. There are two aspects to consider. The first is the neurophysiology of the participants as they witness the event, seeing the Maskil perform the full prostration and give voice to the prayer. One might imagine more than a few mirror neurons firing at the sight of the leader prostrate on the floor even though this was a voluntary gesture on the part of the leader. Thus we can assume that participants in the ritual who see the Maskil prostrate

---

62. For a helpful discussion of the affective dimensions of embodiment, see Harkins, *Reading with an "I,"* 37–46.

63. My discussion of mirror neurons is largely reliant on the work of Antonio Damasio, *Self Comes to Mind: Constructing the Conscious Brain* (New York: Pantheon, 2010), 102–106.

64. Damasio, *Self Comes to Mind*, 104. "We can perform four-way translation among 1) actual movement, 2) somatosensory representations of movement, 3) visual representations of movement, and 4) memory" (106).

65. This has been argued by one of the pioneers in the study of mirror neurons, Marco Iacoboni. For a popular yet learned account, see his *Mirroring People: The Science of Empathy and How We Connect with Others* (New York: Picador, 2009).

himself also simulate this action in their own minds, and that this would be accompanied by the emotional response associated with the posture. In the words of Rappaport: "Intensification of emotion is an aspect of consciousness alteration, and it almost goes without saying that the significata of ritual representations—the general points of the ritual—are generally capable of arousing strong emotions, thus altering consciousness."[66] Thus the performance in liturgy also makes a difference. In ritual performance, as part of the rules of the game for active and willing participants, the community "subsumes individual intentional states and aligns them with intentions of others."[67] The second aspect to consider in understanding the congregational response is the cultural embeddedness of the ritual gesture; a gesture with a certain cultural context in the present and a specific cultural history. How then can we conceive of community formation in relation to the leadership of the Maskil as he performs this ritual prostration and supplication?

Synchronic and Diachronic Cultural Codes of Meaning

In the broader Hellenistic context, we should understand this prayer posture as countercultural: it is counter both to pagan Greek religious practice and to the majority of Judean Hellenists. During the Hellenistic era, prayer was typically offered standing, with arms outstretched to the deity, a posture that did not suggest obeisance and subservience but instead preserved dignity and honor before the gods.[68] Standing for prayer is also the normative posture in the work of Josephus, who includes many additional prayers in his *Jewish Antiquities*, not to mention his account of the Jewish war against Rome.[69]

Self-lowering—whether kneeling, bowing, or prostrating—was of course, then and now, considered the common gesture of submission to one socially or institutionally superior in terms of power and authority.[70] Prostration was for slaves and subjugated prisoners. The biological body cannot be severed entirely from culturally constructed meanings. The

---

66. Rappaport, *Ritual and Religion*, 258–259.

67. Roy Rappaport, "Ritual," *International Encyclopedia of Communications*, vol. 3 (1989): 466–472.

68. Prayer was occasionally offered kneeling as well; Simon Pulleyn, *Prayer in Greek Religion* (New York: Oxford University Press, 1997), 189–190.

69. Tessel M. Jonquière, *Prayer in Josephus*, AJEC 70 (Leiden: Brill, 2007), 270.

70. Jennifer A. Glancy, *Corporal Knowledge: Early Christian Bodies* (New York: Oxford University Press, 2010), 16.

relationship to the deity is conceived along the lines of interpersonal gestures in human society. The posture should be understood in relation to
the language in this hymn that situates the pray-er as a lowly human, a
source of impurity, a worm of the dead, a creature of dust, and so on, the
well-known *Niedrigkeitsdoxologie*. The Maskil's prostration demonstrates
the lowly anthropology of the pray-er without benefit of divine righteousness and revelation.

The synchronic cultural contrast during the Hellenistic-Roman period
could be elaborated, but there is more to say in relation to the canonical
messages about the social body of the Maskil, not only in relation to the
contemporary cultural context of the Yahad but also in relation to the traditional legacy of scripture. In the Hebrew Bible, two kinds of self-lowering
are evident in connection with prayer.[71] The most common posture is indicated by the word *histahaweh*, which is typically translated as a form of the
verb meaning "to prostrate or bow down."[72] The posture that is connected
with the Maskil in the Hodayot, however, is both rarer and more extreme;
it is designated by the intensive *hithpael* of *n-p-l*. Notably, the use of this
verb in the *hithpael* occurs only twice in the Tanakh, both in connection
with a prayer of confession, thus signaling a ritual use.[73] When Moses is
recounting the rupture in covenant caused by the worship of the golden
calf, he describes prostrating himself and interceding on behalf of Aaron
and the people for forty days (Deut 9:15–21). The second occurrence also
has a Mosaic cast: Ezra, the new Moses of the return from exile, prostrates
himself before the temple as part of his intercessory confession on behalf
of Israelites who have intermarried (Ezra 10:1). Prostration is thus paradigmatic of the virtuous leader and heir to Moses, who prostrates himself
in confessional intercession on behalf of others. Indeed, another notable
example of prostration accompanied by confession appears at the beginning of the book of Jubilees, a work that seems to have been among the
scriptures of the Yahad movement. Moses is at Sinai, and God reveals to
him Israel's history, including its future exile. With combined echoes of

71. I have discussed this issue more fully in Judith H. Newman, "Embodied
Techniques: The Communal Formation of the Maskil's Self," *Dead Sea Discoveries* 22,
no. 3 (2015): 249–266.

72. Uri Ehrlich, *The Nonverbal Language of Prayer: A New Approach to the Study of
Jewish Liturgy*, trans. Dena Ordan, TSAJ 105 (Tübingen: Mohr Siebeck, 2004), 44.

73. Prostration accompanied by lengthy confession of sin was a distinctly Judean
posture during the Hellenistic-Roman era. The act of bowing one's face to the ground
and doing obeisance before a king or another kind of overlord is a frequent action
described in the Tanakh, yet the formulation is different, e.g., 2 Sam 9:6. All this
is not to say that the cultural significance of bodily stance was static, as Ehrlich has
made clear.

Deuteronomy 9 and Psalm 51, Moses immediately prostrates himself and intercedes for forty days, praying for God to create a pure heart and provide a holy spirit for them lest they be ensnared by the spirit of Beliar (Jub 1:19–21). We can understand then one canonical message imbedded in the Maskil's prostration lies in his emulation of Moses in his supreme act of intercession as leader of Israel.

The scripture-saturated members of the Yaḥad and its leader sought not only to read scriptures but to ingest, interpret, embody, and enact them as well. This full prostration can also be understood as yet another way in which the Yaḥad sought to differentiate itself from both pagan Greeks and from other Jewish communities, especially their Greek-speaking fellows in the land and abroad.

4.4 THE RITUALIZATION OF THE HODAYOT

1QHᵃ and the Hodayot Manuscripts

Now that we have considered the liturgical body of the Maskil in his performance, it remains to assess the body of psalms in collections of hodayot. What is the nature of this textual collection of prayers? Was the collection understood as scripture by the Yaḥad, like the Psalms familiar to us from the Tanakh? Answering these questions involves considering both the manuscript evidence and the hodayot's content. There are two signs that suggest the importance of hodayot to the community that preserved the scrolls: their appearance in multiple manuscripts, and the distinctive character of 1QHᵃ.

Eight manuscripts of hodayot were found at Qumran, two in Cave 1 and six in Cave 4.[74] While the wording of individual psalms seems to have been consistent in the roughly one-third that overlap in more than one manuscript, the manuscripts do not reflect a stable collection over time in terms of order and number. There are also four manuscripts with hodayot that do not contain overlapping text with the others (4Q433, 433a, 4Q440, 4Q440a). As Angela Harkins has observed, "The various orders and arrangement of the hodayot among the different manuscripts from Caves 1 and 4 indicate that it was a living prayer collection that grew and changed over time, and not in predictable linear ways."[75] Harkins has argued that the

---

74. Stegemann and Schuller, *1QHodayotᵃ*, esp. 86–87, 178–179, 202–203, and 300–301.

75. Harkins, *Reading with an "I,"* 271.

oldest scroll (4Q428), for example, dating from 100–50 BCE, was an earlier form of the collection now known in 1QH^a but contained only the psalms found in 1QH^a 9–26, that is, what is commonly understood as an introductory creation psalm in col. 9, the Teacher Hymns, and the second group of Community Hymns.[76]

The physical character of the youngest and largest scroll, 1QH^a, which has been our particular focus, provides important clues about their significance and use and the evolution of the collection. 1QH^a is also the best preserved, with its thirty poems inscribed on seven sheets of parchment in twenty-eight columns on a scroll that is 35 centimeters high (approximately 13.75 inches) with a reconstructed length of 4.5 meters (about 14.75 feet).[77] It has a very large writing block, with 41–42 lines per column, which is almost twice as large as the next-biggest Hodayot manuscript.[78]

In his extensive work on the scribal scrolls, Emanuel Tov has identified thirty manuscripts that he describes as "*de luxe.*" He defines them as *de luxe* on the basis of wide top and bottom margins, a high quality of leather, fine calligraphy, and a low number of corrections or other scribal insertions.[79] While aspects of Tov's categorization are problematic, 1QH^a would be included in a group that reflects expensive and painstaking preparation.[80] As Émil Puech observes: "The impeccable material crafting of the scroll, which to our knowledge is unique among the manuscripts that have been found,

76. Harkins, "A New Proposal for Thinking about 1QH^a Sixty Years After Its Discovery," in *Texts from Cave 1 Sixty Years After Their Discovery: Proceedings of the Sixth Meeting of the International Organization of Qumran Studies in Ljubljana*, ed. Daniel K. Falk, Sarianna Metso, Donald W. Parry, and Eibert J. C. Tigchelaar, STDJ 91 (Leiden: Brill, 2010), 101–134. There is not a consensus on the character of 4Q428.

77. 4Q429 seems to have been a short scroll of eight columns. 4Q432 is the only papyrus scroll of the Hodayot that seems to have included only the so-called Teacher Hymns and dates to the last quarter of the first century BCE like 1QH^a. See Eileen Schuller in *Qumran Cave 4.XX: Poetical and Liturgical Texts*, Part 2, ed. Esther Chazon et al., DJD 29 (Oxford: Clarendon, 1999).

78. Emmanuel Tov, *Scribal Practices and Approaches Reflected in the Texts Found in the Judean Desert*, STDJ 54 (Leiden: Brill, 2004), 89. Other Hodayot scrolls range from 12 lines to 27/28 lines in height; for a concise overview of the character of the manuscripts, see Eileen M. Schuller, "Recent Scholarship on the *Hodayot* 1993–2010," *Currents in Biblical Research* 10 (2011): 119–162, at 122–131.

79. Tov, *Scribal Practices*, 126–129, 88–89.

80. See the critical evaluation by David Andrew Teeter, *Scribal Laws: Exegetical Variation in the Textual Transmission of Biblical Law in the Late Second Temple Period*, FAT 92 (Tübingen: Mohr Siebeck, 2014), 234–236. Teeter rightly finds a problem with Tov's conjoining the physical format of the manuscript with putative affiliation of a manuscript tradition ("proto-rabbinic text of scripture") and amount of corrections in the scroll, features that have no necessary correlation.

would in itself show the great esteem and importance the scribe-copyist accorded to this text, on a level with the great biblical manuscripts."[81]

The exact use of the Hodayot by the movement has been the subject of debate.[82] Given the complex textual history of the Hodayot, identifying how they were used requires qualification. Different scrolls of hodayot may have served different purposes at the same time, much as in contemporary settings the Book of Psalms is used for private prayer, for responsive readings in corporate worship, for communal study, and for reciting communally, whether chanting, in plainsong or some other means of vocalization. Some have proposed a private use for the first-person hymns and thanksgivings, and this should certainly not be ruled out.

Leather scrolls were expensive and time-consuming to prepare, so the large and elegant character of the 1QH[a] scroll suggests a special use beyond an individual. In light of both the connection to the chief leader of the Yaḥad and its size, it seems evident that large-format scrolls such as 1QH[a] had a public, communal use. I have worked under the assumption that the Maskil (or a maskil) performed the psalms ascribed to him in a communal gathering.[83]

In addition to the large format of the 1QH[a] manuscript, features internal to the contents of the scroll argue for a communal use. The collection of hymns in the 1QH[a] manuscript is at once liturgical and didactic.[84] Some of the psalms are conventionally liturgical in the sense that they are directed

---

81. Émil Puech, "Hodayot," *Encyclopedia of the Dead Sea Scrolls*, vol. 1, ed. Lawrence H. Schiffman and James C. VanderKam (Oxford: Oxford University Press, 2000), 365.

82. Daniel K. Falk, "The Scrolls and the Study of Ancient Jewish Liturgy," in *Oxford Handbook of the Dead Sea Scrolls*, ed. Timothy Lim and John J. Collins (New York: Oxford University Press, 2010), 630–631.

83. This does not rule out the possibility that other literate members of the community also performed some of the hymns in 1QH[a]. So, too, other collections of the hodayot may well have been used for private, individual study, either for reflection, for meditation, or, perhaps more likely, for training of the Maskil or other members of the *yaḥad*. Svend Holm-Nielsen proposed their use in the entry and covenant renewal ceremony described in the Community Rule because of the similarities in wording found in community hymns in columns 1QH[a] 4, 6, 8, and 20; *Hodayot*, 344–345. Carol Newsom, while not addressing the role of the Maskil superscriptions, has suggested that some of the community hymns may have served as a collection of models for oral performance; *The Self as Symbolic Space*, 203. See as well the different possibilities suggested by Eileen Schuller, including "when the Many gathered to 'watch together for a third of each night of the year . . . to bless together' (1QS 6:8)"; "Hodayot," in *Eerdmans Dictionary of Early Judaism*, 749, as discussed earlier in this chapter.

84. Daniel K. Falk, "Petition and Ideology," 142. Russell C. D. Arnold thinks the Hodayot may have been used in different contexts, "both in liturgical ways and in instructional settings"; *The Social Role of Liturgy in the Religion of the Qumran Community*, STDJ 60 (Leiden: Brill, 2006), 232.

as corporate worship toward God.[85] The so-called Self-Glorification Hymn (1QH[a] 25:34–27:4?ff.), one of the four also ascribed to the Maskil, offers the most overt example of this. It contains exhortation to rejoice, give praise, bless, and exalt (1QH[a] 26:10–14, 26), and to proclaim and declare the greatness of God (1QH[a] 26:26, 41) "in the *yaḥad* [or 'unified'] assembly."

The hodayot in 1QH[a] are also didactic, in the sense that they serve as teaching to those who hear them or who witness and participate in their recitation. Two passages in the 1QH[a] scroll point to a didactic purpose. One is part of the longer superscription in which the Maskil is mentioned. The psalm is composed "that the simple may understand . . . forever . . . and that humankind ['*enosh*] may understand concerning . . ." (1QH[a] 5:13). Though fragmentary, there is a clear indication that what follows is teaching for the benefit of the "simple" and humanity more broadly. This communal instructional use is reinforced also on the basis of 1QH[a] 9:36–38, which includes an exhortation in a series of plural imperatives. It begins with a phrase that suggests a didactic purpose and communal setting: "Hear, O sages and those who ponder knowledge," and also includes sectarian terminology, referring to "those who perfect the way." Silent reading by an individual is not in view. The exhortation to "hear" clearly suggests that the psalm was read aloud in a community.

The Maskil as Authorizer of the Hodayot

The Hodayot of 1QH[a] served purposes of both worship and instruction. We can also see that this collection takes on a particular character through the inclusion of an additional passage that describes the Maskil's duties:

> [For the Instruc]tor (Maskil), [thanksgiving and prayer for prostrating oneself and supplicating continually (להתנפל והתחנן תמיד) at all times: with the coming of

---

85. Esther Chazon has identified a number of features in 1QH[a] that argue for their communal liturgical use; "Liturgical Function in the Cave 1 Hodayot Collection," in *Qumran Cave 1 Revisited: Texts from Cave 1 Sixty Years After Their Discovery: Proceedings of the Sixth Meeting of the IOQS in Ljublyana*, ed. D. W. Parry, D. K. Falk, S. Metso, and E. J. C. Tigchelaar, STDJ 91 (Leiden: Boston, 2010), 135–149. These include the formula of "taking a stand before" God with the angels in 1QH[a] 11:22, 19:16, and 26:36; the clustered use of blessings near the end of long hymns; plural summonses to praise; and the lists of appointed times for the Maskil, the spiritual, liturgical leader of the Yaḥad, to offer prayers in 1QH[a] 20:7–13. The passage is quite similar to columns 9 and 10 of 1QS, which describe the Maskil's responsibilities and times of prayer, including an entry into the covenant twice.

light for [its] dominion]; at the midpoints of the day with respect to its arrangement according to the rules for the great light; when it turns to evening and light
goes forth at the beginning of the dominion of darkness at the time appointed
for night; at its midpoint, when it turns toward morning; and at the time that it
is gathered in to its dwelling place before (the approach of) light, at the depar-
ture of night and the coming of day, continually, at all the birthings of time, the
foundations of the seasons, and the cycle of the festivals in the order fixed by
their signs, for all their dominion in proper order, reliably, at the command of
God. (1QHᵃ 20:7–12)

The passage makes clear not only that the Maskil is the chief intercessor,
the one uniquely charged with prostrating and supplicating, but also that
this intercession is to be performed on a continual basis around the cosmic
clock. 1QHᵃ 20:7–14 is a passage that is akin to the end of the Community
Rule in describing the Maskil's responsibility for the regulation of times
for prayer. The heavenly bodies were as much a part of the divine order
and its foreordained cycle as human bodies. The Maskil's prostration is
not a one-time, occasional, or spontaneous practice but is to be habitu-
ated in sync with the cyclical movement of the celestial bodies, obedient
to the divine command for marking prayer times and festivals. The law
of the cosmos should thus accord with the law engraved on the Maskil's
tongue (1QS 10:6, 8, 11). Knowledge about the temporal cycle and how
liturgy corresponded to the divinely created was crucial to obedience to
divine law.

This particular rubric is considerably longer than other superscriptions
to the Maskil, which raises the question of its significance. The inclusion
of such a long rubric serves a purpose greater than simply communicating
instructions to the Maskil. Part of the wisdom inculcated—the canonical
message of this collection as a whole—is the knowledge of the Maskil's
place in aligning worship with the divinely created order of temporal cycles.
It establishes his role as a liturgical maestro within this textual collection
of psalms. To recall the analysis of Catherine Bell in our discussion of 2
Corinthians in Chapter 3, we see here not only the textualization of ritual
but the ritualization of text. This textual collection is ritualized by inclusion of the responsibilities of the Maskil vis-à-vis the cosmic time scheme.
By lodging a description of the Maskil's duties in relation to the collection
of psalms and their timing, the text indicates him as the indispensable performer of these texts. The final result of this interplay of text and rite was
the production of texts that are in effect authorized by the Maskil even if
he is not their *author* in the more literal sense of the term.

The Maskil's authorization also occurs through sacralization. At the end of the long rubric in column 20, the Maskil makes another confession of knowledge:

> And I, the Maskil, I know you, my God, by the spirit that you have placed in me. Faithfully have I heeded your wondrous secret counsel. By your holy spirit you have opened up knowledge within me through the mystery of your wisdom and the fountainhead of your power [. . .] in the midst of those who fear you, for abundant kindness. (1QHᵃ 20:14b–17a)

The Hodayot thus may be considered a matter not simply of divine inspiration but also of human exhalation. The two are in a sense the same, according to the distinctive anthropological perspective of the sect, in which the ability to offer praise is understood to result from a purified state free from sin. The Maskil, however, is uniquely in possession of divine holy spirit within him that reveals esoteric knowledge "in the midst of those who fear you."

Just as the 1QS recension of the Community Rule seems to be the end result of a long process of redaction, so too the Cave 1 collection of the Hodayot reflects the culmination of a longer process, though in this case it is a process of anthologizing discrete poems and hymns.[86] The attribution of Yaḥad texts to the Maskil seems to have expanded over time, with gradually more texts connected with this figure. As Charlotte Hempel observes: "We may therefore witness a very sizeable current of literary activity that spans across a great many scrolls by associating earlier material with the office of the/a *maskil*."[87]

CONCLUSION

The connection of the Maskil to the Hodayot collection brings us full circle to where this chapter began. In thinking about the attribution to a leader, the multiple manuscripts of Hodayot are akin to the non-sectarian psalms that appear in multiple manuscripts among the scrolls. All the psalms

---

86. Eileen Schuller described 1QHᵃ as "a compilation of smaller discrete collections," in "Some Contributions of the Cave Four Manuscripts (4Q427–432) to the Study of the Hodayot," *Dead Sea Discoveries* 8 (2001): 278–287, at 279.

87. Charlotte Hempel, "The *Treatise of the Two Spirits* and the Literary History of the *Rule of the Community*," in *Dualism in Qumran*, ed. Geza Xeravits, LSTS (London: T. & T. Clark, 2010), 102–120, at 116.

eventually become connected to David. A striking passage included in the great psalms scroll 11Q5 describes Israel's David not as a king but as a scribe and sage. He is said to have composed 4,050 psalms and songs for days and festivals throughout the fifty-two weeks of the year, all of which he "spoke through prophecy given to him by the Most High" (11Q5 27:10–11). The passage provides a missing link in understanding the changing role of David and the hermeneutical shift whereby words addressed to God as prayers come to be understood as scripture. The Psalms came to be viewed as inspired words formulated to shape the lives of individuals and communities.[88] There are of course a number of differences that make the analogy inexact. The collections of non-sectarian psalms at Qumran comprise the full range of genres known from the later Psalter. The Maskil is an unnamed figure and not a classic leader of all Israel. The Maskil is not said to write psalms; rather, it is the embodied performance of specific psalms connected to him that shape the hierarchical community of the Yaḥad. But the sapientialization of the psalms in the Hodayot collection and their connection to the Maskil, an inspired sage, is a prominent similarity.

In offering confessional psalms, prostrating, and petitioning, the Maskil trains members of the Yaḥad in a particular embodied ethos. Prostration of the liturgical leader was a strong visual cue to the congregation of the role of the leader among them to embody the virtue of humility. He is humble like Moses, and so prostrates, in order that the whole congregation can stand *bayyaḥad* with the angels. This entailed mastering the tradition of the ancestors, but also augmenting it through interpretation in the key of the Yaḥad's indigenous psychology. The wisdom of the past included preeminently the Torah of Moses and the Prophets, but also the esoteric knowledge of cosmic mysteries revealed to the elect.

The interpretation of earlier texts results in scripturalization. These psalms are understood to be placed on the tongue of the Maskil, who has holy spirit within him and displays and pronounces his knowledge. The Maskil is thus producing a form of teaching that, once written on scrolls in the preserved manuscripts, itself becomes authoritative writing for the Yaḥad movement. His poetic teaching is the sum total of accumulated study of the Torah and Prophets, that part of preparing the way of the Lord by study of the Torah and the Prophets. The Hodayot thus provide

---

88. James L. Kugel, "David the Prophet," in *Poetry and Prophecy*, ed. James L. Kugel (Ithaca, NY: Cornell University Press, 1990), 45–55.

a window into the processes that transformed literary texts into formative scriptures. The intimate and intricate relationship between liturgy and scriptural interpretation, wisdom and prophecy cannot be entirely disentangled nor separated from a consideration of its continuing performed enactment.

Conclusion

Praying is a peculiar practice. It does not come naturally. One has to be taught how to pray: the name of one's god, which words to say, how to comport oneself physically, on what occasions to offer prayer, what forms of address to use, whether to lament one's plight or confess one's faults or those of others, whether to bless, praise, or thank. Even the most "spontaneous" of prayers evince common forms of address and certain patterns. Voicing a prayer supposes, of course, that someone is listening, whether human or divine. Praying presumes a relationship with others or the Other. In his brief treatise *On Prayer*, Marcel Mauss, the influential anthropologist and teacher of Pierre Bourdieu, argues for the social and traditional nature of all prayers, whether communal or individual, private or public, spoken or silent. In short, as Mauss observed, prayer is a social act. It is also an embodied act. Should one kneel or stand? Are the eyes open or closed? Are the hands open or clasped? Voice requires breath and the ability to make sound. Should the prayer be offered sotto voce or loudly proclaimed, chanted to a tune or murmured? In his words, prayer "is a fragment of a religion. In it one can hear the echo of numberless phrases; it is a tiny piece of literature, it is the product of the accumulated efforts of men and women, over generations. . . . An invocation such as the beginning of the Lord's Prayer is the fruit of the work of centuries."[1] Like the Lord's Prayer, engraved on the hearts of Christians, the expression "easy as Ashrei" to

---

1. Marcel Mauss, *On Prayer*, trans. S. Leslie (New York: Berghahn Books, 2003), 33. The original French version of this short essay was his abortive doctoral thesis, which is now housed at the Institute of Social and Cultural Anthropology at Oxford University.

describe the familiarity of Psalm 145 to Jews comes from its daily recital in the liturgy. While both prayers are now offered on their own or as part of ritual services, in earlier times both were lodged in scriptural contexts.

While the Torah of Moses and prophetic books were recognized as authoritative during the Hellenistic-Roman period, there was not one stable set of scriptural texts with fixed and final wording normative for all Jewish communities. The collection of texts and their shape was still in flux. I have combined this now well-established finding of scholarship with evidence for the growing importance of prayer and liturgical activity in the post-exilic period. Prayer was understood to be a principal means of communication with the divine and a spur to revelation when the worshipper was away from the Jerusalem Temple; it served as a complement to or even substitute for Temple sacrifice. It was also a means of self and community formation. A chief feature of formal prayers found both within and independent of cultural texts is their interpretive use of earlier scripture. The creative interpretation of scripture in prayers reinforced the authority of scripture while simultaneously keeping it open. Such liturgical communities were diversely constituted throughout Judea and the diaspora, giving rise to the ongoing, richly varied expressions of Judaism, and Christianity, that we still know today.

In this book, I have sought to illuminate the embodied performative contexts in which scripture can be said to have taken shape. I have adopted a definition of "liturgical" broader than the contemporary understanding of a communal prayer rite in order to include embodied practices around prayer and the learning of scripture. A liturgical habitus, to draw on the concept of Pierre Bourdieu, was cultivated through both individual and communal prayer, reading, and performance. Such ongoing performances were an integral feature of the transmission of cultural texts and their transformation into "scriptural" texts. Oral performance of prayer in connection with the reading and study of scripture were also occasions of interpretation, the results of which we see in scribal transmission and extension of texts. Different instantiations of "indigenous psychology" shaped such interpretation as well as the communal settings in which text was enacted. The liturgical elements and aspects of performance that are represented in the texts themselves serve both to authorize the text as scripture and to establish a setting that enables its extension. In the late Second Temple period, the ongoing interpretation of scripture in communal contexts, mediated in part through prayers, hymns, and other poetic texts, can help to explain its open-ended and pluriform character.

I have argued that the practice of prayer was central both in the formation of individuals and communities as well as in the transformation of literary texts into scripture during the Hellenistic-Roman period. This happened through the ongoing performance of prayer and texts by various learned mediators, "liturgical bodies," in the community. While I have maintained that the contexts for seeing this transformation are most easily discernible and substantiated in the Hellenistic-Roman period, particularly in light of the evidence from the Dead Sea Scrolls, the entwinement of worship and scripture has a long history. In the composition of literature, one finds prayers, hymns, blessings, and songs included as part of the narrative to illustrate and emphasize piety. In the transmission of important cultural texts, whether during their recital or in the subsequent recopying by learned scribes, prayers and hymns were often adapted and inserted at opportune points in the story. At the description of a great event, like the crossing of the Red Sea, or at the consecration marking the completion of the building of the Jerusalem Temple, hymns and prayers were included in scripture as a means of teaching while inculcating particular theological perspectives. The exposure to such influential texts and the learning of such lessons served to shape a liturgical habitus. While the scriptures are ancient in origin, they continued to evolve well into the Common Era even as new works were composed. Whereas the Song of Miriam amounts to a single verse in Exod 15:21, a reworking of the Pentateuch in 4Q365 provides a longer song of triumph. The book of Jubilees, interwoven with prayers and blessings, itself shows vital interpretive engagement with a fluid Pentateuch. The making of scriptures did not occur on a narrow teleological path in the discrete cubicles of individual scribes.

My hope is that this work offers a new perspective, not only because of the anthropological and neurocognitive frameworks enlisted in painting a holistic portrait of scripture creation in communal contexts but also by virtue of the breadth of literature considered in moving beyond works that later entered the Tanakh. I have evaluated an anthology of wisdom sayings, narrative prophetic works, a conflation of letters, and a collection of psalms. The book thus cuts across boundaries of genre.

Different genres reflect different patterns of augmentation. Sirach is an anthological collection of proverbial sayings, yet in contrast to Proverbs, its scribal author models a pious pedagogy that makes both daily worship and the internalization and amplification of wisdom a part of the ongoing task of the budding sage. Daniel and Baruch provide prophetic narratives in which the role of confession in relation to ending the exile is contested through their respective story lines. By interpreting Jeremianic oracles and composing some anew, the book of Baruch authorizes itself as both an etiology of confessional prayer practice and a continuation of Jeremiah's prophetic work. Interpretive tradition is thus revealed as a generative component of new scripture. In forging new transethnic congregations, the letters of Paul interpreted traditional Judean scriptures in light of contemporary cultural practices emerging from a new revelatory understanding. 2 Corinthians is distinctive in its concern for elevating Paul's apostolic status as one who embodies Christ's death in his own suffering.

The Hodayot, as psalms, exhibit a similarity to the non-sectarian psalm collections in their authorization by a learned figure, the Maskil, who was considered an inspired sage and liturgical maestro. Unlike David, the Maskil has no august role in Israel's history. He is a contemporary leader born of the needs of a new movement. The Hodayot display a higher degree of scripturalization in their erudite reworking of scripture understood through the indigenous psychology of the Yaḥad than do the psalms. That the Hodayot never entered anyone's Bible could be due to the demise of the Yaḥad movement in the wake of the Jewish wars with Rome.

I have by no means presented a complete catalogue of scripture formation. Understanding texts as divinely revealed was a crucial element in differentiating scripture from other texts, but the perception of divine revelation varied. In this book, we have considered cases of visionary revelation from angelic figures, the revelatory study of text, the messianic revelation in a messianic figure, and a teacher of esoteric divine knowledge. Many other texts sharing similar dynamics of worship, interpretive discernment, and performance might be considered scripture for other communities in antiquity. Examples include sapiential texts such as the Wisdom of Solomon and 4Q Instruction, the historiographies of 1 and 2 Maccabees, and texts of a more legal bent such as the Temple Scroll. The communal context within which these were forged is not so clearly evident, so the full account of scripture development remains obscure.

The open-ended character of scriptures "before the Bible" has implications for understanding life "after" the Bible. It is important to note that I have not meant in this book to undermine the value of a biblical canon. Delimiting a canon is an important, even essential matter for defining a community. Communities, whether religious or political, benefit from limiting the number of writings they consult for meaning and for value formation. Yet the factors that went into shaping the final borders of biblical canons of Jews and Christians in antiquity occurred in light of later historical events, after the fall of the Temple and connected with the rise of Christianity as a religion of empire after Constantine. But that tale is for another book and another time.

BIBLIOGRAPHY

Ackroyd, Peter. *Exile and Restoration: A Study of Hebrew Thought of the Sixth Century* B.C. The Old Testament Library. Philadelphia: Westminster John Knox Press, 1968.

Aitken, Ellen Bradshaw. *Jesus' Death in Early Christian Memory: The Poetics of the Passion.* Novum Testamentum et Orbis Antiquus 53. Göttingen: Vandenhoeck & Ruprecht, 2004.

Alexander, Elizabeth Shanks. *Transmitting Mishnah: The Shaping Influence of Oral Tradition.* Cambridge: Cambridge University Press, 2006.

Alexander, Elizabeth Shanks. "Women's Exemption from Shema and Tefillin and How These Rituals Came to Be Viewed as Torah Study." *Journal for the Study of Judaism in the Persian, Hellenistic, and Roman Periods* 42 (2011): 531–579.

Alexander, Loveday. "The Living Voice: Scepticism Towards the Written Word in Early Christian and in Graeco-Roman Texts." In *The Bible in Three Dimensions: Essays in Celebration of Forty Years of Biblical Studies in the University of Sheffield*, ed. David J. A. Clines, Stephen E. Fowl, and Stanley E. Porter, 221–247. Journal for the Study of the Old Testament: Supplement Series 87. Sheffield: Sheffield Academic Press, 1990.

Amihay, Aryeh. *Theory and Practice in Essene Law.* New York: Oxford University Press, 2016.

Angel, Joseph L. "Maskil, Community, and Religious Experience in the *Songs of the Sage* (4Q510–511)." *Dead Sea Discoveries* 19 (2012): 1–27.

Arnal, William. "The Collection and Synthesis of 'Tradition' and the Second-Century Invention of Christianity." *Method and Theory in the Study of Religion* 23 (2011): 193–215.

Arnold, Russell C. D. *The Social Role of Liturgy in the Religion of the Qumran Community.* Studies on the Texts of the Desert of Judah 60. Leiden: Brill, 2006.

Ascough, Richard S. "Translocal Relationships Among Voluntary Associations and Early Christianity." *Journal of Early Christian Studies* 5 (1997): 223–241.

Ascough, Richard S. "What Are They Now Saying About Christ Groups and Associations?" *Currents in Biblical Research* 13, no. 2 (2015): 207–244.

Assmann, Jan. "Collective Memory and Cultural Identity." *New German Critique* 65 (1995): 125–133. (Originally published in *Kultur und Gedächtnis*, ed. Jan Assmann and Tonio Hölscher, 9–19. Frankfurt/Main: Suhrkamp, 1988.)

Balentine, Samuel. "'I Was Ready to Be Sought Out by Those Who Did Not Ask.'" In *Seeking the Favor of God*, volume 1, *The Origins of Penitential Prayer in Second Temple Judaism*, ed. Mark J. Boda, Daniel K. Falk, and Rodney A. Werline, 1–20. Society of Biblical Literature Early Judaism and Its Literature 22. Atlanta: SBL, 2006.

Barclay, John M. G. *Paul and the Gift*. Grand Rapids, MI: Eerdmans, 2015.

Barton, John. *Oracles of God: Perceptions of Ancient Prophecy in Israel After the Exile*. London: Darton, Longman, and Todd, 1986.

Beentjes, Pancratius C. *The Book of Ben Sira in Hebrew: A Text Edition of All Extant Hebrew Manuscripts and a Synopsis of All Parallel Hebrew Ben Sira Text*. Leiden: Brill, 1997.

Becker, Eve-Marie. *Letter Hermeneutics in 2 Corinthians: Studies in "Literarkritik" and Communication Theory*. London: T. & T. Clark International, 2004.

Bell, Catherine. *Ritual Theory, Ritual Practice*. New York: Oxford University Press, 2009.

Bell, Catherine. "The Ritualization of Text and the Textualization of Ritual in the Codification of Taoist Liturgy." *History of Religions* 27, no. 4 (1988): 366–392.

Berlin, Adele. *Lamentations*. The Old Testament Library. Louisville, KY: Westminster John Knox Press, 2002.

Berlin, Adele. "Qumran Laments and the Study of Lament Literature." In *Liturgical Perspectives: Prayer and Poetry in Light of the Dead Sea Scrolls*, ed. Esther G. Chazon, 1–17. Studies on the Texts of the Desert of Judah 48. Leiden: Brill, 2003.

Bernstein, Moshe. "'Rewritten Bible' A Generic Category Which Has Outlived Its Usefulness?" *Textus* 22 (2005): 169–196.

Betz, Hans Dieter. *Corinthians 8 and 9*. Philadelphia: Fortress, 1985.

Bieringer, Reimund. "The Comforted Comforter: The Meaning of παρακαλέω or παράκλησις Terminology in 2 Corinthians." *HTS Teologiese Studies/Theological Studies* 67, no. 1 (2011). doi: 10.4102/hts.v67i1.969.

Blumell, Lincoln H. "The Medium and the Message: Some Observations on Epistolary Communication in Antiquity from the Papyri." *Journal of Greco-Roman Christianity and Judaism* 10 (2014): 24–67.

Boda, Mark J. "Confession as Theological Expression." In *Seeking the Favor of God*, volume 1, *The Origins of Penitential Prayer in Second Temple Judaism*, ed. Mark J. Boda, Daniel K. Falk, and Rodney A. Werline, 21–45. Society of Biblical Literature Early Judaism and Its Literature 22. Atlanta: SBL, 2006.

Boda, Mark J., Daniel K. Falk, and Rodney A. Werline, eds. *Seeking the Favor of God*, volume 3, *The Impact of Penitential Prayer Beyond Second Temple Judaism*. Society of Biblical Literature Early Judaism and Its Literature 23. Atlanta: SBL, 2009.

Bogaert, Pierre-Maurice. "Le nom de Baruch dans la littérature pseu-dépigraphique: l'apocalypse syriaque et le livre deutérocanonique." In *La littéra-ture juive entre Tenach et Mischna: quelques problèmes*, ed. Willem C. van Unnik, 56–72. Leiden: Brill, 1974.

Bogaert, Pierre-Maurice. "Le personage de Baruch et l'histoire du livre de Jérémie: Aux origines du livre deutérocanonique de Baruch." In *International Congress on New Testament Studies*, ed. Elizabeth A. Livingstone, 73–81. Berlin: Akademie, 1982.

Bourdieu, Pierre. *Distinction: A Social Critique of the Judgement of Taste*. Cambridge, MA: Harvard University Press, 1984. (Originally published in French as *La Distinction: Critique Sociale du Jugement*. Paris: Éditions de Minuit, 1979.)

Brakke, David. "Scriptural Practices in Early Christianity: Towards a New History of the New Testament Canon." In *Invention, Rewriting, Usurpation: Discursive Fights over Religious Traditions in Antiquity*, ed. Jörg Ulrich, Anders-Christian Jacobsen, and David Brakke, 263–280. Early Christianity in the Context of Antiquity 11. Berlin: Peter Lang, 2012.

Brakke, David, Michael L. Satlow, and Steven Weitzman, eds. *Religion and the Self in Antiquity*. Bloomington: Indiana University Press, 2005.

Brand, Miryam T. *Evil Within and Without: The Source of Sin and Its Nature as Portrayed in Second Temple Literature.* Journal of Ancient Judaism: Supplements 9. Göttingen: Vandenhoeck & Ruprecht, 2013.

Brooke, George J. "Between Authority and Canon: The Significance of Reworkng the Bible for Understanding the Canonical Process." In *Reworking the Bible: Apocryphal and Related Texts at Qumran,* ed. Esther G. Chazon, Devorah Dimant, and Ruth Anne Clements, 85–104. Studies on the Texts of the Desert of Judah 58. Leiden: Brill, 2005.

Brooke, George J. "Canonisation Processes of the Jewish Bible in the Light of the Qumran Scrolls." In *"For It Is Written": Essays on the Function of Scripture in Early Judaism and Christianity,* ed. Jan Dochhorn, 13–35. Early Christianity in the Context of Antiquity 12. Frankfurt am Main: Peter Lang, 2011.

Brooke, George J. *Exegesis at Qumran: 4Q Florilegium in Its Jewish Context.* Journal for the Study of the Old Testament: Supplement Series 29. Sheffield: JSOT Press, 1985.

Brooke, George J. "The Formation and Renewal of Scriptural Tradition." In *Biblical Traditions in Transmission: Essays in Honour of Michael A. Knibb,* ed. Charlotte Hempel and Judith M. Lieu, 39–59. Supplements to the Journal for the Study of Judaism in the Persian, Hellenistic, and Roman Periods 11. Leiden: Brill, 2006.

Brooke, George J. "Miqdash Adam, Eden, and the Qumran Community." In *Gemeinde ohne Tempel = Community Without Temple: Zur Substituierung und Transformation des Jerusalemer Tempels und seines Kults im Alten Testament, antiken Judentum und frühen Christentum,* ed. Beate Ego, Armin Lange, und Peter Pilhofer, 285–301. Tübingen: Mohr Siebeck, 1999.

Brooke, George J. "Parabiblical Prophetic Narratives." In *The Dead Sea Scrolls After Fifty Years: A Comprehensive Assessment,* volume 1, ed. J. VanderKam and P. W. Flint, 271–301. Leiden: Brill, 1998–1999.

Brooke, George J. "Prophecy and Prophets in the Dead Sea Scrolls: Looking Backwards and Forwards." In *Prophets, Prophecy, and Prophetic Texts in the Dead Sea Scrolls,* ed. M. H. Floyd and R. D. Haak, 151–165. Library of Hebrew Bible/Old Testament Studies 427. New York: T. & T. Clark, 2006.

Brooke, George J. "The Qumran Scrolls and the Demise of the Distinction Between Higher and Lower Criticism." In *Reading the Dead Sea Scrolls: Essays in Method.* Society of Biblical Literature Early Judaism and Its Literature 39. Atlanta: SBL, 2013.

Brooke, George J. "Reading, Searching, Blessing." In *The Temple in Text and Tradition: A Festschrift in Honour of Robert Hayward,* ed. R. Timothy McLay, 140–156. London: Bloomsbury, 2015.

Brooke, George J. "The Rewritten Law, Prophets and Psalms: Issues for Understanding the Text of the Bible." In *The Bible as Book: The Hebrew Bible and the Judaean Desert Discoveries,* ed. Edward D. Herbert and Emanuel Tov, 31–40. London: The British Library and Oak Knoll Press, 2002.

Brown, Peter. *The Body and Society: Men, Women, and Sexual Renunciation in Early Christianity.* Princeton, NJ: Princeton University Press, 1988.

Burke, David G. *The Poetry of Baruch: Reconstruction and Analysis of the Original Hebrew Text of Baruch 3:9–5:9.* Society of Biblical Literature Septuagint and Cognate Studies 10. Chico, CA: Scholars Press, 1982.

Camp, Claudia. *Ben Sira and the Men Who Handle Books.* Sheffield: Sheffield Phoenix, 2013.

Carmignac, Jean. "Les citations de l'Ancien Testament et spécialement des Poèmes du Serviteur, dans les Hymnes de Qumran." *Revue de Qumran* 2 (1959–1960): 357–394.

Carr, David M. *The Formation of the Hebrew Bible: A New Reconstruction*. New York: Oxford University Press, 2011.

Carr, David M. *Writing on the Tablet of the Heart: Origins of Scripture and Literature*. New York: Oxford University Press, 2005.

Chazon, Esther G. "Liturgical Function in the Cave 1 Hodayot Collection." In *Qumran Cave 1 Revisited: Texts from Cave 1 Sixty Years After Their Discovery: Proceedings of the Sixth Meeting of the IOQS in Ljublyana*, ed. D. W. Parry, D. K. Falk, S. Metso and E. J. C. Tigchelaar, 135–149. Studies on the Texts of the Desert of Judah 91. Leiden: Boston, 2010.

Chazon, Esther G. "Liturgy Before and After the Temple's Destruction: Change or Continuity?" In *Was 70 CE a Watershed in Jewish History? On Jews and Judaism Before and After the Destruction of the Second Temple*, ed. Daniel R. Schwartz and Zeev Weiss, 371–392. Ancient Judaism and Early Christianity 78. Leiden: Brill, 2012.

Chazon, Esther G. "Tradition and Innovation in Sectarian Religious Poetry." In *Prayer and Poetry in the Dead Sea Scrolls and in Related Literature: Essays in Honor of Eileen Schuller on the Occasion of Her 65th Birthday*, ed. Jeremy Penner, Ken M. Penner, and Cecilia Wassen, 55–68. Studies on the Texts of the Desert of Judah 98. Leiden: Brill, 2012.

Chazon, Esther G. "The Words of the Luminaries and Penitential Prayer in Second Temple Times." In *Seeking the Favor of God*, volume 2, *The Development of Penitential Prayer in Second Temple Judaism*, ed. Mark J. Boda, Daniel K. Falk, and Rodney A. Werline, 177–186. Society of Biblical Literature Early Judaism and Its Literature 22. Atlanta: SBL Press. 2007.

Chazon, Esther G., Torleif Elgvin, Esther Eshel, Daniel Falk, Bilhah Nitzan, Elisha Qimron, Eileen Schuller, David Seely, and Eibert Tigchelaar, eds. *Qumran Cave 4.XX: Poetical and Liturgical Texts*, Part 2. Discoveries in the Judean Desert 29. Oxford: Clarendon, 1999.

Cirafesi, Wally. "'Taken from Dust, Formed from Clay': Compound Allusions and Scriptural Exegesis in 1QHodayot^a 11:20–37; 20:27–39 and Ben Sira 33:7–15." *Dead Sea Discoveries* 24 (2017): 1–31.

Cohn, Yehudah B. *Tangled Up in Text: Tefillin in the Ancient World*. Brown Judaic Studies 131. Providence, RI: Brown Judaic Studies, 2008.

Collins, John J. "The Angelic Life." In *Metamorphoses: Resurrection, Body and Transformative Practices in Early Christianity*, ed. Turid Karlsen Seim and Jorunn Økland, 291–310. Ekstasis 1. Berlin: De Gruyter, 2009.

Collins, John J. *Daniel: A Commentary on the Book of Daniel*. Hermeneia. Minneapolis: Fortress, 1993.

Collins, John J. *Daniel with an Introduction to Apocalyptic Literature*. Ed. Rolf Knierim and Gene M. Tucker. The Forms of the Old Testament Literature 20. Grand Rapids, MI: Eerdmans, 1984.

Connerton, Paul. *The Spirit of Mourning: History, Memory and the Body*. New York: Cambridge University Press, 2011.

Corley, Jeremy. "Searching for Structure and Redaction in Ben Sira." In *The Wisdom of Ben Sira: Studies on Tradition, Redaction, and Theology*, ed. Angelo Passaro and Giuseppe Bellia, 21–48. Deuterocanonical and Cognate Literature Studies 1. Berlin: De Gruyter, 2008.

Corwin, Anna. "Changing God, Changing Bodies: The Impact of New Prayer Practices on Elderly Catholic Nuns' Embodied Experience." *Ethos* 40 (2012): 390–410.

Crenshaw, James L. "The Restraint of Reason, the Humility of Prayer." In *The Echoes of Many Texts: Reflections on Jewish and Christian Traditions: Essays in Honor of Lou H. Silberman*, ed. William G. Dever and J. E. Wright, 81–97. Brown Judaic Studies 313. Atlanta: Scholars Press, 1997.

Cribiore, Raffaella. *Gymnastics of the Mind: Greek Education in Hellenistic and Roman Egypt*. Princeton, NJ: Princeton University Press, 2001.

Csordas, Thomas J, ed. *Embodiment and Experience: The Existential Ground of Culture and Self*. New York: Cambridge University Press, 1994.

Csordas, Thomas J. *Language, Charisma, and Creativity: The Ritual Life of a Religious Movement*. Berkeley: University of California Press, 1997.

Dagenais, John. *The Ethics of Reading in Manuscript Culture: Glossing the* Libro de buen Amor. Princeton, NJ: Princeton University Press, 1994.

Damasio, Antonio. *Self Comes to Mind: Constructing the Conscious Brain*. New York: Pantheon, 2010.

Davies, Philip R. "The Hebrew Canon and the Origins of Judaism." In *The Historian and the Bible: Essays in Honor of Lester L. Grabbe*, ed. Philip R. Davies and Diana V. Edelman, 194–206. London: T. & T. Clark, 2010.

Davies, Philip R. "Loose Canons, Reflections on the Formation of the Hebrew Bible." *Journal of Hebrew Scriptures* 1, no. 5 (1997). http://www.jhsonline.org/cocoon/JHS/a005.html.

Davies, Philip R. *Scribes and Schools: The Canonization of the Hebrew Scriptures*. London: SPCK, 1998.

Davis, Kipp. "Prophets of Exile: 4Q *Apocryphon of Jeremiah C*, Apocryphal Baruch, and the Efficacy of the Second Temple." *Journal for the Study of Judaism in the Persian, Hellenistic, and Roman Periods* 44, nos. 4–5 (2013): 497–529.

Davis, Kipp. "Torah-Performance and History in the *Golah*: Rewritten Bible or 'Representational' Authority in the *Apocryphon of Jeremiah C*." In *Celebrating the Dead Sea Scrolls: A Canadian Collection*, ed. P. Flint, J. Duhaime, and K. Baek, 467–495. Early Judaism and Its Literature 30. Atlanta: SBL Press, 2011.

Deichgräber, Reinhard. *Gotteshymnus und Christushymnus in der frühen Christenheit: Untersuchungen zur Form, Sprache und Stil der frühchristlichen Hymnen*. Studien zur Umwelt des Neuen Testaments 5. Göttingen: Vandenhoeck & Ruprecht, 1967.

Dimant, Devorah. "The Apocryphon of Jeremiah." Paper presented at the first meeting of the International Organization for Qumran Studies, Paris, 1992.

Dimant, Devorah. "From the Book of Jeremiah to the Qumranic *Apocryphon of Jeremiah*." *Dead Sea Discoveries* 20 (2013): 452–471.

Dimant, Devorah. *Qumran Cave 4.XXI: Parabiblical Texts, Part 4: Pseudo-Prophetic Texts*. Discoveries in the Judean Desert 30. Oxford: Clarendon Press, 2001.

Dimant, Devorah. "Time, Torah, and Prophecy at Qumran." In *History, Ideology, and Bible Interpretation in the Dead Sea Scrolls: Collected Studies*, 301–314. Forschungen Zum Alten Testament 90. Tübingen: Mohr Siebeck, 2014.

Doering, Lutz. *Ancient Jewish Letters and the Beginning of Christian Epistolography*. Wissenschaftliche Untersuchungen zum Neuen Testament 298. Tübingen: Mohr Siebeck, 2012.

Doering, Lutz. "Jeremia in Babylonien und Ägypten: Mündliche und schriftliche Toraparänese für Exil und Diaspora nach 4Q*Apocryphon of Jeremiah C*." In *Frühjudentum und Neues Testament im Horizont Biblischer Theologie: Mit einem*

Anhang zum Corpus Judaeo-Hellenisticum Novi Testamenti, ed. W. Kraus and K. W. Niebuhr, 50–79. Tübingen: Mohr Siebeck, 2003.

Donaldson, Terence L. *Paul and the Gentiles: Remapping the Apostle's Convictional World.* Philadelphia: Augsburg Fortress, 1997.

Downs, David J. *The Offering of the Gentiles.* Wissenschaftliche Untersuchungen zum Neuen Testament 2.248. Tübingen: Mohr Siebeck, 2008.

Eckhardt, Benedikt. "The Eighteen Associations of Corinth." *Greek, Roman and Byzantine Studies* 56 (2016): 646–662.

Ehrlich, Uri. *The Nonverbal Language of Prayer: A New Approach to the Study of Jewish Liturgy.* Trans. Dena Ordan. Texts and Studies in Ancient Judaism 105. Tübingen: Mohr Siebeck, 2004.

Esler, Philip F. *The First Christians and Their Social World.* London: Routledge, 1994.

Falk, Daniel K. "Biblical Adaptation for 4Q392 *Works of God* and 4Q393 *Communal Confession.*" In *The Provo International Conference on the Dead Sea Scrolls: Technical Innovations, New Texts, and Reformulated Issues,* ed. Donald W. Parry and Eugene Ulrich, 126–146. Studies on the Texts of the Desert of Judah 30. Leiden: Brill, 1999.

Falk, Daniel K. *Daily Sabbath, and Festival Prayers in the Dead Sea Scrolls.* Studies on the Texts of the Desert of Judah 27. Leiden: Brill, 1998.

Falk, Daniel K. "Material Aspects of Prayer Manuscripts at Qumran." In *Literature or Liturgy? Early Christian Hymns and Prayers in Their Literary and Liturgical Context in Antiquity,* ed. Clemens Leonhard and Hermut Löhr, 33–87. Wissenschaftliche Untersuchungen zum Neuen Testament II 363. Tübingen: Mohr Siebeck, 2014.

Falk, Daniel K. "Petition and Ideology in the Dead Sea Scrolls." In *Prayer and Poetry in the Dead Sea Scrolls and in Related Literature: Essays in Honor of Eileen Schuller on the Occasion of Her 65th Birthday,* ed. Jeremy Penner, Ken M. Penner, and Cecilia Wassen, 135–159. *Studies on the Texts of the Desert of Judah 98.* Leiden: Brill, 2012.

Falk, Daniel K. "Scriptural Inspiration for Penitential Prayer." In *Seeking the Favor of God,* volume 2, *The Development of Penitential Prayer in Second Temple Judaism,* ed. Mark J. Boda, Daniel K. Falk, and Rodney A. Werline, 127–157. Society of Biblical Literature, Early Judaism and Its Literature 22. Atlanta: SBL Press, 2007.

Falk, Daniel K. "The Scrolls and the Study of Ancient Jewish Liturgy." In *Oxford Handbook of the Dead Sea Scrolls,* ed. Timothy Lim and John J. Collins, 630–631. New York: Oxford University Press, 2010.

Fauconnier, Gilles, and Mark Turner. *The Way We Think: Conceptual Blending and the Mind's Hidden Complexities.* New York: Basic Books, 2002.

Feinberg, Todd E. *From Axons to Identity: Neurological Explorations of the Nature of Identity.* New York: W. W. Norton, 2009.

Fischer, Georg, and A. Vonach. "Tendencies in the LXX Version of Jeremiah." In *Der Prophet wie Mose: Studien zum Jeremiahbuch,* 64–72. Wiesbaden: Harrassowitz, 2011.

Fishbane, Michael. *Biblical Interpretation in Ancient Israel.* Oxford: Clarendon Press, 1988.

Fitzgerald, John T. *Cracks in an Earthen Vessel: An Examination of the Catalogues of Hardships in the Corinthian Correspondence.* Society of Biblical Literature Dissertation Series. Atlanta: Scholars Press, 1988.

Fletcher-Louis, Crispin H. T. *All the Glory of Adam: Liturgical Anthropology in the Dead Sea Scrolls.* Studies on the Texts of the Desert of Judah 42. Leiden: Brill, 2002.

Flint, Peter W. "The Daniel Tradition at Qumran." In *The Book of Daniel: Composition and Reception*, volume 2, ed. John J. Collins, Peter W. Flint, and Cameron VanEpps, 329–367. Leiden: Brill, 2001.

Flood, Gavin. *The Ascetic Self: Subjectivity, Memory, and Tradition*. New York: Cambridge University Press, 2004.

Floyd, Michael. "Penitential Prayer in the Second Period from the Perspective of Baruch." In *Seeking the Favor of God*, volume 2, *The Development of Penitential Prayer in Second Temple Judaism*, ed. Mark J. Boda, Daniel K. Falk, and Rodney A. Werline, 51–81. Early Judaism and Its Literature 22. Atlanta, GA: SBL Press, 2007.

Fraade, Steven D. "Interpretive Authority in the Study Community at Qumran." *Journal of Jewish Studies* 44 (1993): 46–69.

Fraade, Steven D. "Literary Composition and Oral Performance in the Early Midrashim." *Oral Tradition* 14 (1999): 33–51.

Frennesson, Bjørn. *"In a Common Rejoicing": Liturgical Communion with Angels in Qumran*. Uppsala: Uppsala University Library, 1999.

Friesen, Steve. "Paul and Economics: The Jerusalem Collection as an Alternative to Patronage." In *Paul Unbound: Other Perspectives on the Apostle*, ed. Mark P. Given, 27–54. Peabody, MA: Hendrickson, 2010.

Gallagher, Shaun. "Philosophical Conceptions of the Self: Implications for Cognitive Science." *Trends in Cognitive Sciences* 4, no. 1 (2000): 14–21.

Gamble, Harry Y. *Books and Readers in the Ancient Church: A History of Early Christian Texts*. New Haven, CT: Yale University Press, 1995.

Gauthier, Philippe. *Les cités grecques et leurs bienfaiteurs (IVe–Ier avant J.-C): Contribution à l'histoire des institutions*. Suppléments du bulletin de correspondence hellénique 12. Athènes: École Française d'Athènes, 1985.

Gilbert, Maurice. "Methodological and Hermeneutical Trends in Modern Exegesis on the Book of Ben Sira." In *The Wisdom of Ben Sira: Studies on Tradition, Redaction, and Theology*, ed. Angelo Passaro and Giuseppe Bellia, 1–20. Deuterocanonical and Cognate Literature Studies 1. Berlin: De Gruyter, 2008.

Gilbert, Maurice. "Prayer in the Book of Ben Sira." In *Prayer from Tobit to Qumran*, ed. R. Egger-Wenzel and J. Corley, 117–135. International Society for the Study of Deuterocanonical and Cognate Literature 1. Berlin: De Gruyter, 2004.

Glancy, Jennifer. *Corporal Knowledge: Early Christian Bodies*. New York: Oxford University Press, 2010.

Goering, Greg. *Wisdom's Root Revealed: Ben Sira and the Election of Israel*. Supplements to the Journal for the Study of Judaism in the Persian, Hellenistic, and Roman Periods 139. Leiden: Brill, 2009.

Goldstein, Jonathan. "The Apocryphal Book of I Baruch." *Proceedings of the American Academy for Jewish Research* 46–47 (1979–1980): 179–199.

Goodman, Martin. *The Ruling Class of Judaea: The Origins of the Jewish Revolt Against Rome A.D. 66–70*. Cambridge: Cambridge University Press, 1987.

Gordley, Matthew E. *Teaching Through Song in Antiquity*. Wissenschaftliche Untersuchungen zum Neuen Testament 2.302. Tübingen: Mohr Siebeck, 2011.

Gottwald, Norman K. *Studies in the Book of Lamentations*. SCM's Studies in Biblical Theology 14. London: SCM Press, 1954.

Gowan, Donald E. "The Exile in Jewish Apocalyptic." In *Scripture in History and Theology: Essays in Honor of J. Coert Rylaarsdam*, ed. A. W. Merrill and T. W. Overholt, 205–223. Pittsburgh Theological Monograph Series 17. Pittsburgh: Pickwick, 1977.

Gregory, Bradley C. "The Postexilic Exile in Third Isaiah." *Journal of Biblical Literature* 126, no. 3 (2007): 475–496.

Greenberg, Moshe. *Biblical Prose Prayer as a Window into the Popular Religion of Israel.* Berkeley: University of California Press, 1983.

Grossman, Maxine. "Cultivating Identity: Textual Virtuosity and 'Insider' Status." In *Defining Identities: We, You, and the Other in the Dead Sea Scrolls*, ed. Florentino García Martínez and Mladen Popović, 1–11. Studies on the Texts of the Desert of Judah 70. Leiden: Brill, 2008.

Grossman, Maxine, ed. *Rediscovering the Dead Sea Scrolls: An Assessment of Old and New Approaches and Methods.* Grand Rapids, MI: Eerdmans, 2010.

Gunneweg, Antonius H. J. *Das Buch Baruch.* JSHRZ III. Gütersloh: Gütersloher Verlaghaus, 1980.

Gygax, Marc Domingo. *Benefaction and Rewards in the Ancient Greek City: The Origins of Euergetism.* New York: Cambridge University Press, 2016.

Hall, David D., ed. *Lived Religion in America: Toward a History of Practice.* Princeton, NJ: Princeton University Press, 1997.

Halvorson-Taylor, Martien. *Enduring Exile: The Metaphorization of Exile in the Hebrew Bible.* Supplements to Vetus Testamentum 141. Leiden: Brill, 2010.

Harkins, Angela Kim [as Angela Kim]. "Authorizing Interpretation in Poetic Compositions in the Dead Sea Scrolls and Later Jewish and Christian Traditions." *Dead Sea Discoveries* 10 (2003): 26–58.

Harkins, Angela Kim. "The Community Hymns Classification: A Proposal for Further Differentiation." *Dead Sea Discoveries* 15 (2008): 121–154.

Harkins, Angela Kim. "How Should We Feel About the Teacher of Righteousness?" *Is There a Text in This Cave? Studies in the Textuality of the Dead Sea Scrolls in Honour of George J. Brooke*, ed. Ariel Feldman, Maria Cioată, and Charlotte Hempel, 493–514. Studies on the Texts of the Desert of Judah 119. Leiden: Brill, 2017.

Harkins, Angela Kim. "A New Proposal for Thinking About 1QHᵃ Sixty Years After Its Discovery." In *Texts from Cave 1 Sixty Years After Their Discovery: Proceedings of the Sixth Meeting of the International Organization of Qumran Studies in Ljubljana*, ed. Daniel K. Falk, Sarianna Metso, Donald W. Parry, and Eibert J. C. Tigchelaar, 101–134. Studies on the Texts of the Desert of Judah 91. Leiden: Brill, 2010.

Harkins, Angela Kim. *Reading with an "I" to the Heavens: Looking at the Qumran Hodayot Through the Lens of Visionary Traditions.* Ekstasis 3. Berlin: De Gruyter, 2012.

Hasselbalch, Trine Bjørnung. *Meaning and Context in the Thanksgiving Hymns: Linguistic and Rhetorical Perspectives on a Collection of Prayers from Qumran.* Early Judaism and Its Literature 42. Atlanta: SBL Press, 2015.

Hawley, Robert. "On *Maskil* in the Judean Desert Texts." *Henoch* 28 (2006): 43–77.

Hempel, Charlotte. "Community Structures in the Dead Sea Scrolls: Admission, Organization, Disciplinary Procedures." In *The Dead Sea Scrolls After Fifty Years: A Comprehensive Assessment*, volume 2, ed. Peter W. Flint and James C. VanderKam, 67–92. Leiden: Brill, 1999.

Hempel, Charlotte. "From Maskil(im) to Rabbim." In *Biblical Traditions in Transmission: Essays in Honour of Michael A. Knibb*, ed. Charlotte Hempel and Judith Lieu, 133–156. Leiden: Brill, 2006.

Hempel, Charlotte. *The Qumran Rule Texts in Context: Collected Studies.* Texts and Studies in Ancient Judaism 154. Tübingen: Mohr Siebeck, 2013.

Hempel, Charlotte. "The Qumran Sapiential Texts and the Rule Books." In *The Wisdom Texts from Qumran and the Development of Sapiential Thought*, ed. Charlotte

Hempel, Armin Lange, and Hermann Lichtenberger, 277–295. Bibliotheca Ephemeridum Theologicarum Lovaniensium 159. Leuven: Peeters, 2002.

Hempel, Charlotte. "Reflections on Literacy, Textuality, and Community in the Qumran Dead Sea Scrolls." In *Is There a Text in This Cave? Studies in the Textuality of the Dead Sea Scrolls in Honour of George J. Brooke*, ed. Ariel Feldman, Maria Cioată, and Charlotte Hempel, 69–82. Studies on the Texts of the Desert of Judah 119. Leiden: Brill, 2017.

Hempel, Charlotte. "The *Treatise of the Two Spirits* and the Literary History of the *Rule of the Community*." In *Dualism in Qumran*, ed. Géza Xeravits, 102–120. Library of Second Temple Studies. London: T. & T. Clark, 2010.

Henrich, Joseph. "The Evolution of Costly Displays, Cooperation, and Religion: Credibility Enhancing Displays and Their Implications for Cultural Evolution." *Evolution and Human Behavior* 30 (2009): 244–260.

Henze, Matthias. "*4 Ezra* and *2 Baruch*: Literary Composition and Oral Performance in First-Century Apocalyptic Literature." *Journal of Biblical Literature* 131 (2012):181–200.

Henze, Matthias, ed. *A Companion to Biblical Interpretation in Early Judaism*. Grand Rapids, MI: Eerdmans, 2012.

Henze, Matthias. *Jewish Apocalypticism in Late First Century Israel: Reading 2 Baruch in Context*. Texts and Studies in Ancient Judaism 142. Tübingen: Mohr Siebeck, 2011.

Henze, Matthias. "The Use of Scripture in the Book of Daniel." In *A Companion to Biblical Interpretation in Early Judaism*, ed. Matthias Henze, 279–307. Grand Rapids, MI: Eerdmans, 2012.

Hobsbawm, Eric. "Introduction: Inventing Traditions." In *The Invention of Tradition*, ed. Eric Hobsbawm and Terence Ranger, 1–15. Cambridge: Cambridge University Press, 1983.

Hofius, Otfried. "Der Gott allen Trostes": παράκλησις und παρακαλέω in 2 Kor 1, 3–7." In *Paulusstudien*, ed. Otfried Hofius, 244–254. Wissenschaftliche Untersuchungen zum Neuen Testament 51. Tübingen: Mohr Siebeck, 1989.

Holm-Nielsen, Svend. *Hodayot: Psalms from Qumran*. Acta Theologica Danica 2. Aarhus: Universitetsforlaget, 1960.

Horsley, Richard A. *Revolt of the Scribes: Resistance and Apocalyptic Origins*. Minneapolis: Fortress, 2010.

Horsley, Richard A. *Scribes, Visionaries and the Politics of Second Temple Judea*. Louisville, KY: Westminster John Knox Press, 2007.

Horsley, Richard A., and Patrick Tiller. "Ben Sira and the Sociology of the Second Temple." In *Second Temple Studies III: Studies in Politics, Class and Material Culture*, ed. Philip R. Davies and John M. Halligan, 74–107. Journal for the Study of the Old Testament: Supplement Series 340. Sheffield: Sheffield Academic Press, 2002.

Hughes, Frank W. "Rhetoric of Reconciliation: 2 Corinthians 1.1–2.13 and 7.5–8.24." In *Persuasive Artistry: Studies in New Testament Rhetoric in Honor of George A. Kennedy*, ed. Duane F. Watson, 336–350. The Library of New Testament Studies 50. Sheffield: JSOT Press, 1991.

Hughes, Julie A. *Scriptural Allusions and Exegesis in the Hodayot*. Studies on the Texts of the Desert of Judah 59. Leiden: Brill, 2006.

Iacoboni, Marco. *Mirroring People: The Science of Empathy and How We Connect with Others*. New York: Picador, 2009.

Jaffee, Martin S. *Torah in the Mouth: Writing and Oral Tradition in Palestinian Judaism, 200 BCE–400 CE*. New York: Oxford University Press, 2001.

Jassen, Alex P. *Mediating the Divine: Prophecy and Revelation in the Dead Sea Scrolls and Second Temple Judaism*. Studies on the Texts of the Desert of Judah 68. Leiden: Brill, 2008.

Johnson, Mark. *The Meaning of the Body: Aesthetics of Human Understanding*. Chicago: University of Chicago Press, 2007.

Jokiranta, Jutta. *Social Identity and Sectarianism in the Qumran Movement*. Studies on the Texts of the Desert of Judah 105. Leiden: Brill, 2013.

Jonquière, Tessel M. *Prayer in Josephus*. Ancient Judaism and Early Christianity 70. Leiden: Brill, 2007.

Kabasele Mukenge, André. "Les citations interne en *Ba.* 1, 15–3, 8. Un procédé rédactionnel et actualisant." *Le Muséon* 108 (1995): 211–237.

Kabasele Mukenge, André. *L'unité littéraire du livre de Baruch*. Etudes Bibliques 38. Paris: Librairie Gabalda, 1998.

Kaplan, Jonathan. "Comfort, O Comfort, Corinth: Grief and Comfort in 2 Corinthians 7:5–13a." *Harvard Theological Review* 104, no. 4 (2011): 433–45.

Kartveit, Magnar. *The Origin of the Samaritans*. Supplements to Vetus Testamentum 128. Leiden: Brill, 2009.

Kelber, Werner H. *The Oral and the Written Gospel: The Hermeneutics of Speaking and Writing in the Synoptic Tradition, Mark, Paul, and Q*. Bloomington: Indiana University Press, 1997.

Kelber, Werner H., and S. Byrskog, eds. *Jesus in Memory: Traditions in Oral and Scribal Perspectives*. Waco, TX: Baylor University Press, 2009.

Kermode, Frank. *The Sense of an Ending: Studies in the Theory of Fiction*. New York: Oxford University Press, 1967.

Kessler, Martin. "Jeremiah Chapters 26–45 Reconsidered." *Journal of Near Eastern Studies* 27 (1968): 81–88.

Kittredge, Cynthia Briggs. "Rethinking Authorship in the Letters of Paul." In *Walk in the Ways of Wisdom*, ed. Shelly Matthews, Cynthia Briggs Kittredge, and Melanie Johnson-Debaufre, 318–333. Harrisburg, PA: Trinity Press International, 2003.

Klawans, Jonathan. *Impurity and Sin in Ancient Judaism*. New York: Oxford University Press, 2000.

Klein, Anja. "From the 'Right Spirit' to the 'Spirit of Truth': Observations on Psalms 51 and 1QS." In *The Dynamics of Language and Exegesis at Qumran*, ed. Devorah Dimant and Reinhard G. Kratz, 171–191. Forschungen zum Alten Testament 2.35. Tübingen: Mohr Siebeck, 2009.

Klinzing, Georg. *Die Umdeutung des Kultus in der Qumrangemeinde und im Neuen Testament*. Studien zur Umwelt des Neuen Testaments 7. Göttingen: Vandenhoeck & Ruprecht, 1971.

Kloppenborg, John S. "Literate Media in Early Christ Groups: The Creation of a Christian Book Culture." *Journal of Early Christian Studies* 22 (2014): 21–59.

Kneucker, J. J. *Das Buch Baruch*. Leipzig: Brackhaus, 1879.

Knibb, Michael A. "The Community of the Dead Sea Scrolls: Introduction." *Dead Sea Discoveries* 16 (2009): 297–308.

Knibb, Michael A. "The Exile in the Intertestamental Period." *Heythrop Journal* 17 (1976): 253–272.

Knohl, Israel. "Between Voice and Silence: The Relationship Between Prayer and Temple Cult." *Journal of Biblical Literature* 115 (1999): 17–30.

Koch, Klaus. *Deuterokanonische Zusätze zum Danielbuch: Entstehung und Textgeschichte.* AOAT 38/1–2. Neukirchen-Vluyn: Neukirchener Verlag, 1987.

Kosmala, Hans. "Maśkîl." *Journal of the Ancient Near Eastern Society of Columbia University* 5 (1973): 235–241.

Kratz, Reinhard. "The Teacher of Righteousness and His Enemies." In *Is There a Text in This Cave? Studies in the Textuality of the Dead Sea Scrolls in Honour of George J. Brooke,* ed. Ariel Feldman, Maria Cioată, and Charlotte Hempel, 515–532. Studies on the Texts of the Desert of Judah 119. Leiden: Brill, 2017.

Krueger, Derek. *Liturgical Subjects: Christian Ritual, Biblical Narrative, and the Formation of the Self in Byzantium.* Divinations. Philadelphia: University of Pennsylvania Press, 2014.

Kugel, James L. "David the Prophet." In *Poetry and Prophecy,* ed. James L. Kugel, 45–55. Ithaca, NY: Cornell University Press, 1990.

Kugel, James L. "Early Interpretation: The Common Background of Late Forms of Biblical Exegesis." In *Early Biblical Interpretation,* ed. James L. Kugel and Rowan A. Greer. Library of Early Christianity 3. Philadelphia, PA: Westminster, 1986.

Kugel, James. L. *In the Valley of the Shadow: On the Foundations of Religious Belief (and Their Connection to a Certain, Fleeting State of Mind).* New York: Free Press, 2012.

Kugel, James L. "Is There But One Song?" *Biblica* 63 (1982): 329–350.

Kugel, James L. *Joseph in Potiphar's House: The Interpretive Life of Biblical Texts.* San Francisco: Harper San Francisco: 1990.

Kugel, James. L, ed. *Prayers That Cite Scripture: Biblical Quotation in Jewish Prayers from Antiquity Through the Middle Ages.* Cambridge, MA: Harvard University Center for Jewish Studies, 2006.

Kugel, James L. *Traditions of the Bible: A Guide to the Bible as It Was at the Start of the Common Era.* Cambridge, MA: Harvard University Press, 1998.

Kugel, James L. "Wisdom and the Anthological Temper." *Prooftexts* 17 (1997): 9–32.

Kuhn, Heinz-Wolfgang. *Enderwartung und gegenwärtiges Heil: Untersuchungen zu den Gemeindeliedern von Qumran.* Studien zur Umwelt des Neuen Testaments 4. Göttingen: Vandenhoeck & Ruprecht, 1966.

LaCocque, André. "The Liturgical Prayer in Daniel 9." *Hebrew Union College Annual* 47 (1976): 119–142.

LaCocque, André. *Le livre de Daniel.* Neuchâtel: Delachaux et Niestlé, 1976.

LaCoste, Nathalie. "Waters of the Exodus: A Material Analysis of the Exodus Narrative in Hellenistic Egypt." PhD dissertation, University of Toronto, 2016.

Lakoff, George. *Women, Fire, and Dangerous Things: What Categories Reveal About the Mind.* Chicago: University of Chicago Press, 1987.

Lakoff, George, and Mark Johnson. *Metaphors We Live By.* Chicago: University of Chicago Press, 1980.

Lakoff, George, and Mark Johnson. "Why Cognitive Linguistics Requires Embodied Realism." *Cognitive Linguistics* 13, no. 3 (2002): 245–263.

Lambert, David A. *How Repentance Became Biblical: Judaism, Christianity, and the Interpretation of Scripture.* New York: Oxford University Press, 2016.

Lambert, David A. "Was the Dead Sea Sect a Penitential Movement?" In *Oxford Handbook of the Dead Sea Scrolls,* ed. Timothy Lim and John J. Collins, 501–513. New York: Oxford University Press, 2010.

Lange, Armin. "The Textual History of the Book of Jeremiah in Light of Its Allusions and Implicit Quotations in the Qumran *Hodayot.*" In *Prayer and Poetry in the Dead Sea Scrolls and in Related Literature: Essays in Honor of Eileen Schuller on the Occasion of Her 65th Birthday*, ed. Jeremy Penner, Ken M. Penner, and Cecilia Wassen, 251–284. Studies on the Texts of the Desert of Judah 98. Leiden: Brill, 2012.

Lange, Armin. *Weisheit und Prädestination: Weisheitliche Urordnung und Prädestination in den Textfunden von Qumran*. Studies on the Texts of the Desert of Judah 18. Leiden: Brill, 1995.

Lee, Briana (Bo Yeon). "'Jeremiah' and the Fate of Jerusalem and Its Temple: From Destruction to Restoration." PhD dissertation, University of Toronto, 2016.

Leipoldt, Johannes, and Siegfried Morenz. *Heilige Schriften: Betrachtungen zur Religionsgeschichte der antike Mittelmeerwelt*. Leipzig: O. Harrossowitz, 1953.

Levenson, Jon D. *Resurrection and the Restoration of Israel: The Ultimate Victory of the God of Life*. New Haven, CT: Yale University Press, 2008.

Lienhardt, Godfrey. *Divinity and Experience: The Religion of the Dinka*. Oxford: Oxford University Press, 1961.

Liesen, Jan. *Full of Praise: An Exegetical Study of Sir 39, 12–35*. Supplements to the Journal for the Study of Judaism in the Persian, Hellenistic, and Roman Periods 64. Leiden: Brill, 1999.

Lim, Timothy H. *The Formation of the Jewish Canon*. New Haven, CT: Yale University Press, 2013.

Lührmann, Dieter. "Ein Weisheitspsalm aus Qumran (11QPs^a XVIII)." *Zeitschrift für die alttestamentliche Wissenschaft* 80 (1968): 87–97.

Luhrmann, Tanya M. *When God Talks Back: Understanding the American Evangelical Relationship with God*. New York: Vintage, 2012.

Lundbom, Jack R. "Baruch, Seraiah, and Expanded Colophons in the Book of Jeremiah." *Journal for the Study of the Old Testament* 36 (1986): 89–114.

Macintyre, Alasdair. *After Virtue*. Notre Dame, IN: University of Notre Dame Press, 1981.

Macumber, Heather. "Angelic Intermediaries: The Development of a Revelatory Tradition." PhD dissertation, University of Toronto, 2012.

Magness, Jodi. *The Archaeology of Qumran and the Dead Sea Scrolls*. Grand Rapids, MI: Eerdmans, 2012.

Maier, Harry O. *Picturing Paul in Empire: Imperial Image, Text, and Persuasion in Colossians, Ephesians, and the Pastoral Epistles*. London: Bloomsbury, 2013.

Malina, Bruce J. *The New Testament World: Insights from Cultural Anthropology*. Rev. ed. Louisville, KY: Westminster John Knox Press, 1993.

Marböck, Johannes. "Structure and Redaction History of the Book of Ben Sira: Review and Prospects." In *The Book of Ben Sira in Modern Research: Proceedings of the First International Ben Sira Conference 28–31 July 1996, Soesterberg, Netherlands*, ed. P. Beentjes, 61–80. Beihefte zur Zeitschrift für die alttestamentliche Wissenschaft 255. Berlin: De Gruyter, 1997.

Marshall, J. T. "The Book of Baruch." In *Hastings' Dictionary of the Bible*, volume 1, 251–254.

Martin Hogan, Karina, Matthew Goff, and Emma Wasserman, eds. *Pedagogy in Ancient Judaism and Early Christianity*. Early Judaism and Its Literature 41. Atlanta: SBL Press, 2017.

Matera, Frank. *2 Corinthians: A Commentary*. The New Testament Library Series. Louisville, KY: Westminster John Knox Press, 2003.

Matlock, Michael D. *Discovering the Traditions of Prose Prayers in Early Jewish Literature*. Library of Second Temple Studies 81. New York: Bloomsbury, 2012.

Mauss, Marcel. *On Prayer*. Trans. S. Leslie. New York: Berghahn Books, 2003.

McDonald, Lee Martin. "Biblical Canon." *Oxford Bibliographies in Biblical Studies*, last revised April 29, 2015. doi: 10.1093/OBO/9780195393361-0017. http://

www.oxfordbibliographies.com/view/document/obo-9780195393361/obo-
9780195393361-0017.xml.

McKnight, Scot. "Collection for the Saints." In *Dictionary of Paul and His Letters*, ed. Gerald F. Hawthorne and Ralph P. Martin, 143–147. Downers Grove, IL: InterVarsity Press, 1993.

McLay, Timothy. "The Old Greek Translation of Daniel IV–VI and the Formation of the Book of Daniel." *Vetus Testamentum* 55 (2005): 304–323.

McNamara, Patrick. *The Neuroscience of Religious Experience*. New York: Cambridge University Press, 2009.

Metso, Sarianna. *The Serekh Texts*. Library of Second Temple Studies 62. New York: T. & T. Clark, 2007.

Meyer, Nicholas A. *Adam's Dust and Adam's Glory in the Hodayot and the Letters of Paul*. Novum Testamentum, Supplements 168. Leiden: Brill, 2016.

Miller, Eric. "The Self-Glorification Hymn Reexamined." *Henoch* 31 (2009): 307–324.

Minor, Mitzi L. *2 Corinthians*. Macon, GA: Smyth & Helwys, 2009.

Mintz, Alan. *Ḥurban: Responses to Catastrophe in Hebrew Literature*. New York: Columbia University Press, 1984.

Moore, Carey A. *Daniel, Esther and Jeremiah: The Additions*. Trans., intro., and commentary by Carey Moore. Anchor Bible 44. New York: Doubleday, 1977.

Moxnes, Halvor. "Honor and Shame." *Biblical Theology Bulletin* 23 (1993): 167–176.

Mroczek, Eva. *The Literary Imagination in Jewish Antiquity*. New York: Oxford University Press, 2016.

Najman, Hindy. "Configuring the Text in Biblical Studies." In *A Teacher for All Generations: Essays in Honor of James C. VanderKam*, volume 1, ed. E. F. Mason, S. I. Thomas, A. Schofield, and E. Ulrich, 3–22. Supplements to the Journal for the Study of Judaism in the Persian, Hellenistic, and Roman Periods 153. Leiden: Brill, 2012.

Najman, Hindy. *Seconding Sinai: The Development of Mosaic Discourse in Second Temple Judaism*. Supplements to the Journal for the Study of Judaism in the Persian, Hellenistic, and Roman Periods 77. Leiden: Brill, 2003.

Najman, Hindy, and Konrad Schmid, eds. *Jeremiah's Scriptures*. Supplements to the Journal for the Study of Judaism in the Persian, Hellenistic, and Roman Periods. Leiden: Brill, 2015.

Nasrallah, Laura Salah. "Grief in Corinth: The Roman City and Paul's Corinthian Correspondence." In *Contested Spaces: Houses and Temples in Roman Antiquity and the New Testament*, ed. David L. Balch and Annette Weissenrieder, 109–140. Mohr Siebeck, 2012.

Newman, Judith H. "Covenant Renewal and Transformational Scripts in the Performance of the Hodayot and 2 Corinthians." In *Jesus, Paulus, und die Texte von Qumran*, ed. Jörg Frey, Enno Edzard Popkes, and Sophie Tätweiler, 291–330. Tübingen: Mohr Siebeck, 2015.

Newman, Judith H. "Embodied Techniques: The Communal Formation of the Maskil's Self." *Dead Sea Discoveries* 22, no. 3 (2015): 249–266.

Newman, Judith H. "Prayer of Manasseh." In *Seeking the Favor of God*, volume 2, *The Development of Penitential Prayer in Second Temple Judaism*, ed. M. J. Boda, D. K. Falk, and R. A. Werline, 105–125. Early Judaism and Its Literature 22. Atlanta, GA: SBL Press, 2007.

Newman, Judith H. *Praying by the Book: The Scripturalization of Prayer in Second Temple Judaism*. Society of Biblical Literature Early Judaism and Its Literature 14. Atlanta: Scholars Press, 1999.

Newsom, Carol A. "Deriving Negative Anthropology Through Exegetical Activity." In *Is There a Text in This Cave? Studies in the Textuality of the Dead Sea Scrolls in Honour of George J. Brooke*, ed. Ariel Feldman, Maria Cioată, and Charlotte Hempel, 258–274. Studies on the Texts of the Desert of Judah 119. Leiden: Brill, 2017.

Newsom, Carol A. "Flesh, Spirit, and the Indigenous Psychology of the Hodayot." In *Prayer and Poetry in the Dead Sea Scrolls and in Related Literature: Essays in Honor of Eileen Schuller on the Occasion of Her 65th Birthday*, ed. Jeremy Penner, Ken M. Penner, and Cecilia Wassen, 339–354. Studies on the Texts of the Desert of Judah 98. Leiden: Brill, 2012.

Newsom, Carol A. "Models of the Moral Self: Hebrew Bible and Second Temple Judaism." *Journal of Biblical Literature* 131 (2012): 5–25.

Newsom, Carol A. "A Response to Norman K. Gottwald, 'Social Class and Ideology in Isaiah 40–55: An Eagletonian Reading.'" *Semeia* 59 (1992): 73–78.

Newsom, Carol A. "The Sage in the Literature of Qumran: The Functions of the Maśkîl." In *The Sage in Israel and the Ancient Near East*, ed. John G. Gammie and Leo G. Perdue, 373–382. Winona Lake, IN: Eisenbrauns, 1990.

Newsom, Carol A. *The Self as Symbolic Space: Constructing Identity and Community at Qumran*. Studies on the Texts of the Desert of Judah 52. Leiden: Brill, 2004.

Nicholson, Ernest W. *Deuteronomy and Tradition*. Oxford: Blackwell, 1967.

Niditch, Susan. *Oral World, Written Word: Ancient Israelite Literature*. Library of Ancient Israel. Louisville, KY: John Knox Press, 1996.

Nikolova, Svetlina. "The Composition and Structure of Ben Sira in the Oldest Slavonic Translation." In *The Bible in Slavic Tradition*, ed. A. Kulik, C. MacRobert, S. Nikolova, M. Taube, and C. Vakareliyska, 243–256. Studia Judaeoslavica 9. Leiden: Brill, 2016.

Nitzan, Bilhah. *Qumran Prayer and Religious Poetry*. Translated by Jonathan Chipman. Studies on the Texts of the Desert of Judah 12. Leiden: Brill, 1994.

Nitzan, Bilhah. "Repentance in the Dead Sea Scrolls." In *The Dead Sea Scrolls After Fifty Years*, volume 2, ed. Peter W. Flint and James C. VanderKam, 145–170. Leiden: Brill, 1999.

Norenzayan, Aya, Azim F. Shariff, Aiyana K. Willard, Edward Slingerland, Will M. Gervais, Rita A. McNamara, and Joseph Henrich. "The Cultural Evolution of Prosocial Religions." *Behavioral and Brain Sciences* (2016): 1–65.

O'Brien, Peter Thomas. *Introductory Thanksgivings in the Letters of Paul*. Supplements to Novum Testamentum 49. Leiden: Brill, 1977.

Pace, Sharon. *Daniel*. Macon, GA: Smyth and Helwys, 2008.

Pajunen, Mika S. "The Praise of God and His Name as the Core of the Second Temple Liturgy." *Zeitschrift für die alttestamentliche Wissenschaft* 127 (2015): 475–488.

Palmer, Carmen. "The *Gēr* in the Dead Sea Scrolls: Exploring Attitudes Toward Gentiles." PhD dissertation, University of Toronto, 2016.

Pannkuk, Justin L. "Are There למשכיל Sections in the Hodayot? Evidence from Cave 4 (1)." *Revue de Qumran* 28 (2016): 3–13.

Penner, Jeremy. *Patterns of Daily Prayer in Second Temple Period Judaism*. Studies on the Texts of the Desert of Judah 104. Leiden: Brill, 2012.

Perdue, Leo G. "Baruch Among the Sages." In *Uprooting and Planting: Essays on Jeremiah for Leslie Allen*, ed. John Goldingay, 260–290. The Library of Hebrew Bible/Old Testament Studies 459. Edinburgh: T. & T. Clark, 2007.

Perdue, Leo G. *The Sword and the Stylus: An Introduction to Wisdom in the Age of Empires*. Grand Rapids, MI: Eerdmans, 2008.

Perdue, Leo G. *Wisdom and Cult: A Critical Analysis of the Views of Cult in the Wisdom Literatures of Israel and the Ancient Near East.* Society of Biblical Literature Dissertation Series 30. Missoula, MT: Scholars, 1977.

Perdue, Leo G. *Wisdom Literature: A Theological History.* Louisville, KY: Westminster John Knox, 2007.

Pfann, Stephen J. "4QDaniel^d (4Q115): A Preliminary Edition with Critical Notes." *Revue de Qumran* 17, no. 65 (1996): 37–71.

Pietersma, Albert. "From Greek Isaiah to Greek Jeremiah." In *Isaiah in Context: Studies in Honour of Arie van der Kooij on the Occasion of His Sixty-Fifth Birthday,* ed. Michaël van der Meer, Percy van Keulen, William Th. van Peursen, and Bas ter Haar Romney, 359–387. Supplements to Vetus Testamentum 138. Leiden: Brill, 2010.

Pietersma, Albert. "Jeremiah and the Land of Azazel." In *Studies in the Hebrew Bible, Qumran, and Septuagint: Presented to Eugene Ulrich,* ed. Peter Flint, Emanuel Tov, and James VanderKam, 403–413. Supplements to Vetus Testamentum 101. Leiden: Brill, 2006.

Pietersma, Albert, and Benjamin G. Wright. *A New English Translation of the Septuagint.* New York: Oxford University Press, 2007.

Plantinga-Pauw, Amy. *Proverbs and Ecclesiastes: A Theological Commentary on the Bible.* Louisville, KY: Westminster John Knox Press, 2015.

Porter, Stanley. *Paul's Letter Collection: Tracing the Origins.* Minneapolis: Fortress, 1994.

Portier-Young, Anathea E. *Apocalypse Against Empire: Theologies of Resistance in Early Judaism.* Grand Rapids, MI: Eerdmans, 2011.

Puech, Émil. "Hodayot." In *Encyclopedia of the Dead Sea Scrolls,* volume 1, ed. Lawrence H. Schiffman and James C. VanderKam. Oxford: Oxford University Press, 2000.

Puech, Émil. "Quelques aspects de la restauration du Rouleau des Hymnes (IQH)." *Journal of Jewish Studies* 39 (1988): 38–55.

Pulleyn, Simon. *Prayer in Greek Religion.* New York: Oxford University Press, 1997.

Rajak, Tessa. "Benefactors in the Greco-Jewish Diaspora." In *Geschichte-Tradition-Reflexion: Festschrift für Martin Hengel zum 70. Geburtstag,* volume 1, ed. Hubert Cancik, Hermann Lichtenberger, and Peter Schäfer, 305–319. Tübingen: Mohr, 1996.

Rapapport, Roy A. "Ritual." In *International Encyclopedia of Communications,* volume 3 (1989): 466–472.

Rapapport, Roy A. *Ritual and Religion in the Making of Humanity.* New York: Cambridge University Press, 1999.

Reed, Annette Yoshiko. "Interrogating 'Enochic Judaism': 1 Enoch as Evidence for Intellectual History, Social Reality, and Literary Tradition." In *Enoch and Qumran Origins: New Light on a Forgotten Connection,* ed. Gabriele Boccaccini, 336–344. Grand Rapids, MI: Eerdmans, 2005.

Reif, Stefan C. "Prayer in Early Judaism." In *Prayer from Tobit to Qumran,* ed. Renate Egger-Wenzel and Jeremy Corley, 439–464. International Society for the Study of Deuterocanonical and Cognate Literature 1. Berlin: De Gruyter, 2004.

Reitemeyer, Michael. *Weisheitslehre als Gotteslob: Psalmentheologie im Buch Jesus Sirach.* Bonner biblische Beiträge 127. Berlin: Philo, 2000.

Reitemeyer, Michael. "'With All Your Heart': Praise in the Book of Ben Sira." In *Ben Sira's God: Proceedings of the International Ben Sira Conference, Durham-Ushaw College 2001,* ed. Renate Egger Wenzel, 199–213. Zeitschrift für die alttestamentliche Wissenschaft 321. Berlin: De Gruyter, 2002.

Rendsburg, Gary and Jacob Binstein. *The Book of Ben Sira.* www.bensira.org.

Rey, Jean-Sébastien. "La transmission des sentence proverbiales dans les différents témoins hébreux du livre du Siracide." In *Corpus anciens et bases de données*, ed. Marie-Sol Ortola, 27–39. Analyse linguistique et interculturelle des énoncés sapientiels et de leur transmission de l'Orient à l'Occident et de l'Occident à l'Orient 2. Nancy: Presses Universitaires de Nancy, 2012.

Reymond, Eric. "New Hebrew Text of Ben Sira Chapter 1 in MS A (TS 12.863) (1)." *Revue de Qumran* 103, no. 26 (2014): 327–344.

Roetzel, Calvin J. "2 Corinthians." In *The Blackwell Companion to the New Testament*, ed. David E. Aune, 437–443. Oxford: Wiley-Blackwell, 2010.

Saldarini, Anthony J. *The Book of Baruch*. The New Interpreter's Bible 6. Nashville, TN: Abingdon Press, 2001.

Sampley, J. Paul. *2 Corinthians. The New Interpreter's Bible* 11. Nashville, TN: Abingdon Press, 2000.

Sanders, James A. *Canon and Community: A Guide to Canonical Criticism*. Philadelphia: Fortress, 1984.

Schaller, Joseph J. "Performative Language Theory: An Exercise in the Analysis of Ritual." *Worship* 62 (1988): 415–432.

Scheper-Hughes, Nancy and Margaret M. Lock. "The Mindful Body: A Prolegomenon to Future Work in Medical Anthropology." *Medical Anthropology Quarterly* n.s. 1, no. 1 (March 1987): 6–41.

Schjødt, Uffe, Hans Stødkilde-Jørgensen, Armin W. Geertz, and Andreas Roepstorff. "Highly Religious Participants Recruit Areas of Social Cognition in Personal Prayer." *Social Cognitive and Affective Neuroscience* 4 (2009): 199–207.

Schmid, Konrad. "The Canon and the Cult: The Emergence of Book Religion in Ancient Israel and the Gradual Sublimation of the Temple Cult." *Journal of Biblical Literature* 131, no. 2 (2012): 289–305.

Schmitz, Otto. "παρακαλέω/παράκλησις." In *Theological Dictionary of the New Testament*, volume 5, ed. Gerhard Kittel and Gerhard Friedrich, trans. Geoffrey W. Bromiley, 773–779. Grand Rapids, MI: Eerdmans, 1968.

Schniedewind, William. *How the Bible Became a Book: The Textualization of Ancient Israel*. Cambridge: Cambridge University Press, 2005.

Schofield, Alison. *From Qumran to the Yaḥad: A New Paradigm of Textual Development for the Community Rule*. Studies on the Texts of the Desert of Judah 77. Leiden: Brill, 2009.

Scholem, Gershom. *The Messianic Idea in Judaism and Other Essays on Jewish Spirituality*. New York: Schocken, 1971.

Schubert, Paul. *The Form and Function of the Pauline Thanksgivings*. Beihefte zur Zeitschrift für die alttestamentliche Wissenschaft 20. Berlin: A. Töpelmann, 1939.

Schuller, Eileen. "Hodayot." In *Eerdmans Dictionary of Early Judaism*: 747–749.

Schuller, Eileen. "Petitionary Prayer and the Religion of Qumran." In *Religion in the Dead Sea Scrolls*, ed. John J. Collins and Robert Kugler, 29–45. Studies in the Dead Sea Scrolls and Related Literature. Grand Rapids, MI: Eerdmans, 2000.

Schuller, Eileen. "Recent Scholarship on the *Hodayot* 1993–2010." *Currents in Biblical Research* 10 (2011): 119–162.

Schuller, Eileen. "Some Contributions of the Cave Four Manuscripts (4Q427–432) to the Study of the Hodayot." *Dead Sea Discoveries* 8 (2001): 278–287.

Schuller, Eileen. "Some Observations on Blessings of God in Texts from Qumran." In *Of Scribes and Scrolls: Studies on the Hebrew Bible, Intertestamental Judaism*

and Christian Origins Presented to John Strugnell on the Occasion of his Sixtieth
Birthday, ed. Harold W. Attridge, John J. Collins, and Thomas H. Tobin, 133–
143. Resources in Religion 5. Lanham, MD: University Press of America, 1990.

Schuller, Eileen, and Carol A. Newsom. *The Hodayot (Thanksgiving Psalms): A
Study Edition of 1QH^a*. Early Judaism and Its Literature 36. Atlanta: SBL
Press, 2012.

Schuller, Eileen, and Hartmut Stegemann, eds. *Qumran Cave 1.III: 1QHodayot ^a and
4QHodayot ^{a-f}*. Translation of texts by Carol Newsom. Discoveries in the Judean
Desert 40. New York: Oxford University Press, 2009.

Schwartz, Seth. *Were the Jews a Mediterranean Society? Reciprocity and Solidarity in
Ancient Judaism*. Princeton, NJ: Princeton University Press, 2010.

Scott, James M. "Exile and Self-Understanding of Diaspora Jews in the Greco-Roman
Period." In *Exile: Old Testament, Jewish and Christian Conceptions*, ed. J. M. Scott,
173–218. Supplements to the Journal for the Study of Judaism in the Persian,
Hellenistic, and Roman Periods 56. Leiden: Brill, 1997.

Segal, Michael. *Dreams, Riddles, and Visions Textual, Contextual, and Intertextual
Approaches to the Book of Daniel*. Beihefte zur Zeitschrift für die alttestamentliche Wissenschaft 455. Berlin: De Gruyter, 2016.

Segal, Moshe Zvi. *Sefer Ben Sirah Hashalem*. 2nd ed. Jerusalem: Bialik, 1958.

Seow, Choon-Leong. *Daniel*. Westminster Bible Companion. Louisville, KY: Westminster
John Knox, 2003.

Skehan, Patrick W., and Alexander A. Di Lella. *The Wisdom of Ben Sira*. The Anchor Bible
39. New York: Doubleday, 1987.

Smend, Rudolf. *Die Weisheit Jesus Sirach Erklärt*. Berlin: Reimer, 1906.

Smith-Christopher, Daniel. "The Book of Daniel." *The New Interpreter's Bible*, volume 7.
Nashville, TN: Abingdon, 1996.

Snyder, H. Gregory. *Teachers and Texts in the Ancient World: Philosophers, Jews and
Christians*. London: Routledge, 2000.

Sommer, Benjamin. *A Prophet Reads Scripture: Allusion in Isa 40–66*. Stanford,
CA: Stanford University Press, 1998.

Sosis, Richard. "Religion and Intragroup Cooperation: Preliminary Results of a
Comparative Analysis of Utopian Communities." *Cross-Cultural Research* 34
(2000): 70–87.

Sosis, Richard, and Candace S. Alcorta. "Signaling, Solidarity, and the Sacred:
The Evolution of Religious Behavior." *Evolutionary Anthropology* 12 (2003):
264–274.

Steck, Odil H. *Das apokryphe Baruchbuch: Studien zur Rezeption und Konzentration "kanonischer" Überlieferung*. Forschungen zur Religion und Literatur des Alten und
Neuen Testaments 160. Göttingen: Vandenhoeck & Ruprecht, 1993.

Steck, Odil, Reinhard Kratz, and Ingo Kottsieper. *Das Buch Baruch. Der Brief des Jeremie,
Zusätze zu Ester und Daniel*. Göttingen: Vanderhoeck & Ruprecht, 1998.

Stipp, Hermann-Josef. "Offene Fragen zu Übersetzungskritik des antiken griechischen
Jeremiabuches." *Journal of Northwest Semitic Languages* 17 (1991): 117–128.

Stock, Brian. *The Implications of Literacy: Written Language and Models of Interpretation
in the Eleventh and Twelfth Centuries*. Princeton, NJ: Princeton University Press,
1983.

Stoner, Ryan. "A Sacrifice of Time: Work, Worship and the Embodiment of Sabbath in
Ancient Judaism." PhD dissertation, University of Toronto, 2014.

Stowers, Stanley K. *Letter Writing in Greco-Roman Antiquity.* Louisville, KY: Westminster John Knox, 1986.

Stuckenbruck, Loren T. *The Myth of Rebellious Angels: Studies in Second Temple Judaism and New Testament Texts.* Tübingen: Mohr Siebeck, 2014. Reprinted: Grand Rapids, MI: Eerdmans, 2017.

Stuckenbruck, Loren T., and Wendy E. S. North. *Early Jewish and Christian Monotheism.* London: T. & T. Clark, 2004.

Tanzer, Sarah. "Biblical Interpretation in the Hodayot." In *A Companion to Biblical Interpretation in Early Judaism,* ed. Matthias Henze, 255–275. Grand Rapids, MI: Eerdmans, 2012.

Tanzer, Sarah. "The Sages at Qumran: Wisdom in the *Hodayot*." PhD dissertation, Harvard University, 1987.

Taylor, Charles. *Sources of the Self: The Making of Modern Identity.* Cambridge, MA: Harvard University Press, 1989.

Teeter, David Andrew. *Scribal Laws: Exegetical Variation in the Textual Transmission of Biblical Law in the Late Second Temple Period.* Forschungen Zum Alten Testament 92. Tübingen: Mohr Siebeck, 2014.

Thackeray, Henry St. John. *The Septuagint and Jewish Worship: A Study in Origins. The Schweich Lectures 1920.* London: British Academy, 1921.

Thrall, Margaret E. *2 Corinthians 1–7: A Critical and Exegetical Commentary on the Second Letter to the Corinthians,* volume 1. International Critical Commentary Series. Edinburgh: T. & T. Clark, 1994.

Tigchelaar, Eibert. "Constructing, Deconstructing and Reconstructing Fragmentary Manuscripts: Illustrated by a Study of 4Q184 (4QWiles of the Wicked Woman)." In *Rediscovering the Dead Sea Scrolls: An Assessment of Old and New Approaches and Methods,* ed. Maxine L. Grossman, 26–47. Grand Rapids, MI: Eerdmans, 2010.

Tigchelaar, Eibert. "Editing the Hebrew Bible: An Overview of Some Problems." In *Editing the Bible: Assessing the Task Past and Present,* ed. John S. Kloppenborg and Judith H. Newman, 41–65. Society of Biblical Literature Resources for Biblical Study 69. Atlanta: Society of Biblical Literature, 2012.

Tigchelaar, Eibert. "Lady Folly and Her House in Three Qumran Manuscripts: On the Relation Between 4Q525 15, 5Q16, and 4Q184 1." *Revue de Qumran* 23, no. 91 (2008): 271–281.

Toorn, Karel van der. *Scribal Culture and the Making of the Hebrew Bible.* Cambridge, MA: Harvard University Press, 2007.

Tov, Emmanuel. *The Book of Baruch.* Missoula, MT: Scholars Press, 1975.

Tov, Emmanuel. "The Literary History of the Book of Jeremiah in the Light of Its Textual History." In *Empirical Models for Biblical Criticism,* ed. J. H. Tigay, 211–237. Philadelphia: University of Pennsylvania Press, 1985.

Tov, Emmanuel. *Scribal Practices and Approaches Reflected in the Texts Found in the Judean Desert.* Studies on the Texts of the Desert of Judah 54. Leiden: Brill, 2004.

Tov, Emmanuel. *The Septuagint Translation of Jeremiah and Baruch: A Discussion of an Early Revision of the LXX of Jeremiah 29–52 and Baruch 1:1–3:8.* Harvard Semitic Monographs 8. Missoula, MT: Scholars Press, 1976.

Tov, Emmanuel. "The Significance of the Texts from the Judean Desert for the History of the Text of the Hebrew Bible: A New Synthesis." In *Qumran Between the Old and New Testaments,* ed. Frederick H. Cryer and Thomas L. Thompson, 277–309. Journal for the Study of the Old Testament: Supplement Series 290. Sheffield: Sheffield Academic Press, 1998.

Tov, Emmanuel. *Textual Criticism of the Hebrew Bible*. Rev. and expanded ed. Minneapolis, MN: Fortress, 2012.

Trobisch, David. *The First Edition of the New Testament*. New York: Oxford University Press, 2000.

Tull-Willey, Patricia. *Remember the Former Things: The Recollection of Previous Texts in Second Isaiah*. Society of Biblical Literature Dissertation Series 161. Atlanta: Scholars Press, 1997.

Ulrich, Eugene. *The Dead Sea Scrolls and the Developmental Composition of the Bible*, 215–227. Supplements to Vetus Testamentum 169. Leiden: Brill, 2015.

Ulrich, Eugene. *The Dead Sea Scrolls and the Origins of the Bible*. Grand Rapids, MI: Eerdmans, 1999.

Ulrich, Eugene. "The Text of Daniel in the Qumran Scrolls." In *The Book of Daniel: Composition and Reception*, volume 2, ed. John Joseph Collins, Peter W. Flint, and Cameron VanEpps, 573–585. Leiden: Koninklijke Brill NV, 2001.

Urbanz, Werner. *Gebet im Sirachbuch: Zur Terminologie von Klage und Lob in der griechischen Texttradition*. Herders biblische Studien 60. Freiburg: Herder, 2009.

Veyne, Paul. *Bread and Circuses: Historical Sociology and Political Pluralism*. Trans. Brian Pearce. London: Penguin, 1992. (Translation of *Le Pain et le cirque*. Paris: Seuil, 1976.)

von Gall, August F. *Die Einheitlichkeit des Buches Daniel*. Giessen: Ricker, 1895.

Von Rad, Gerhard. *Das Formgeschichtliche Problem des Hexateuchs*. Stuttgart: Kohlhammer, 1938.

Von Weissenberg, Hanne, and Elisa Uusimäki. "Are There Sacred Texts in Qumran? The Concept of Sacred Text in Light of the Qumran Collection." In *Is There a Text in This Cave? Studies in the Textuality of the Dead Sea Scrolls in Honour of George J. Brooke*, ed. Ariel Feldman, Maria Cioată, and Charlotte Hempel, 21–41. Studies on the Texts of the Desert of Judah 119. Leiden: Brill, 2017.

Wambacq, Bernard N. "Les prières de Baruch (i 15–ii 19) et de Daniel (ix 5–19)." *Biblica* 40 (1959): 463–475.

Wan, Sze-kar. "Collection for the Saints as Anticolonial Act: Implications of Paul's Ethnic Reconstruction." In *Paul and Politics: Ekklesia, Israel, Imperium, Interpretation*, ed. Richard A. Horsley, 191–215. Harrisburg, PA: Trinity Press International, 2000.

Ward, Richard F. "Pauline Voice and Presence as Strategic Communication." *Semeia* 65 (1995): 95–107.

Wassén, Cecilia, and Jutta Jokiranta. "Groups in Tension: Sectarianism in the Damascus Document and the Community Rule." In *Sectarianism in Early Judaism: Sociological Advances*, ed. David J. Chalcraft, 205–245. London: Equinox, 2007.

Watson-Jones, Rachel E., and Cristine H. Legare. "The Social Functions of Group Rituals." *Current Direction in Psychological Science* 25 (2016): 42–46.

Watts, James W. "Scripturalization and the Aaronide Dynasties." *Journal of Hebrew Scriptures* (2013): 13.6. doi:10.5508/jhs.2013.v13.a6. http://www.jhsonline.org/Articles/article_186.pdf.

Weinfeld, Moshe. *Deuteronomy and the Deuteronomic School*. Oxford: Clarendon Press, 1971.

Weitzman, Steven. "Mediterranean Exchanges: A Response to Seth Schwartz, 'Were the Jews a Mediterranean Society?'" *The Jewish Quarterly Review* 102 (2012): 491–512.

Welborn, Lawrence L. "Paul and Pain: Paul's Emotional Therapy in 2 Corinthians 1.1–2.13; 7.5–16 in the Context of Ancient Psychagogic Literature." *New Testament Studies* 57 (2011): 547–570.

Welborn, Lawrence L. "Paul's Appeal to the Emotions in 2 Corinthians 1.1–2.13; 7.5–16." *Journal for the Study of the New Testament* 82 (2001): 31–60.

Werline, Rodney. "The Experience of God's *Paideia* in the Psalms of Solomon." In *Experientia*, volume 2: *Linking Text and Experience*, ed. Colleen Shantz and Rodney A. Werline, 17–44. Society of Biblical Literature Early Judaism and Its Literature 35. Atlanta: SBL, 2012.

Werline, Rodney A. *Penitential Prayer in Second Temple Judaism: The Development of a Religious Institution*. Society of Biblical Literature Early Judaism and Its Literature 13. Atlanta: Scholars Press, 1998.

Westermann, Claus. "Struktur und Geschichte der Klage im Alten Testament." *Zeitschrift für die alttestamentliche Wissenschaft* 66 (1954): 44–80.

White Crawford, Sidnie. *Rewriting Scripture in Second Temple Times*. Studies in the Dead Sea Scrolls and Related Literature. Grand Rapids, MI: Eerdmans, 2008.

Wiles, Gordon P. *Paul's Intercessory Prayers: The Significance of the Intercessory Prayer Passages in the Letters of St. Paul*. New York: Cambridge University Press, 1974.

Wright, Benjamin G. "Ben Sira on the Sage as Exemplar." In *Praise Israel for Wisdom and Instruction: Essays on Ben Sira and Wisdom, the Letter of Aristeas and the Septuagint*, 165–178. Journal for the Study of Judaism in the Persian, Hellenistic, and Roman Periods 131. Leiden: Brill, 2008.

Wright, Benjamin G. *No Small Difference: Sirach's Relationship to Its Hebrew Parent Text*. Society of Biblical Literature Septuagint and Cognate Studies 26. Atlanta: Scholars Press, 1989.

Wright, Benjamin G. "Torah and Sapiential Pedagogy in the Book of Ben Sira." In *Wisdom and Torah: The Reception of "Torah" in the Wisdom Literature of the Second Temple Period*, ed. Bernd U. Schipper and D. Andrew Teeter, 157–186. Supplements to the Journal for the Study of Judaism in the Persian, Hellenistic, and Roman Periods 163. Leiden: Brill, 2013.

Wright, J. Edward. *Baruch Ben Neriah: From Biblical Scribe to Apocalyptic Seer*. Columbia: University of South Carolina Press, 2003.

Zahn, Molly. *Rethinking Rewritten Scripture: Composition and Exegesis in the 4QReworked Pentateuch Manuscripts*. Studies on the Texts of the Desert of Judah 95. Leiden: Brill, 2011.

Ziegler, J. *Sapientia Iesu Filii Sirach*. Septuaginta Vetus Testamentum Graecum Auctoritate Societas Litterarum Gottingensis editum volume XII/2. Göttingen: Vandenhoeck & Ruprecht, 1965.

Zsengellér, J. "Does Wisdom Come from the Temple." *Studies in the Book of Ben Sira*, ed. G. Xeravits and J. Zsengellér, 135–149. Supplements to the Journal for the Study of Judaism in the Persian, Hellenistic, and Roman Periods 127. Leiden: Brill, 2008.

AUTHOR INDEX

SUBJECT INDEX

anthology, anthological, 20, 43, 45, 143
apostolic authority, 86, 98–100, 104
associations, 79–80
authorship, 26n5, 85, 102n64

Baruch, 19–20, 53–57, 60–75, 95–96,
    113, 117–118, 143
  book of, 53, 60, 71, 96, 143
  Jeremiah-Baruch, 20, 55, 74
Ben Sira (figure), 24n1, 44–45, 51, 110,
    113, 115–116. *See also* Sirach (text)
benefaction, 76–78, 80, 89, 100. *See also*
    collection
blessing, 32n25, 59, 69n45, 85–89,
    91–92, 98–100, 104, 108–109,
    111–112, 119, 124, 135n85, 143
  divine, 59
  introductory, 20, 76, 86n30,
    97–98, 100
  priestly, 59, 112
body, 1, 4, 9n20, 12–14, 16–17, 23,
    30–31, 33n27, 38, 46, 55, 58, 76,
    86, 99–101, 104, 105n70, 128–130
  body-in-the-world, 12
  eucharistic, 75–76, 85, 105
  liturgical, 6–7, 9, 11, 13, 19,
    105n70, 132
  mindful, 12–13, 23, 28n11,
    33–34, 128
  scribal, 6, 23
  social, 12–13, 131
  three senses, 12, 30n19

canon, 3–6, 7n14, 14, 102n64, 144
charis (gift), 77–79, 81, 83–85
collection
  as benefaction, 76–78
  as costly display, 81–83, 85

as eucharistic liturgy, 83–85
for Jerusalem, 20, 76–77, 100
as vertical movement, 83–85
collective memory, 6, 91
conceptual metaphors, 12, 83
confession, 1, 20, 25–26, 29, 32,
    35–37, 50, 53–58, 60–63, 68–70,
    73–75, 83, 96, 108, 117, 120–122,
    125–127, 131, 137, 143. *See
    also* prayer
confessional prayer, 19–20, 53–59,
    63, 65–66, 69, 70, 96, 125–127,
    131, 143
confessional psalms, 138
consolation, 60, 86–100
Corinth, 77, 89–90
Corinthians, the, 75, 79, 81–82, 84, 86,
    88–91, 99, 104
cultural memory, 20, 89, 91, 96, 98, 100,
    104, 108n1

Dead Sea Scrolls, 2, 4, 9–10, 14, 88n34,
    107, 108n1, 109n2, 143.
    See also Qumran
diakonia, 77n3, 83–84
dispositions, 33n27

embodied, 12, 14, 33–34, 36–37, 50, 75,
    86, 100, 104, 127, 138, 141–142
  action, 50, 128, 141
  cognition, 11
  socially, 60
embodiment, 6, 9, 11–14, 16, 129n62
enactment, 24, 36, 42, 46, 76,
    95–96, 139
etiology, 69, 74, 143
eucharist(ic), 76, 83, 85, 105
exile (Babylonian), 93–95

SOURCES INDEX